Lord of Creation

Brendan O'Malley is Dean of Chapel and a tutor at the University of Wales, Lampeter. Of Irish descent, Scottish birth and education and of Welsh adoption, his interests lie particularly in Celtic, monastic and pastoral spirituality. In his younger years he was a Cistercian monk. He is now a Canon of St David's Cathedral. His previous publications include the award-winning *The Animals of St Gregory* (Paulinus Press, 1981); *A Pilgrim's Manual*, St David's (Paulinus Press, 1985); *A Welsh Pilgrim's Manual* (Gomer Press, 1989); *God at Every Gate* (Canterbury Press and Morehouse Publishing, 1997); *Celtic Blessings* (Canterbury Press and Twenty-Third Publications, 1998); *A Celtic Eucharist* (Canterbury Press and Morehouse Publishing, 2001); *A Celtic Primer* (Canterbury Press and Morehouse Publishing, 2002).

The Companion to A Celtic Primer,
the complete Celtic worship resource and collection

Lord of Creation

A Resource for Creative Celtic Spirituality

Edited and compiled by
Brendan O'Malley

CANTERBURY PRESS
Norwich

First published in 2005 by the Canterbury Press Norwich
(a publishing imprint of Hymns Ancient & Modern Limited,
a registered charity)
St Mary's Works, St Mary's Plain,
Norwich, Norfolk, NR3 3BH

www.scm-canterburypress.co.uk

British Library Cataloguing in Publication data

A catalogue record for this book is available
from the British Library

ISBN 1-85311-619-X

Typeset by Regent Typesetting, London
Printed and bound by
Biddles Ltd, www.biddles.co.uk

Contents

Lord of the Elements Workshop

Most of the sections in this book are suitable for all ages, particularly the meditation exercises, Prayer Beads and the workshop Lord of the Elements.

I would like to express my gratitude to my three wonderful assistants at the University of Wales, Lampeter, David Rhydderch, Karen Asmuss and Laura Jarvis; for their patience and humour in the early stages of preparing the typescript. Also to Lynda Cadman and Rebecca Jarman who typed up the final draft, then to Christine Smith, publisher, and the staff of Canterbury Press.

silence

hold

in your

heart

the true place

of understanding.

a

stillness

which is alive

as the

heart

of a

rose.

anon.

To
Bishop Graham Chadwick

An Inspiration

LORD of
CREATION

come LORD CHRIST, king of the earth,
lead us as we walk with you
that the earth may be healed.

come, holy spirit hovering over the water
and guide us as we sail to you,
that the waters may flow with life.

come, you angels of the fire and light
and show us how to dance with you,
that in the light may be born the
flame of love.

come, you breath of the air,
and inspire us with the breath of you,
that the air may reverberate with the
sound of the word.

come, lady mary and the saints of heaven
and help us to pray with you,
that the earth may be redeemed through
the love of christ.

BRENDANUS SCOTUS

Introduction

O God, *Lord of Creation,* I invoke you. You are my gracious counsellor. Do not turn your face toward me, for you are my judgement without betrayal.

You are my King, you are my law, yours is my flesh, my body. I love you, blessed Christ, for my soul is yours tonight.

Let me not conceal it, O King. May I be in your royal dwelling all my days. May I eat the feast from your table. Do not leave me behind, O God.

Early Irish Lyric[1]

This book is offered as a resource in creative Celtic spirituality, it is my hope that each section may be used as a basis for the practical and imaginative teaching of the spiritual life relating to the whole person in body, mind and spirit.

Why the term Celtic? The early Celts certainly never called themselves 'Celts' but rather used various tribal names. The ancient Irish, Scots and Welsh were of similar race but would not have seen themselves as belonging to neat national states in the modern sense of the term. Their difference was more to do with language – it still is! Whether oral or written, language is central to a proper understanding of Celtic culture and spirituality. Nevertheless, one is able intuitively to absorb the essence of Celtic spirituality from researching the spirituality of the Bible, the writing of the Fathers of the early Church, the Desert Fathers, the cult of the saints, folklore, story, archaeology, anthropology and art as well as reading the liturgy, poetry and prose culled mainly from monastic sources. It is really about being sensitive to what could be described as the 'Celtic stream of things'; we can add materials derived from our own interpretation, understanding and knowledge of Celtic Christianity and apply it in a modern idiom to a virtual tapestry, combining both old and new.

That is not to say that just about anything goes in this matter! No, the Celtic saints were a very tough breed indeed; more warrior than sweet and gentle, meek and mild. St David, St Columba *et al.*, lived extremely ascetic lives involving extreme self-discipline and were, by our modern standards, harsh to their disciples. Their life stories were written by hagiographers not in the least intent on writing accurate biography as much as using the saints' story as a focus on, for example, in the Life of St David, what it means to be an ascetic, that is well exercised in the whole of his person and therefore strong. Saints, like St David, were the celebrities of their day, representing what a people should aspire to.

The Celtic saints were people attracted to asceticism, hard work and the word of God. They loved the Scriptures and they were deeply influenced by the book of Psalms, the books of wisdom and the New Testament. Travelling the world seeking the one God and the place of their resurrection, they saw creation, from God's viewpoint, as one. They were part of a whole dancing harmony, masters of creation, 'the fish of the sea, the birds of heaven and all living animals on their earth' (Genesis 1.28–31).

Through the creative work of their hands, interior prayer and learning the Word of God they interrelated with the uncreated energy of God present within all created being: 'In him we live and move and have our being' (Acts 17.28).

The writing of the Christian Celts is full of a deep awareness of the cosmic unity among all creatures. Theirs was a cosmology that can be traced back to the early Christian mystics:

> I am the wind that breathes upon the sea,
> I am the wave on the ocean.
> I am the murmur of leaves rustling,
> I am the rays of the sun,
> I am the beam of the moon and stars,
> I am the power of the trees growing,
> I am the bud breaking into blossom,
> I am the movement of the salmon swimming,
> I am the courage of the wild boar fighting,
> I am the speed of the stag running,
> I am the strength of the ox pulling the plough,
> I am the sap of the mighty oak tree,
> And I am the thoughts of all people
> Who praise my beauty and grace.

From the Black Book of Carmarthen, *early Welsh*[2]

The cosmos-centred Christian Celts prayed before, during and after any work engaged upon, whether tilling a field, milking a cow or fishing at sea. It was through their interior contemplative prayer that they were able to touch the indwelling at the centre within the daily task as well as in ruminating on Holy Scripture, and contemplating the central mystery of their faith, namely, the Incarnation. By faith they knew that God the Father had sent his only Son to communicate, through his material body and through the rest of material creation, with us.

Through matter, the historical Jesus Christ has been able to communicate God's great love for humankind. By creating the world the fullness of God is manifest through sharing his life with us by making us into his adopted children.

It is through the reconciling Christ that we are brought back to God, and not only us but the whole of creation which is 'crying out as if in the pangs of childbirth and waiting for the people of God to appear' (Romans 8). The created universe waits with eager expectation for this revelation. St Paul demonstrates the dominion of Christ over all creation, visible and invisible. All created being is created by him and are in his care. They have been created for him and are being brought into completion through the action of divine love. The Cosmic Christ is bringing all created being back to the Father through his Church, for:

> He is the image of the invisible God, the firstborn of all creation, for in him all things in heaven and on earth were created, things visible and invisible, whether thrones or dominions or rulers or powers – all things have been created through him and for him. He himself is before all things, and in him all things hold together. He is the head of the body, the Church, he is the beginning, the firstborn from the dead, so that he might come to have first place in everything. For in him all the fullness of God was pleased to dwell and through him God was pleased to reconcile to himself all things, whether on earth or in heaven, by making peace through the blood of his cross.
>
> *Colossians 1.15–20*

Christ's light, love and power is struggling to come to birth within the heart of all creation. We, the brothers and sisters of Jesus, are gifted to bring this into effect.

Jesus the Christ is Lord of Creation, and all things belong to him:

> He has put all things under his feet and made him, as the ruler of everything, the head of the Church; which is his body, the fullness of him who fills the whole creation.
>
> *Ephesians 1.22–23*

We have been baptized into his body, the mystical body of Christ, and we are a new creation, in Christ, inserted into the universe to reconcile and bring it into oneness according to the will of God. We are to co-operate with God's very own uncreated energies of love – his gifts to us – to bring the gift of creation into its fullness:

> So if anyone is in Christ, there is a new creation: everything old has passed away; see, everything has become new! All this is from God, who reconciled us

to himself through Christ, and has given us the ministry of reconciliation; that is, in Christ God was reconciling the world to himself, not counting their trespasses against them, and entrusting the message of the reconciliation to us. So we are ambassadors for Christ, since God is making his appeal through us; we entreat you on behalf of Christ, be reconciled to God.

2 Corinthians 5.17–20

We are to reach the fullness of God through all created activity under the influence of the Spirit of Jesus, the Cosmic Christ. It is by God-in-action, the grace which is God's presence as activating love, that energizes all creatures and brings them into being (Psalm 33.5–90).

In the book of Habakkuk there is a description of God's energies:

> God came from Teman.
> The Holy One from Mount Paran.
> His glory covered the heavens,
> And the earth was full of his praise.
>
> The brightness was like the sun;
> Rays came forth from his hand,
> Where his power lay hidden.

Habakkuk 3.3–4

It is through the power of grace which flows from the essence of the Godhead and yet is distinct from the actual essence of God, that the whole Trinity acts out its loving relationship toward created being. Grace in the biblical sense is God 'going forth from himself'. It is a dynamic, energetic force, never static, but revealing itself in the events of each day; it shines through the whole universe with transforming love as God goes forth to us in uncreated energies of love. It is God at the heart of matter.

The Cosmic Christ is the Spirit of the risen Jesus Christ within all that exists. The activating energies of the Cosmic Christ are constantly working within the whole universe as transforming love calling to us as we seek to find the face of God; by virtue of the Incarnation. If we want to know creation, we must love the Incarnation.

None of the foregoing is new. It is a process theology stemming from the Holy Scriptures to the early Greek Fathers who were deeply imbued with the biblical *hesed* tradition of God's loving kindness for all his creatures. This mystical theology reveals the hidden beauty within the heart of creation, something known to the early Christian mystics of the Eastern Church and brought to the Celtic fringes through the influence of the pseudo-Dionysius, Gregory of Nyssa,

Lord of Creation

Maximus the Confessor, Cassian, Gregory the Great, St Martin of Tours, Ninian, Columba, Patrick, Tírechán and others. They taught us to contemplate God as love in all things and love him through seeking to know him, love him and serve him in this world and in the next. For these mystics, the unknowable God is present within and open to being experienced by the Christian.

Essentially, it is the desire to know God and to love him that matters and the experience of this desire is already a prayer. It is ardent, it is also patient. It grows under the trial of time. One must learn to wait for God in order to love him the more. 'He who with his whole soul, desires God, certainly possesses the One he loves' (St Gregory the Great, *In Evangelia*, 30.1). To describe this present and yet absent God who is deep within our hearts and yet overwhelmingly transcendent – infinite yet always present in creation – we could learn from Brother Lizard culled from the pages of St Gregory's Morals on the Book of Job and found in my bestiary *The Animals of Saint Gregory*:

> Often a man has a fountain of inward liquid but does not drink from it. It's not that he cannot understand, it is just that he won't apply himself to the reading of Holy Writ. He knows that he has the ability to understand by studying, yet he disdains all study of the lessons of truth. He knows that the words of Divine utterance are great, but won't put himself out in order to understand them. On the other hand, another man has a thirst for knowledge and doesn't have the ability; love draws him to meditation, but his dull sense withstands him and he often finds out, through earnestness of love, that Divine Law which the cleverer man remains ignorant of through carelessness. The quick witted learn nothing of God from disdaining Him, while the dull follow after Him with warm affection.
>
> *Moralia 6.12*

Brother Lizard was of the slower sort. He had few apparent gifts; he was not attractive to look at nor was he clever or quick-witted. Everything he did was accomplished with painstaking endeavour. He was the monastery cook and from his kitchen he poured out his love in the service of others. He had a happy heart and his attitude was transmitted in his work, so that the simple fare he served took on the element of a sacrament. Through his work, his love was made visible. In his work, he found the reality of himself, something no one else could know.

It was sacramental because the more sensitive he was to God in prayer, the more aware he was of the encounter with God in creation. He realized the creative power of God through the work of his hands. Through prayer, he sanctified his work and in this way he himself became a sacrament or gesture of God to his brethren in Christ. Lizard's cooking became part of his ritual, his loving awareness of and reverence for Spirit in matter, and in others. 'Let the brethren serve one another . . . for this service brings increase of reward and of charity' (Rule of Saint Benedict).

His loving awareness that all of creation is made sacred by the incarnation of Christ and his reverence for all the materials he handled as signs of God's love, to be used to further that love and so co-create the world in Christ, deepened, the more he encountered Christ in work and prayer.

As any opportunity to give or witness to Love presented itself, Brother Lizard would step forward and serve that need and in so doing would advance slowly towards his Maker. In this way he advanced in the footsteps of Love and the footsteps of God were imprinted upon his heart; they became his way of life. Although he could not see God he tracked Him by His footsteps. This was his prayer, 'I humbly follow after Thee with all my heart and thy right hand is my support' (Psalm 63.8) and:

As a hind longs for the running streams,
So do I long for thee, O God.
With my whole being I thirst for God
The living God.
When shall I come to God and
Appear in his presence?

Psalm 42.1–3

In his thirst, which was the prayer of Lizard, he saw all things in Christ and Christ in all things and these fast became the footsteps whereby Lizard would climb higher and attain the heights of the Palace of the King of Heaven. He did not scorn the practice of the least thing which would aid the understanding of love. He did not have wings like his spiritually gifted Brothers Eagle, Hawk or Heron, nor did he pretend to fly in prayer as Brother Ostrich did, but slowly proceeded by virtue of the few gifts given him.

Brother Lizard knew that he would not reach his perfection as a Lizard, until he had reached the dwelling of the unclouded light. The desire of Brother Lizard's life (and this was already prayer) was for the lights of the City of God.

From a long way off he would contemplate their beauty and that of their and his Creator and although at a distance from his beloved, he possessed the one he loved. 'He who with his whole soul, desires God, certainly already possesses the one he loves' (Saint Gregory, *In Evangelia* 30.1).

One day, he and Brother Eagle decided to seek God in the heights of their souls. Though inspired by him, Brother Lizard was aware that he was not the spiritual athlete Brother Eagle was and so, in his painstaking way, he set off in search of the City of God in the mountain of his heart. He slowly climbed with

Lord of Creation

his hands. 'The Lizard climbs with his hands and is in Kings' palaces' (Prov. 30.28), Solomon had said, and with this inspiration he lifted himself level by level. As he journeyed he remembered the confession of Saint Augustine who looked for God in the image of the earth; and the earth answered, 'I am not He'; all created things on the earth confessed the same. He asked the sea and the deeps and they replied, 'We are not thy God, seek above us'. He asked the air around him and all that moved in it and the inhabitants replied that they were not God either. He asked the heavens, sun, moon, stars – nor, said they, were they the God he sought. He asked the same question of everything that surrounded him and they all replied, 'He made us'. His questioning them was his thoughts on them, and their form of beauty gave the answer, 'Not I made myself but God', and Augustine looked inside himself and asked himself, 'Who are you?' and answered: 'A man, and look how in me there is a soul and body, one outside, the other within. By which of these do I seek God? I have searched for Him in a bodily way from earth to Heaven, so far as I could send messengers by the beams of my eyes. But the better way is the inner, for all the messengers of the body reported to it the answers of heaven and earth and all that dwelt therein who said we are not God, but he made us' (*Confessions of Saint Augustine*).

Brother Lizard moved away from these images for they were obstacles to the Pure Being who cannot be known by human intelligence, when it is surrounded and assailed by images or concepts; and while ascending out of himself he was able to look below at the bodily images which had filled his heart in prayer. The more he ascended towards God, the deeper into his being he went; without the intermediary of images he scaled the mountain towards God.

Higher and higher he went. He could not see the Eagle below. The Eagle had sat in a bush because he knew that he could fly into the Light in an instant and so did not have to exert himself too early in the day. The noon-day sun came and he slept, although he lulled himself into a feeling of well-being by thinking that he was inwardly awake. Afternoon came and still Brother Eagle postponed flight. Although Eagle's tendency was towards the light and he had the gifts to reach the eternal, yet he was blinded by his negligence which turned him in towards himself and not outwards towards God.

Meanwhile, slow, dull Lizard had reached the walls of the Eternal Kingdom and was lifted by Love into the knowledge of the Light; but his soul was dazzled by so much light, and he could not take it all in. It was consuming him, and he fell back, weakened by the light and weighed down by his sins. He crept back down the mountain of his soul and rejoined his brothers with an even deeper humility than before.

The Animals of St Gregory[3]

The apophatic experience depicted here is on the understanding that we cannot say an awful lot about God because for although he is immanent he is at the same time transcendent. If we could understand God he would cease to be God. His overwhelming transcendence brings darkness to our reasoning. We know more about what God is not than about what he is (read Job 28.1–28). This is the experience of Br Lizard in the story. Presence and transcendence are in apophatic theology. We best understand by faith, albeit experienced in darkness. Lizard learned that God as he is in himself is blinding to the mind and is experienced as dazzlement – he simply could not take it all in. Lizard found that the closer we are to union with God, the more blinding God becomes. We cannot know God rationally, only by way of intuition and inner vision. Therefore we withdraw to be quiet, detached and silent in contemplative prayer. The grace that we receive through interior prayer or the uncreated energy of God is deposited and stored up, as it were, to be used as fuel for growth in prayer which is a growth in awareness of God, especially as he lives and acts through his infinite love within us.

The Celtic saints were aware of this God who through his uncreated energies within them and the whole of creation is eternally immanent in Spirit and yet, this Holy Spirit, the Cosmic Christ, transcends the whole universe of created matter toward the ultimate and eternal perfection of the universe, because it is immanent in the whole of it. This is deeply biblical in its inspiration following the teaching of the Divine Word, which is continuously in the act of creating the universe and who takes on matter in the human form of Jesus the Christ, who in his risen, life-giving spirit as the Cosmic Christ gives life to humankind which is his extended body, the mystical body of Christ.

God pursues us, his people, as he stretches out his 'two hands – Jesus Christ and the Holy Spirit', as St Irenaeus said in the second century. The incarnational activity of Jesus Christ in the cosmos is known as the Logos of God in each event, in each creature. It is the principle of harmony that shows us the relationship of a given creature to God's total order of salvation.

The Logos of God according to Maximus the Confessor is the universal key to understanding, as well as the key to understanding the universe. The Celt was able to contemplate the Logos working within creation to bring it to spiritual fulfilment within the divine mind. For the contemplative person, their experience was to receive the Spirit of the risen Jesus, the Cosmic Christ and to experience all being as co-existing according to the eternal mind of God.

Celtic Christianity is an embodied spirituality as can be understood in the lives of the saints and the writing of the scribes. It has a tremendous sense of place, hospitality and the extended family, the Celtic Christian community. As noted before, it has a deep and abiding sense of the immanent presence and power of God, as well as of God as transcendent Being.

Lord of Creation

What can this spirituality, which can only really be seen as 'Celtic' because it was practised by the Celtic peoples, give us today?

We live in a society that has largely lost touch with the environment and which is searching for a spirituality relating it to creation; a society that rarely attends Church, if at all, and when a community does that, then it loses its sense of religion which is the link between the heavenly and the earthly; a society that has little hospitality and no table liturgy because families rarely sit down at table together, not even on a Sunday; a society that does not say grace before meals, or pray at any moment during the day as our Celtic Christian forefathers did. We sometimes say 'weren't they lucky to have that way of life'. No, they were not lucky, they learned their faith on their mothers' knees and in the fields or at sea or in the workshop of their fathers. Today, they would be lucky to receive any Christian education at school! People are searching for roots in family life, the country and the environment. They seek a theology of work and prayer in their search for the One Thing Necessary, the Lord of Creation.

Here is to be found an attempt to help bring about an embodied spirituality through lessons and meditations on how to pray using the whole person. A series of exercises are given to enable both teacher and pupil to experience through the heart and body a contemplative awareness of the indwelling God at the heart of matter. The end result aims to be both a cosmological and mystical means for transformation.

The Welsh have a saying: *Telyneg yw Duw nid traethawd*, that is 'God is a lyrical poem, not an essay', the realization of which is a blessing!

Brendan O'Malley
Lampeter 2004

Divine
Light

O God, you who made
the SUN, are the SUN
of my SOUL and I LOVE
your RADIANCE.
I LOVE you, O LIGHT eternal;
grant that I may see you
in the BRIGHTNESS of YOUR GLORY.

DIVINE LIGHT, proceeding from
the splendour of the TRINITY
flood my HEART with your LOVE,
my MIND and my SOUL and
every PART of me,
till I shall be ILLUMINED and one with
the LIGHT OF CHRIST within me.

BRENDANUS SCOTUS

How to Use this Book

I have always found it easier to teach people how to pray by showing them how to experience the presence of God through the heart, which means through the body, grounded and in tune with the uncreated energy of God. This is not 'airy-fairy' nonsense, but a practical means for recovering an almost lost experience of the incarnate God who lives and moves and breathes in us wherever we encounter this in people, the Holy Scriptures or in creation.

When the reader in the early Church or in the medieval monastery read the Scriptures he read them aloud and in a low tone, so that the sentence was not only seen by the eyes but heard by the ears. The result was a 'muscular memory of the words pronounced and an aural memory of the words heard', as I was taught as a young monk by the great Benedictine Jean Leclercq. It is relatively easy to teach young people to meditate through teaching them how to 'breathe' their prayer, use their imagination in the early stages or do sitting, walking or dance meditation. All of this is holistic and deeply biblical in its provenance.

In modern times we have separated ourselves from the natural world around us and treated it as an object and not as a fellow creature. God has been seen as transcendent, 'up there', as against immanent and shining through all created matter. God, through grace, goes out of himself in his uncreated energies sharing his love and life with us. He is within us and above us, 'Your body, you know, is the temple of the Holy Spirit' (1 Corinthians 6.19). Jesus, the Christ, found his Father in nature all around him as well as within the temple of his body.

This resource is for use individually and/or in groups. It may be used by a retreat or workshop leader to enable people to get in touch with their inner life and therefore in touch with Christ in whose image and likeness they are created. Here we experience God's life working within the human context of our every-day life and enabling us to find the place of reconciliation between matter and spirit; the human heart: 'for anyone who is in Christ, there is a new creation; the old creation is gone, and now the new one is here. It is all God's work of handing on their reconciliation' (2 Corinthians 5.17). It is essentially a book written to being people to an experience of 'oneness' in body, mind and spirit, as taught and sought after in the Celtic spiritual tradition.

Í am but a little child,
yet my man he shall be laid
on the LORD of the
world.
the king of the elements himself
shall REST upon my heart
and i will give him peace.

ST BRIGID

Praying with the Whole Person

It is useful to meditate on the following quotation from Anthony Bloom describing the statue *The Thinker* by Rodin: 'It is clear that this man does not think only with his brain. He thinks with his whole being, his whole body is concentrated in thought; he thinks with all his muscles, with all his members, even with the position of his body. This is man transformed into the incarnation of thought.'

We need to express ourselves in body language in order to feel free. For example, to free the self-expression of a child is to give the child a language, which goes beyond what he or she has understood intellectually. When a child spontaneously carries a plan into effect, something happens, something changes in the child. Undeveloped areas in their being are developed.

We must emphasize the importance of genuine, spontaneous expressive movement – something not unreflecting or unforeseen. Whatever form it may take, it frees us from conformity so that we may be open to something different; to become and then to be, to exist – in the full sense of the word. It is quite true that I can pray anywhere, playing, walking or working, or in the car when saying the Jesus Prayer or praying the Jesus Breath. I can pray in the middle of a crowd or when in the company of another who is, frankly, boring me. There is nothing to stop me. No one knows what is going on inside me. No one knows that I am praying.

But I can also, to make a prayer, a real prayer, put my body into a beautiful attitude and make a beautiful movement. I can use my hands, my arms and legs, my whole body. Without saying a word, I can return to God quite a lot. I take up a beautiful position, a position in which I feel comfortable.

I can stay still, but not stiff.
I breathe deeply.
I am quiet, at ease.
I shut my eyes.

At this moment only one thing matters to me:

God is in me.
I do not see him,
but he is present.

I attend to his presence.
I am in control of my body,
I am in control of my mind;
I am, all of me, present to God.

Slowly, I make a movement
with my hands, with my arms.
I look at my hands carefully.

These hands of mine are speaking,
speaking to God.
They are lifted to him,
in the shape of a cup,
to receive what he says
opened wide,
they offer themselves:
they give themselves.

Here I am, Lord,
standing before you,
with my hand high, like a tree,
stretching out towards the sky.

You fill me with wonder.
I love you.
I am proud to be your child.

The human body is a rhythmic phenomenon within the dance of creation; whether resting, walking, standing, sitting, kneeling or dancing it is a vital part of the cosmic dance, the whole created order of things which tumble forth from the hand of our Creator God.

We are conditioned to believe that prayer is an intellectual, mind, emotional happening which needs expression only in words. In the Western tradition it has been located in the psyche or seen as a form of telepathic brain activity. The Eastern Christian tradition sometimes expresses it as 'standing before God with the mind in the heart'. Remember the song 'These boots are made for walking, and that is what they do'? Well, the body is made for prayer and that is what it does! The human body is a temple of the Holy Spirit (1 Corinthians 6.19–20) and made for the glory of God. Through our faces and bodies we express our moods and feelings in word and song.

The body has its own language, for example, one small gesture, such as making the sign of the cross, is a beautiful thing, which says more than volumes of words. Physical movement can express spiritual intentions whether it be the sign of the cross or bowing, genuflecting, walking, prostrating or dancing. The body in this manner becomes an animated, living sacrament, effecting what it symbolizes, for example, bowing the head rhythmically as the supplicant breathes the Jesus Prayer: 'Lord Jesus Christ, Son of God, have mercy on me, a sinner.' Prayer needs our bodies that we may become vehicles of grace and act out the intention of our hearts.

In the liturgy we give shape to the prayer of the community when Christ stands in our midst. It is important to remember that at the heart of the whole Christian gospel is the doctrine that 'the Word became flesh and dwelt among us'. At the centre of all Christian prayer is the essential truth that the whole human person, spirit, mind and body has been saved, made whole and healed. Through our bodies we express our prayer and through corporal works of mercy, that is sharing and caring for others: 'By their fruits you shall know them' (Matthew 7.20).

Unfortunately the language of people's bodies in the Church is not always a helpful expression of the community at prayer. Some kneel with eyes closed and head buried in their hands or pew. Others sit or stand at will. Some make the sign of the cross while others won't, either through shyness or because they do not want to be thought physical and 'catholic'. Why do we not use them better? On a typical Sunday in church all we need is a head, a mouth, a bottom and our feet. The legs, arms, torso and hands never get a look in except to help a hand reach to a hymn book!

The first Christians prayed with arms outstretched in the form of the cross. Tertullian (AD 200) wrote:

We Christians pray with eyes raised to heaven and hands outstretched because we are innocent, bareheaded, because we have no need to blush . . . We are not satisfied to raise our hands as the pagans do, but we stretch them out in the remembrance of our Lord's passion . . . We do not lift up our hands ostentatiously (like the pagans), but modestly and with moderation.

At the celebration of the Eucharist the president prays standing with outstretched arms much in the manner of these early Christians as depicted in icons and paintings entitled *orans*. Today, in the liturgy, we often stand during the Eucharistic Prayer and at the gospel and Nicene creed. Irenaeus (AD 150) explains why: 'On Sunday we remain standing as if to show that Christ has raised us again, and that by his grace he has delivered us from sin and death.' Standing at prayer we are in solidarity with the risen Christ, ourselves in a risen state, free and joyful, confident and happy. Standing is the opposite position to that of kneeling. It is also a sign of respect which is why we stand at the gospel and the creed.

Another sign of respect is the 'bow'. The most solemn form of bow is a deep or profound bow from the waist. The simplest form is an inclination from the head forward and down. The solemn bow is still used in some monastic orders rather than a genuflection, which is to go down on one knee. It is interesting to note that this form of body-prayer-language is also seen in the courtroom life when officials nod or bow to the judge or magistrate when they pass in front of them, a derivation of the courtesy or bow upon being introduced to royalty. We should bow at the words in the creed where mention is made of the Incarnation of Our Lord Jesus Christ, and at the words of the institution, in the Eucharistic Prayer: 'This is my Body' and 'This is my Blood'.

Standing to pray is a very ancient custom pre-dating Christianity. It was customary in all the main religions as it was in the Jewish faith. Jews and pagans both knelt for prayer as well, but Christians seldom did, except as an act of supplication or penance. The knowledge that we rise with Christ is the main reason for our standing at prayer. To stand before God with the mind in the heart is still practised in the liturgy of the Eastern Orthodox Church. Indeed, the elderly are the only people who sit on the few benches or seats available during a long two-to three-hour liturgy. To stand before God is a sign of respect still retained in the Western Church during the gospel and creed. It is also an acknowledgement of our dignity as a son or daughter of God rather than an unworthy sinner with buried head in penitence.

We stand at the celebration of the Holy Eucharist during the following parts:

1 From the beginning of the Eucharist to the end of the collect
2 For the gospel
3 For the creed
4 From the sign of peace until the invitation to communion

Sitting is commended for:

1 The readings (except the gospel)
2 The sermon
3 The intercessions/bidding prayer (some prefer to kneel)
4 The offertory
5 After communion for a period of silent prayer

Some people prefer to kneel during the intercessory prayers. We may kneel during the distribution of Holy Communion and after receiving it for a silent prayer. Note that we may kneel or stand while receiving Holy Communion according to local custom.

In the early Church Christians gave the sign of peace (1 Peter 5.14) as a sign of friendship, bonding and forgiveness. Nowadays we show mutual forgiveness and charity by a light hand clasp. It is very important to note that the peace we are passing on is the peace of Christ. Therefore when 'passing the peace' or 'pax' as it was called in ancient times, it may be advisable to say 'The peace of Christ' to whomever we may be giving it.

Christians have made the sign of the cross since the second century. Before giving up their lives the early martyrs crossed themselves. The fingers make the sign by drawing a cross from the forehead to chest, and from the left shoulder to the right. When blessing oneself with holy water or when blessed water is sprinkled over the head, we may cross ourselves, renewing our baptismal promises interiorly: as the water is sprinkled over us, washing, cleansing, flowing over us as a sign of forgiveness and the overflowing love of God.

Many Christians make the sign of the cross at the beginning of the proclamation of the gospel. It is generally done in a slightly different manner from the usual way: the sign is made with the thumb of the right hand. A small cross is made on the forehead, and then lightly on the lips, before tracing the cross on the chest at heart level. We are to hear the gospel and understand it in our minds, proclaim it with our lips and believe it in our hearts. In other words we are to embody and practise it with the whole of our lives; for we are redeemed in mind, spirit and body.

Praying with the whole person is good for you. In our age, where there is adoration of eternal youth, good health has become a priority. Eat this and drink that and you will have long life. Keep fit and use this special method above all, fight against pollution, the great enemy of health. There is some truth in all this advice, but it is not enough. Good health is not just a matter of the air we breathe or the food we eat. It is a matter of the ideas we have, of the thoughts that simmer in our heads, of our taste for life.

Again, why are so many people suffering from stress, depression and neurosis? Is it because of violence on TV? Pressure of the modern work-place? Public transport and the strain of commuting? The seduction of shopping? Yes, certainly, but that is not the whole story. People are miserable because they do not know why they are here on earth. They have lost the sense and meaning of life. What can help them?

Why not the practice of prayer? Prayer is centred on the source of life, or rather, it proceeds from the Source of life. Prayer is an essential secret which enables me to live life to the full. It says: 'You are loved madly by God. He offers you happiness that will last for ever.' Prayer is divine osteopathy which clicks me into place. It clears my head and enables me to see things as they are. It is the one thing that matters and shows me what really matters. Yes, prayer is healthy. It is life itself. Read the Gospels. Observe Jesus for he, the son of God, used to pray. The air that you breathe is God. You are breathing God in and out. Become aware of that; and stay with that awareness. Prayer is the breathing of the breath of life. It is the strongest spiritual element in all the world.

There is a Christian meditation movement under way which realizes that one can pray, not only with the mind or intellect but also with the breath of the body. Christian mysticism is once again being studied and harnessed to a renewal of desert and Celtic spirituality which is much needed in the new millennium.

The use of the breath, as found in Eastern meditation, centres the activity of prayer deep within the body. Faith makes the prayer of the breath a religious experience. Faith is the experience of the Divine . . . and so breath-prayer, breathing, becomes an exercise of faith.

Breathing Exercise

Take 3 deep breaths
Take 3 light breaths
Take 3 short breaths
Take 3 heavy breaths
Take 3 refined breaths
Take 3 breaths for light
Take 3 breaths for love
Take 3 breaths for peace

Mother Breath Exercise

Inhale to the count of seven – hold for the count of one.
Exhale to the count of seven – hold for the count of one.

INTRODUCTORY MEDITATION

Thanksgiving for our embodiment and an experience of the pulsation of life

The response to this meditation is a silent receptivity in our heart to the emptiness and stillness within our body and within space. Appropriate music may be played.

Breathing down into our belly, the centre of our body . . .
Our heartbeat resonating with the rhythm of the earth,
inhaling and exhaling together the one breath of the universe. (*pause*)

We're going now on a journey through our body, starting with our feet . . . on the in-breath . . .

travelling up through the calves of the legs . . . thighs . . . pelvis . . . ribcage . . . chest . . . arms and hands . . . throat and neck . . . face and head, feeling our head as a physical part of us . . .

giving thanks for those humble parts of ourselves . . . our muscles . . . our bones . . . and our blood.

Being aware of the rhythms of nature within us:
The cycles of rest and activity – of illness and health, of growth from birth, through youth, maternity, old age . . . and death.

Being aware of those twins, pain and pleasure, that are an intrinsic part of our physical nature.

Feeling the suffering and sacrifice that we all face in our lives.
Letting go of thoughts, desires and images . . . coming to a still place inside.

Being with Being
And in the void of space within,
The womb of becoming at the centre of our being,
Opening ourselves to the nothingness out of which everything comes.
In the abundant space within feeling.

The power of the Creating Spirit out into the world in deep rivers of creativity . . . of passion . . . of healing . . . and of justice making . . . with our fellow human beings, and with the earth.

BASIC MEDITATION EXERCISE

Intention

The intention of the exercise is to discover and relate to the still centre within, that is the heart. It may therefore be described as Christ-centred.

Steps to take

The body

The first step concerns the physical body. Our aim is to find a position, which combines relaxation and alertness. For most people this means sitting in a straight-backed chair. The head should be held erect, the hands clasped loosely in the lap or placed palms upwards or flat against the thighs, and the feet firmly on the floor. This position may be modified according to individual needs. What is important is that as far as possible the position of the body should express the intention of the meditator. The physical form so becomes an outward sign of an inner state of being that is of relaxed alertness.

The breath

The body is now in position and we are ready to follow a process of relaxation. It is helpful to relate this to breathing. This is done systematically. Begin with the head and on the out-breath relax the scalp and facial muscles. Do the same with the shoulders, chest, stomach and abdomen, arms, waist, thighs, legs and feet. Finally breathe out several times as though through all the pores of the body, consciously relaxing the whole physical frame. If you become aware of the tightening up of any muscles, return to that part and consciously relax. Take this slowly.

Observation

With the mind's eye now observe your body – relaxed yet alert. Reverence your body, that is, accept it as a unique, God-given vehicle of the real you.

Lord of Creation

The emotions

Allow yourself to become aware of your emotions. They too constitute a body. Unlike the physical body they are not confined in one limited space. They are immensely 'busy' in many areas. However they also directly interfere with the physical body, expressing themselves in 'blocks', for example, muscle tension, pains, etc. at the attempt to relax. Allow yourself to become aware of any areas of emotional tension. Do not try to deal with or repress them. Recognize them: observe, acknowledge and let them go. As with the physical body, the process of stepping back from emotional tension may be related to the breathing, so on each out-breath we let go of the pressures and tensions. For example, one may use the image of smoke rising from the body and being dispersed.

The intellect

The uncontrolled activity of the intellect blocks off true awareness. As with the emotions, so with the intellect, we need to distance ourselves, to step back from the incessant chatter of the brain. To 'try' to do this can be self-defeating. Allow the mind gradually to quieten down. Gently allow it to relate to one thing. So gradually bring the attention to the centre of the chest and allow it to focus there. This can be problematic though, because this area, especially the solar plexus, is often blocked by emotions. To centre the mind it helps to count the breaths, always up to ten and then start again. Be careful not to force the breathing when doing it.

The still centre

We are now identifying the heart of our being. This is the still centre, the place of 'perfect clear perception'.

Refocusing

If and when the attention wanders, as you become aware of this, gently return to the focal point and centre again (the use of a mantra is invaluable). Remember it is the 'intention' that matters. Each return to the centre reinforces this.

Visualization

The concept of the light of Christ or the Christ light, is basic. This light has the qualities both of peace and love. It is that described in the New Testament as the light of the world.

Use of a mantra

To centre, still, and fix the attention, we may use what is called a mantra. A mantra is a word or short phrase, which is said slowly over and over again. The mantra is very important in this form of meditation because its function goes beyond the mere saying of the word, or phrase. The mantra centres the mind and as it were comes to sound in the heart so that one comes almost to feel the mantra at the centre of one's being, releasing its rich associations and meaning within us. Many people praying meditatively use as their mantra the Jesus Prayer: 'Lord Jesus Christ Son of God, have mercy on me.'

This Jesus Prayer is nothing less than a capsule summary of the whole of Christian doctrine. In using it as a mantra one enters into, and opens oneself to, the whole redeeming word of Christ. Every word of the Jesus Prayer is heavy with meaning, every word gives the richest of associations to those who know their Bible. One can use as a mantra a single word such as 'Love', 'Jesus' or *'maranatha'* ('Lord Jesus Christ come!'). Choose one mantra, preferably the Jesus Prayer, and stick to it, alone. One will find that in slowly and continuously repeating it one is taken to a deeper level of consciousness, where one becomes aware of God's presence within, and oneself in God's presence. Dame Julian of Norwich describes the experience in this way:

> God is nearer to us than our own soul; for he is the ground in whom the soul standeth, and he is the mean that keepeth the substance and the sense-nature together so that they shall never dispart. For our soul sitteth in God, in very rest and our soul is kindly rooted in God in endless love.

Meditation is about being with God at a level of experience beyond words. We are what we do with our silence.

Three points to remember

1 Through our baptism, the light of Christ is always present within the heart.
2 Centred in this Holy Light, you are always in complete control.

3 Decide beforehand how long your meditation is to be, and keep to the period you have decided. One should try and aim at at least one fifteen-minute period every day (building it up gradually from five to avoid 'failure').

Perseverance is needed

Because meditation is so simple many people deceive themselves into thinking that they cannot be doing it right, and so they abandon the practice. But meditation requires perseverance, and one will soon come to realize that life would be impoverished without it. Another trap may be to expect 'something' to happen during meditation, for example spiritual experiences/visions, etc. This is not usually the case, neither should it be mistaken for the aim of the exercise.

THE BREATH

In the oriental tradition, this breath is not just the air that fills my lungs giving energy to my little body. Rather is it the breath of the universe.

> Through breathing I arrive at a harmony with the vibrating cosmos. Similar to this in the Western tradition is the breath or the wind or the 'spiratio', which speaks of the Holy Spirit breathing in me, uniting me to all people and to all creation and to the Father. This, in the New Testament, is the 'Spirit of Jesus'.
>
> *William Johnston,* Silent Music

Aspirare – to breathe, to aspire, that is to reach towards a goal
Suspirare – to draw a breath, to suspire, to sigh and long for
Anhelare – to draw breath with difficulty, to pant for
Inspirare – to blow or breathe upon, to inspire or be inspired

All the above Latin terms are expressions of desire, sublimation, prayer and deep capacity for God. These examples of the exercise of the breath and being conscious of the Spirit through the use of the breath are but a small example of the abundant possibilities of how meditation exercises can facilitate an experience of the transcendent through breathing.

> The holy time is quiet as a nun, breathless with adoration.
>
> *William Wordsworth*

Deep in the silence of the adoring heart is a sense of the breathless. We simply hear the breathing of the heart as a metronome keeping time.

When beginning meditation it is recommended that we keep the back straight. We take a deep breath and hold it for a moment before exhaling. It is a good practice to count up to ten on the inhalation, then breathe out for the count of ten and to carry on for some time concentrating on the breath. This has the effect of quieting the imagination as well as the superficial layers of the mind so that we may concentrate at a deeper level of unconscious life. With thoughts and images out of the way we are able to be aware only of the breath at the level of our deepest self. In the Bible, the breath is known as the centre of our being; it is precisely when breath enters into matter that human becomes human being.

What we are breathing is the breath of the cosmos. We are, through the breath, relating to the to-and-fro of the cosmos and in harmony with what the Celts call 'the music of what happens'. We dance with the Spirit, who is *spiratio* and fills the universe, who is God's inner active presence, constantly shaping the body of Christ.

Now this is not pantheism or 'New Age', it is perfectly Christian. It was our Lord Jesus Christ who 'breathed' on his apostles and said: 'Receive the Holy Spirit . . .' Hence also the wind that shook the buildings immediately before the descent of the Holy Spirit upon the apostles. So when we pray the prayer-of-the-breath we are conscious of the presence of the Spirit.

pRAYER is the RespiRAtion of the soul.

God is Breath,
For the breath of the wind is shared by all,
Goes Everywhere, nothing shuts it in,
Nothing holds it prisoner

Maximus the Confessor

A good exercise is to pray down into the heart, on inhalation to name 'Jesus' and on the out-breath the word 'Christ'. If you can do it, breathe in 'light' and out 'light' at the same time. We breathe in Jesus the light of the world and we breathe him out. It all depends on the ability to 'con-centre', to concentrate on each breath. Sense the breath and the light and let each inspiration reach into the deepest, most spiritual, still centre of your being, the I AM. If you do it well your heart will expand with love and you will radiate that love on the out-breath.

By relaxing into this experience of love, then, with each breath, you will develop a healing presence.

Thou mastering me
God! Giver of breath and bread;
World's strand, sway of the sea;
Lord of living and dead.

Gerard Manley Hopkins

We also know of the wind as a destroyer, not only as a life-giver, for example the desert wind, which is responsible for heat and drought, the hot air, which is called poisonous in Israel, and the desert wind clouding the atmosphere, full of fine particles of sand.

There is a deep relationship, too, between wind and breath, which are often called the same; the wind as breath (of man), and breath of God, *pneuma* of God, which combines with the spirit and the fire. The breath of God is the breath of life, the *ruah* (Hebrew) and *spiritus* (Latin) meaning spirit (in female form). The breath can be seen as a 'puff' of wind. It can be used to indicate power and energy as well as spirituality. It can also be the great breath of the universe guiding and controlling the life-principle. In the Indian tradition this is known as *atman* or *prana*.

In many religions and philosophies the breath is given various interpretations. Breath is not only a mechanical-technical process, it is indicative of very early concepts relating to the life of the spirit. Even *anima* and *animus* are related to *anémos* meaning 'breath' and 'wind'.

According to the Old Testament (Genesis 1.2), God aroused to life the man he created by his breath, which symbolizes the Spirit of creation. He is indeed the king of the elements. Let us pursue the multiple meanings in our everyday speech:

- 'To be short of breath' – to have little endurance, not to let go sufficiently
- 'to take a long/deep breath' – to fulfil something, to persist, unshakeable, tough, long-lived
- 'I panted, ran breathless' – fright, fear, death
- 'to allow a pause for breath' (which literally cannot happen) – however points to an excessive hectic breathing and a one-sided life, work, harshness
- 'up to the last drawing of breath' – life and death are connected with breath

Breath Therapy

When you sit, keep your body as erect as possible (like a puppet on a string): and become aware of your breathing.

As you breathe out, relax the muscles, beginning with the head: breathing away the tensions . . .

Relaxing the scalp and the sides of the face . . . and the jaw line where so much tension gathers.

Breathe away the tensions of the shoulders . . . dropping the shoulders and the arms . . . and the hands . . . and the fingers . . . letting them completely relax.

Relax the chest muscles . . . the waist . . . and the thighs . . . and the legs, breathing away the tensions.

Now, as you breathe out . . . breathe out as though you are breathing through the pores of your body . . .

Completely alert and in control . . . at the same time, as much as possible, relaxed.

For a few moments breathe out through all the pores of the body.

Silence.

As this exercise indicates, one's total mental and physical energy is mobilized. This, of course, involves posture, breathing, one's energy, and all the activity of the mind, as well as a great faith and courage that reaches to the deepest recesses of the heart. Thus you mobilize posture, breath, energy – the body becomes an eye. The mind and body are composed, the whole self is unified and concentred. Then you begin to say inwardly your word, for example *maranatha* or your sentence, 'Lord Jesus Christ, Son of God, have mercy on me a sinner' . . . with the mind in the heart.

SITTING MEDITATION

Many sat at the Lord's feet
And listened to what he was saying.

Luke 10.39

Proper sitting is a wonderful way to practise meditation. Learning prayer through the body is a fundamental of true contemplation. It is a way that proceeds from the body to the mind.

We begin by sitting in a correct sitting position. Sit on the edge of a stable chair or bench, feet flat on the ground about shoulder-width apart. The knees should ideally be positioned slightly (really only a little) lower than the hips to help relaxation of this area. Keep your whole spine upright and as much in one straight line as possible, imagining its beginning to be at the top of your head rather than the top of your neck. Do not bend forwards or backwards, especially not in the region of your neck and lower back. To keep your neck straight you may have to tuck in your chin *very* slightly. It can be helpful to imagine that you are a marionette hanging by a thread from the top of your head, suspended upright, but relaxed all around that thread which forms a straight line through your spine. You can place your hands loosely on your thighs either facing up or down or find any other position that will not make your shoulders tense up. While you are arranging your body posture (it also helps to really DO some arranging, moving around ever so slightly to find that correct position!) also start to regulate your breathing which in turn will help to begin composing your mind. Again, this is a method of prayer using the 'whole body'. It is rather simple, though it may require some patient practice at the beginning. The secret is to devote all your strength to *doing* it. You will see that sitting with a *straight spine*, corrects not only your physical posture but also your entire 'body', that is your whole person. It is a strange person whose mind is not composed by straightening of his/her body. When you sit properly your mind becomes orderly; if you arrange the body in an upright, balanced manner, you are able to relax without 'slouching' and that in turn makes it possible to relax the mind while remaining alert/focused. Conversely, when you sit in a slouch your mind slouches, too.

The same thing can be said in regard to breathing. To regulate your breath is to compose your mind. If you breathe slowly and deeply from the abdomen, your mind becomes relaxed and tranquil. If you use a method to compose your mind, it also becomes unified and concentrated.

Standing Meditation

Happy are your people! Happy are these your servants,
who stand before you and hear your wisdom!

2 Chronicles 7

The standing position is perhaps less known as a body prayer position. You can wear light shoes for this, but ideally only socks or bare feet provided it is warm enough where you do your meditation.

Place your feet, shoulder-width apart, flat and firm on level ground. As in the sitting mediation the idea is to achieve an upright, straight and balanced posture. It can help to imagine that you are standing in water, gently supported, but not stiff or, again, that you are a puppet on a thread, suspended by the top of your head with the thread going all the way through your spine and pulled straight down by gravity. Very slightly move back and forward and/or sideways on your feet until you feel your weight equally balanced between them. To straighten out your spine along the imaginary thread you have to tuck in your chin a *little* and drop your tailbone, to get rid of the 'kinks' in the neck and the lower back. This may not be easy at first and feel very strange, even 'wrong', because most of the time our posture is not balanced or straight at all, we do not register it (or better, we register this bad posture as correct, upright, etc.). While remembering the feeling of being suspended from the top of your head, *very slightly* bend your knees to ease the dropping of your tailbone. It is a movement similar to the very first stage of sitting down on a stool behind and directly below you, but really only the very first bit! Around the imaginary axis of the thread you can now also swing left and right, as if someone was twirling the thread. Let your arms swing along gently and try to loosen the big muscles in your thighs, as well as all other muscles. Decrease the motion until you have a balanced, relatively comfortable posture. Since your knees are bent your weight will be above the balls of your feet rather than in their centre. At all times make sure you don't slump your shoulders forward or pull them backwards: Your whole posture should be upright and straight without being forced or stiff. Your arms should be hanging loose to start with but ever so slightly away from the body, give some space between their inside and your body. Later on they may float further out on their own accord, which is a good thing. This whole posture is not easy at first and relaxing your muscles in it may be a tricky task to fulfil as well, for example your thighs have to build up some strength perhaps. So do not start out thinking you can meditate like this for 20 minutes – five minutes is enough to begin with. Then begin to breathe your prayer . . .

It is important to note that five minutes of this exercise can be a long time to begin with, that is, five minutes from the point when you have found your standing position and are actually standing still rather than adjusting your posture. Once you have found your posture, methodically relax your body by breathing away the tensions at the scalp (cf. Basic Meditation Exercise page 26). Work your way down the body to the feet. If a particular area is especially difficult or has started to ache, it is helpful to spend some time breathing into it. For example, the neck and shoulders are often a problem, because here we tend to hold all the everyday tensions. On your in-breath breathe into the neck/shoulder/muscle/joint, and on the out-breath think 'relax', let the tension flow out with your breath.

At all times during your body prayer do not feel that you have to stiffen your posture, rather make very small movements to ease and loosen areas that begin to tense up!

WALKING MEDITATION

Surely the Lord your God has blessed
You in all your ways; he knows
your walking through this great wilderness

Deuteronomy 2.7

Tolkien said that 'Not all who wander are lost'. Too often we walk and see nothing because we are mentally distracted and are oblivious to our surroundings. Many people use the gym or engage in aerobics or other forms of workout without caring for their psyche or their spiritual well-being.

To walk meditatively is to enjoy the environment through its colour, texture, sound, design and apparent beauty as well as through its inner sound, silent music and immediate presence.

My Beloved is the mountains, the solitary wooded valleys, strange
islands . . . silent music.

St John of the Cross

We relax as we stroll and concentrate on the present as we walk, simply held in the consciousness of the unity of all being, held in the intense silence at the centre of an obscure sense of presence.

Apart from this way of walking being a beneficial holistic activity it is also a method for centring, for depth, for becoming one with the Other towards whom we journey inwardly as well as outwardly. Walking meditation opens up deeper layers of consciousness which brings into play the more subtle and mystical areas of our being. The result is a greater sense of interior unity.

Scientists encourage relaxed walking as a beneficial holistic activity. A team of psychologists at the University of Illinois have found that a gentle walk, three times a week, prevents memory loss and boosts performance in the parts of the brain that usually waste away most quickly as a result of ageing. The study showed how subjects who walked between 15 and 60 minutes, three days a week, scored much more highly in tests of mental aptitude than another group who did stretching and toning to stay in shape. Aerobic exercise such as walking is known to increase the supply of oxygen to the brain, a process that slows down as we age, and helps it work more efficiently. According to the Illinois researchers the walkers fared significantly better at tasks controlled by the frontal and prefrontal cortex, the parts of the brain that are responsible for planning, inhibition and short-term memory. Another study at Indiana University revealed that for people suffering from mild to moderate emotional problems, walking can form an efficient part of treatment; even resulting in improvements comparable with those gained from standard psychotherapy.

A medieval English mystic once described meditation as a 'oneing exercise' because it makes us whole. Walking meditation has the effect of bringing the many layers of a human being into an integrated whole. It also makes thin the canvas of creation where he may as George Herbert wrote:

> Look on glass' and' on it may stay his eye; or, if he pleaseth, through it pass, and then the heaven espy.

Walking prayer reminds the pilgrim that he is treading on holy ground, perhaps at first being only dimly aware of the immanent presence of the Lord of creation – the divine life present within and then shining through 'like shook foil', a diaphanous experience. This life is welling up within us, in the innermost recesses of our heart, as we become open to the presence of God not only within ourselves but perceived and sensed in the unfolding of creation. It is 'thin' as the Celts know, the divine veil between human being, creation, and the Lord of creation, the God of Being, who shines through and who is present in the essence of matter and spirit. He is our ceaseless call and longing. He is the sounding wave, the voice of the sea . . .

> It swims with the seal in his laughter.
> The sacrament of being you share with me!
>
> *Ray Howard Jones*

To enter beyond this 'thin veil' is to enter into a felt experience of the kingdom of God, both created and uncreated. It is to go beyond time and space. As we experience the drawing of the veil, subject–object distinction disappears. God is within us and the whole of God's creation is in God; the whole creation is in us too. He is the pulsing life of all, the ceaseless call and longing, the unquenchable thirst, the One Thing Who Matters.

This is about an experience where there is only the divine Now. To be experienced, God must be present to us. His presence is a loving presence. He is the fullness of our desire and is ultimately what we seek in life, therefore he must be experienced as a real presence by his loving action within us.

Lord of Creation

Prayer is a state of being, it is not what we 'do' before God, it is a state of existence rather than action. But when we walk-before-God in meditation we become conscious of the presence of the transcendent holiness of God through the Cosmic Christ, the 'I AM', present within all creation. Aware of our own poverty and emptiness, we surrender ourselves to love, returning gift-for-gift-received, seeking to serve a loving God. We realize that our body is not a body but the temple of the living God. Contemplation is to 'con-temple'. The word 'spirit' refers to the breath and when we breathe our Jesus Prayer, for example, in rhythmic unison with the movement of our body we walk into wholeness, healing and holiness.

A walking meditation

All you have to do is look straight and see the road, and when you see it, don't sit looking at it – walk.

Ayn Rand

It has been said before that although most people consider walking on water to be a miracle, the real miracle is not to walk on air or water, but to walk on earth. This becomes apparent the more conscious we become of the fact that we *are* walking. We must also be conscious of each breath we take as we walk, as well as every feeling and experience that we have in relation to ourselves. We walk in the 'now' and are conscious of everything that happens in the 'now'. Therefore we *experience* the path we are walking on. If we are really engaged in this act of mindfulness we will consider the act of each step we take as an infinite wonder, and our hearts will open like a flower, enabling us to live in the moment; the real presence of the present moment.

As we place each foot on mother earth we do it in the knowledge that creation is wondrous. We are at the centre of a sacramental encounter, the miraculous and mysterious reality of the continuous creativity of the Creator God.

Every day we are caught up in the continuous act of the uncreated love of God giving birth to miracles which we seldom recognize: a blue sky, white clouds, green leaves, the wind and the sea – our own two eyes. All around us life is rushing towards us 'like shook foil'.

There is only one life and that is God's life which he gives us from moment to moment; drawing us to himself with every breath we take . . .

Thomas Merton[4]

Walking meditation exercise

While walking, very, very slowly (ideal for walking round a maze) concentrate on each step – as if it is all you will ever do – lift the left foot one inch off the ground, glide forward smoothly and slowly, place it lovingly on the ground, repeat with the other. Remember, be completely mindful of what you are doing and be aware that you are the connection between heaven and earth during this exercise. You are relaxed yet in control, above all, in the present moment, the still point.

As we walk we practise the sacrament of the present moment by following our breath, breathing in and out the leaves and flowers, sun and air. We enter into communion with the One from whom all creation has its being. We return to the centre . . .

> What I do is live.
> How I pray is breathe.
>
> *Thomas Merton*

We do not walk haphazardly without order or aim, but walk where body, heart, breathing and sight are united in rhythm. It is best to be alone, on a forest path or beside a lake or in open country, above all, alone, advancing with rhythmic steps, opening and closing the eyes in turn (it seems strange, but do try!) four paces with open eyes and four with closed eyes, with a very simple repetitive prayer. Very soon peace invades the body, things become full of silence and take an intensely new appearance, the heart feels only the moment, forgetting its usual operation.

Here the walking does not lead anywhere except to itself, with its rhythm, its movements and its silence – above all to the Presence which gradually invades it. Remember well that you can't go on a journey to find God unless you take God along!

> *An ait a bhfuil do chroi is ann a*
> *Thabharfas do chosa thu.*
> Your feet bring you to where your heart is.
>
> *Ancient Irish proverb*

Another walking exercise

When you walk, become aware for a while of the motion of your legs – get the feel of the movement. This will have a soothing effect.

1 Walk with the head up, chin drawn slightly in, shoulders back and with measured tread.
2 Inhale a complete breath, counting (mentally) 1, 2, 3, 4, 5, 6, 7, 8, learn first the length of your breath, one count for each step, making the inhalation extend over the eight counts.
3 Exhale slowly through the nostrils, counting as before . . . 1, 2, 3, 4, 5, 6, 7, 8. One count a step.
4 Rest between breaths, continual walking and counting 1–8, one count to a step.
5 Repeat until you begin to feel tired. Then rest for a while, and resume at pleasure.
Repeat several times.

One may vary this exercise by retaining the breath during a 1, 2, 3, 4 count, and then exhale in an 8-step count. Practise whichever plan seems agreeable to you.

Summary

1 The principle of the *path* or *way* which signifies that which comes from the feet treading, that is, the road is made as you go.
2 The physical body is the temple of God. In the consideration of the walk the feet are themselves connected to a shrine (the body).
3 It should be recognized that before we can run, we must be able to walk and by the same token, even before we walk we need to breathe, for breath is life. 'What I do is live, how I pray is breathe.'
4 We require dynamic posture in walking – back straight, head perpendicular – 'back breathing'.
5 If we practise 'walking towards the kingdom', no matter what the goal or purpose, walking becomes easier when using holy thoughts or phrases which may be repeated. In this way we build up grace, the dynamic within sacramental ritual.
6 Breathe up the backbone – lessons in meditation should not be lost when the body is in motion.

The practice of the Presence of God is not so much a doctrine as a practice to be used at all times.

a
soft
day

a soft day, thank god.
a wind from the south
with a honey mouth —
a scent of drenching leaves
briar and beech and lime
white elder flower and thyme:
and the soaking grass smells sweet
under my two bare feet:
and the rain drips, drips, drips
drips from the leaves.

a soft day, thank god.
the hills wear a shroud
of silver cloud.
the web of spider weaves
is a glittering wet.
the woodland path is wet;
and the soaking earth smells sweet
under my two bare feet.
and the rain drips, drips, drips
drips from the leaves.

an old irish song [5]

Lord of Creation

CONTEMPLATIVE DANCE

We have played the flute for you,
and you would not dance!

Matthew 11.17

I praise the dance, for it frees people
from the heaviness of matter and binds the isolated to community.
I praise the dance, which demands everything:
health and a clear spirit and a buoyant soul.
Dance is a transformation of space, of time, of people,
who are in constant danger of becoming all brain, will or feeling.
Dancing demands a whole person, one who is firmly anchored in the centre
of his life,
who is not obsessed by lust for people and things and the demon of isolation
in his own ego.
Dancing demands a freed person, one who vibrates with the equipoise of all
his powers.
I praise the dance.
O Man, learn to dance, or else the angels in heaven will not know what to do
with you.

St Augustine[6]

The whole of creation has been envisioned as the dance of God. Humankind focuses the dance of creation through the rhythmic phenomenon of the liturgy, the work of the people. The liturgy, today often referred to as Christian worship, is the practice of public prayer through word, sacrament, movement, silence and intensive prayer. A central intention of the liturgy is to draw us into community and incarnational concern for others and to bring the kingdom to fruition on earth.

Today's liturgy contains many relics from early Church precedents. For example, in biblical Hebrew the word 'company' is derived from 'dance' (*mecholah*, translated as 'company' in the Song of Solomon 6.13 derives from *mecholah*, which means to dance with others in a group). The word 'companion' is also derived from *com-panis* meaning bread-sharer. In the Psalms one is urged to come together to praise the Lord with dancing (Psalms 149 and 150). Much of David's success in building the consciousness of community in early Israel and unifying the tribes is attributed to his ability in leading others in dance and communal celebration. The word 'chorus' means 'dance' and 'stanza' means 'stand' or 'halt'. In the early Church people would stand in position while a soloist or choir sang or danced the stanza, but then during the chorus, all would begin to move.

Dance is rooted in the early liturgies of the Christian community and is an expression of humankind's religious moods. It is a part of the ritual of most of the world's religions and particularly so in the practice of religion in ancient Israel. The Old Testament is full of references to dancing especially in the Psalms: 'Let them praise his name with dancing' (Psalm 149.3).

Unfortunately festive joy, sacred movement, dance and poetry are largely lacking in modern worship. It is an intellectual, wordy, regulated exercise, reflecting liturgical theology rather than poetic expression. The theology of the body needs to be celebrated in movement and sensuality as well as in thought and theology governed by rubrics. If the worship of God is to reflect the whole of life, that is, become holistic, then it must not be solely about word and thought but also joy and dancing and yes, even laughter! Rest and recreation need to be afforded a place in worship giving respite to the stress and strain of work-a-day living opening up new landscapes of the interior world of the soul.

In recent years, the re-appearance of what could be described as Gnosticism, the phenomenon of the New Age movement, could well be interpreted as a reaction to materialism and consumerist excess. The New Agers pick and mix their beliefs from a supermarket of religious practices, therapies and cults, often derived from Eastern as well as Native American Indian religions. They search for remedies for the despair and boredom of the rat-race found in consumerist secular society. When starved of true mystical content, the spiritually famished feed on any fantasy. They invade any cultic phenomenon, even though it may be bereft of the dynamic of essential mysticism, for the sake of a transient experience of momentary happiness.

Time and time again we hear young people complain that institutionalized church worship is boring. Perhaps they need to be better instructed in the timeless archetypal quality of sacred liturgy, or could it not be possible to experiment in the use of deeper contemplative silence for several minutes instead of the Nicene creed or homily? Why not dance instead of a processional or recessional hymn or even dance the Kyrie (to a Taizé chant) or the sign of peace. There are many good CDs, tapes and books available, as well as dance teachers to instruct those languishing under the yoke of liturgical sadness and searching for the freedom of exultation and inner happiness.

Shout for joy to God our strength,
shout to acclaim the God of Jacob!
Start the music and sound the tambourine,
the melodious harp and lyre!

Psalm 81.2–3

For several years, as a parish priest, I presided or rather squatted on a prayer stool at a portable altar roughly the size of a coffee table, over what was known as a liturgical dance Eucharist. It was very much a modern equivalent of the Celtic wanderer with his portable altar, pyx, cross, stole and manual on journey for his place of resurrection. He would stop and celebrate the Eucharist and then move on. This style of liturgy-on-the-move was further developed by pilgrims on their way to the holy places. Today it can be adapted for all manner of festivals and events such as pilgrimages, rogation-tide, holy-well visits and community occasions such as a picnic.

Because this form of Eucharist is not a 'churchy' affair it is possible to use less words and more movement and silence. As with social dancing, liturgical circle dance is out of the ordinary lives of most people and so it is possible to enter into the spirit of the dance more easily.

It is so important to remember that we are not only spirit, but also flesh. Our bodies have a certain beauty and grace, and we are expected to use them for the greater glory of God. They should not be seen as sinful or worthy only of discipline but rather as temples of the Holy Spirit and therefore the natural vehicles of the soul expressing itself outwardly through the body.

We should worship God in the form that God created us, in body *and* soul; with the whole of our being. We cannot pray joyfully apart from the body – indeed, it is possibly better to pray through correct use of the body, that is the breath, recollected movement and dance, wonder and stillness when relating to God's presence in creation. The body is indeed the temple in which the glory of God is sung.

Body prayer can be expressed in various ways. Vocal prayer is one, song is another. And a third is body movement and dance, here we have the whole body praising and praying to God. Song is the joy of the voice; dancing is the joy of the body. Together, singing and dancing, both created by God, must like all his creatures, praise the Lord:

Praise the Lord with trumpet sound
Praise him with the lute and harp!
Praise him with tambourine and dance;
Praise him with strings and pipe,

Praise him with clanging cymbals;
Praise him with clashing loud cymbals,
Let everything that breathes praise the Lord!
Praise the Lord!

Psalm 150

Here we find the Word of God coming forth to us in Psalm 150, demanding that we dance in his praise. Whoever praises the Lord in dance, then, accomplishes his will. Dance itself expresses and promotes prayer. The whole of Christian tradition, rooted in Scripture with Jewish tradition preceding it, created sacred dance as a heritage belonging to the people of God. In the early Church, Clement of Alexandria in the third century speaks of the dancing which accompanies prayer, and explains its meaning:

> Prayer is a dialogue with God. Even if we speak silently while murmuring or without opening our lips, we have prayed internally. God always listens to all internal conversation. That is why we raise our head and hands towards the heavens and move our feet to the last movement of prayer, accompanying the movement of our thoughts toward the unintelligible essence. We endeavour, through that, to detach ourselves from our bodies with our words; we raise our winged souls to the heavens.[7]

Again, Eusebius of Caesarea (AD 339) tells how the victory of Constantine engendered dancing in the Christian community:

> All was filled with light, and it was with smiling faces and sparkling eyes that they regarded one another, scarcely lowering their eyes. With dancing choruses, hymns in the cities and country, they honoured God, the sovereign King.[8]

Gregory of Nazianzen (AD 390), too, explains that dances accompanied the feasts of martyrs:

> We assemble, we hasten together. This is truly a solemn celebration, pleasing to Christ. We honour or we shall truly honour the martyrs; we truly dance some triumphant dances.[9]

Throughout the writings of the early Fathers of the Church we find dancing expressed as a lyricism of the body accompanying the elevation of the soul. There are many references to spiritual dancing as a 'dance of the Holy Spirit'. Methodious of Olympia (AD 312), in *The Banquet*, speaks of celestial dancing in the words of the virgin Agatha:

Lord of Creation

I am a spouse of the Word. I receive in dowry, as a crown and riches from the Father, the gift of incorruptibility. I advance triumphantly through the ages, crowned with flowers, which do not wither, sparkling flowers of wisdom. I dance with Christ, the King without beginning or end.[10]

The gospel to be shared in a Dance Eucharist is Luke 6.23: 'Rejoice and leap for joy.' In Aramaic, which Jesus spoke, the word for 'rejoice' is the word for 'dance'. Dance was the means for coming back to joy (re-joice), as well as expressing it; hence 'leap for joy'. He probably said simply 'Rejoice!', for a Jew would understand that dance was the way to rejoice. That dance was understood by Jews as being the means to rejoice at the time of Jesus is suggested also by a comparison of Matthew 5.11–12 and Luke 6.23:

Blessed are you when people revile you and persecute you and utter all kinds of evil against you falsely on my account. *Rejoice and be glad*, for your reward is great in heaven, for in the same way they persecuted the prophets who were before you.

Blessed are you when people hate you, and when they exclude you, revile you and defame you on account of the Son of Man. *Rejoice* on that day and *leap for joy*, for surely your reward is great in heaven; for that is what their ancestors did to the prophets.

Luke has made explicit to the Greek mind what would have been implicitly understood by the Jews from Matthew's account, hence his addition of 'leap for joy' to the word 'rejoice'. The understanding is that rejoice equals dance lies behind many scriptural passages and translations.

The notion of 'leaping for joy' could be anathema for many Christians. Nevertheless, it could also be possible that souls withdrawn into themselves might be delivered from their stiffness.

You have transformed my tears
into a dance
You have clothed me with joy.

Psalm 30

It is very important that liturgical dance be performed in a disciplined way. Discipline does not imply stiffness. 'Discipline', writes Béjart, the choreographer for whom dancing means so much, 'consists in choosing the essential, be it in the life, in the way of living, of imagining the world. It is when one keeps only the essential and the necessary that one finds suddenly the focus of vitality and of truth.' Béjart again, talking of dance, mentions that 'the body must be deeply moulded to find one's liberty. But beware! This liberty goes *beyond* discipline and just short of it. I believe firmly that the body, to be able to participate in this joy and in this liberty, must pass through various stages of purification.' Béjart sums up: 'What is a dancer? Somebody who can stand up and do anything after having spent twenty years in practising discipline.' This statement is true of the contemplative meditator whose self-discipline enables the constant practice of the presence of God. Discipline frees the soul to be constantly turned towards God as a direct result of being at ease with the body whose litheness reflects the same spiritual desire.

When we walk or dance our prayer we are journeying toward the One. Our going towards him is to announce his coming to us.

> Have you heard his silent step?
> He is coming, coming, coming for ever.
> At every moment, at every age,
> at every night he is coming, coming, coming for ever.
>
> *Tagore,* Gitanjaei

Everything becomes a path towards him and neither pains, nor joys, nor labours, nor leisure, are an obstacle to his approach.

> 'Towards me you come
> unceasingly and always you
> become the nearest.'
>
> *Tagore,* Gitanjaei

As we walk or dance towards the Presence, he gradually invades us.

Basic dance steps

The **Tripudium** (which means 'three steps' or 'transport of joy' (*jubilate* in Latin), which is simply three steps forward and one back, three forward and one back, etc.) is probably the most common dance step. It was used in Christian church processions for one thousand years and fits with hymns of 2/4, 2/3 or 4/4 time. The common way of doing this step was not, as is often the case today, in single file or in round or circle dance but in processions with the dancers abreast with arms linked in row after row . . . moving through the streets and into the church and around in it during the hymns of the service, then out through the streets as a recessional.

It is not a circle dance, which is cyclical, but it advances towards God representing us stepping backwards every now and then! Taking three steps forward and one back indicates how we get there in the end in spite of set-backs in life.

The **Vine** is another important step in circle dance and consists of:

right foot in, then left foot in,
pass right foot over left foot
and right foot behind left foot
step left and repeat.

Alouette

two steps left, one step right
(repeat)
two steps left, two steps right

The normal handhold used in sacred/circle dance is with the right hand held palm upwards (that is, receiving), and the left hand held palm downwards (that is, giving). In the case of some dances this does not apply, as the little fingers link up rather than the whole hand. Hands are either joined with circle dance partners at shoulder height in the 'W-hold' or at hip height in the 'V-hold'. Much more about these various steps, holds, etc. can be found in the booklets recommended below in 'Further Reading'

Further reading

Davies, J. G., *Liturgical Dance: A Historical, Theological and Practical Handbook*, SCM Press: London, 1984. (Excellent text book.)

Blogg, M., *Dance and the Christian Faith*, Hodder & Stoughton: London, 1985. (Dance seen within the disciplines of Scripture, education and art.)

Lamont, G. and R., *Move Yourselves*, Bible Society: Swindon, 1983. (Drama and movement workshops.)

King, J., *The Dancing Circle* (a collection of articles on aspcts of sacred/circle dancing, edited and compiled by Judy King, includes articles by Gabriele Wosien, Friedel Kloke-Eibb, Laura Shannon, Nawal Gadalla, Sting).

Dances of Universal Peace: Spiritual Dance and Walk Book (a wonderful book that serves as an introduction to the early Dance of Universal Peace and Walks Meditation, also including instructions for Dances of Universal Peace).

Dancing Circles: Taizé Dances (Dancing Circles booklet of circle dance steps to your favourite Taizé chants, including Adoramus Te Domine, Confitemini Domino, Veni Sancte Spiritus, Ubi Caritas, Magnificat, Christe Domine Jesus, Nada Te Turbe, Dans Nos Obscurites; ideal for Contemplative Dance Eucharist material).

The above three publications and a current price list is available from: Dancing Circles, 4 The Cross, Wivenhoe, Colchester, CO7 9QN. Tel: 01206824783, email: dancingcircles@hotmail.com

For details of circle dance teachers and workshops, please contact: *Grapevine* (quarterly journal of the circle dance network), c/o Jackie Spearpoint, 63 Oak Farm Road, Birmingham, B30 1ET, Tel. 0121 459 1479, email: Jackie.spearpoint@virgin.net

Lord of the dance

In one of the apocryphal Christian books, the Acts of St John, we learn that after the Last Supper our Lord, Jesus Christ, came down from the table and danced a sacred round with his twelve disciples and 'Having danced these things with us, the Lord went forth. And we, as though beside ourselves, or wakened out of deep sleep, fled each our separate ways.'[11] The second council of Nicaea attacked and condemned the Acts of St John. At the time of the council, the dance round, the Hymn of Jesus with words sung by Christ, was widely believed to be a ritual of imitation with Christ as the mystagogue or teacher of the mysteries.

Why did the early Church Fathers suppress the apocryphal Acts of St John? Sacred dance and holy liturgy involves us bodily, emotionally and intellectually for through the dance of the liturgy my own person and the group are brought into an expected relationship. Even though it may be conceived and born from group and self, that relationship is a new thing with a life of its own, and in turn renews all three . . . the threefold dance of creation and of the Holy Trinity . . . When we dance, when we celebrate, we are writing our theology with our hands and feet and voices, into our bodies.

The danced hymn of praise signifies the fulfilment of the Lord's Supper. The inward dynamic consists in the offering of praise with Christ standing in the centre and the twelve apostles moving around him in a circle. Here the disciples are united with their Master in the mystery of at-one-ment. Sounding through the dance is the voice of Christ and this voice as the original sound at the beginning and end of creation, is there imparting the essence of its mystery through the dance.

In the early Church it was held that angels were always present during the celebration of the Eucharist. They participated with Christ in the performance of the sacred mystery. Christian art has, throughout the centuries, amply illustrated this notion of the singing and dancing angels. Early Fathers of the Church often commented on the dance as a means of worship and of linking the faithful to the angels and blessed souls in Paradise:

> Could there be anything more blessed than to imitate on earth the ring-dance of the angels, and at dawn to raise our voices in prayer and by hymns and songs to glorify the rising creator?
>
> *St Basil, Bishop of Caesarea, fourth century*

THE HYMN OF JESUS

He gathered us together and said: 'before I am delivered over unto them we will hymn the Father, and so go forth to what lies before us.' Then bidding us make as it were a ring, by holding each others' hands, with him in the midst, he said: 'Answer "Amen" to Me.' Then he began to hymn and say:

Glory to you, Father!
And we going round in a ring answered to him:
Amen!
Glory to you, Word (Logos)!
Amen!
Glory to you, Grace (Charis)!
Amen!
Glory to you, Spirit!
Glory to you, Holy One!
Glory to your Glory!
Amen!
We praise you, O Father;
We give thanks to you, O Light;
In whom darkness dwells not!
Amen!
I would be saved; and I would save.
Amen!
I would be loosed; and I would loose.
Amen!
I would be wounded; and I would wound.
I would be consumed for love; and I would consume.
Amen!
I would be begotten; and I would beget.
Amen!
I would eat; and I would be eaten.
Amen!
I would hear; and I would be heard.
Amen!
I would be understood; being all understanding (*nous*).

I would be washed; and I would wash.
Amen!
Grace leads the dance.
I would pipe; dance you all.
Amen!
I would play a dirge; lament you all.
Amen!
The one Eight in One sounds with us.
Amen!
The Twelfth Number above leads the dance.
Amen!
All whose nature is to dance, dance.
Amen!
Who dances not, knows not who comes.
Amen!
I would flee; and I would stay.
Amen!
I would adorn; and I would be adorned.
Amen!
I would be united; and I would unite.
Amen!
I have no dwelling; and I have dwellings.
Amen!
I have no place; and I have places.
Amen!
I have no temple; and I have temples.
Amen!
I am a lamp to you who sees me.
Amen!
I am a mirror to you who understands me.
Amen!
I am a door to you who knocks at me.
Amen!
I am a way to you, a wayfarer.
Amen!
See yourself in me who speaks;
And seeing what I do;
For yours is the Passion of Man
That I am to suffer.
You could not at all be conscious
Of what you suffer,

Were I not sent as your Word by the Father.
Seeing what I suffer,
You saw me as suffering;
And seeing, you did not stand still,
But were moved wholly,
Moved to be wise.
You have me for a couch; rest upon me.
Who I am, you shall know when I depart.
What now I am seen to be, that I am not.
But what I am you shall see when you come.
If you have known how to suffer,
You would have power not to suffer.
Know how to suffer, and you have power not to suffer.
That which you know not, I myself will teach you.
But as for me, if you would know what I was:
In a word I am the word who did dance all things, and
Was not shamed at all.
'twas I who leaped and danced.
But do you understand all, and understanding, say:
Glory to you, father!
Amen!

And having danced these things with us, beloved, the Lord went forth. And we, as though beside ourselves, or wakened out of deep sleep; fled each our several ways.

Compiled from various sources and translations

The icon of the Hymn of Jesus depicted on page 55 is by the artist Margaret Delfanne and owned by the author. An icon is a window into heaven. It is a picture that teaches in simple form spiritual and theological truth. The world is bound by certain laws; time, space, perspective, light and shade. Icons are not depicting this natural world, but a higher reality and an eternal truth. No time, except the present, eternal hour. The laws of the natural world are suspended in favour of higher laws. No shadows, but light room within. Icons are a language to describe the indescribable. To make visible what is invisible. We need to be still before an icon; to come in open, loving expectancy that the Holy Spirit will teach us something of God.

The dance is not immediately apparent; it is a solemn dance; it signifies inward joy; eternal joy. The lively hand of God is echoed in the hand of his Son: the hand that blesses.

Lord of Creation

The three arches symbolize the Trinity and the Church. The drapery on the building symbolizes the Precious Blood.

Judas is diminished in size to signify the shrunken state of his soul: his face in profile symbolizes evil. A serpent issues from his foot, Satan; who is even present in holy places. Judas leaves the company through a small rectangle which symbolizes earth; he enters hell.

The disciples look the same yet different, they are unique persons making one body. Their movement of rhythm gravitates towards Jesus.

St Peter is identified because of the rock at his feet, which signifies the foundation of the Church; the stone that the builders rejected; the very stones that would cry out to praise God; the stone that for some would prove a stumbling block; the stone that was rolled away; and all the stones that feature so abundantly in the Bible. On the altar is the chalice, the cup of precious blood; beneath, Judas holds the bag of coins, the ever present choice of God or Mammon. This is echoed in the two openings above the Company. The icon has for its foundation a cross; the chalice is at the centre of that cross.

Praying with the Whole Person

when we meet
god
without intermediary.

out of the DIVINE UNITY there
shines
into us a simple light;

and this
light
shows us our
darkness
and nakedness
and nothingness.

adapted from john ruysbroeck

Contemplative Dance Eucharist

Dancing the Eucharist is a deeply moving way, in every sense of the word, of celebratory prayer. It is at one and the same time a mode of contemplative prayer and of praise and joy.

It is best to use a portable altar, which has the appearance of a low coffee table at which the celebrant may sit on a prayer stool (if this is beyond the priest, then, a low chair may be used). All that need be placed on the portable altar is a crucifix, small metal or pottery chalice and paten plus purificator. The simpler the better. For vestment wear a broad woven stole. Do not forget to wear loose clothing for ease of movement. Celtic style is best! After all, the inspiration for this modern Celtic liturgy is derived from the early Celtic wanderers who carried cross, pyx, manual for prayer and stole in their scrips (satchels).

Place icons to represent the community of angels and saints in a circle round the outside of the circle of eucharistic dancers who sit on prayer stools or mats in the inner circle. In the centre of the circle place a large cross lying up against a cushion. Flowers, a bowl of water, a stone and a candle may be placed around it to represent creation and the elements. Use your imagination, this is what it is for!

We know so very little about ourselves; very little about our bodies and a lot less, even, about the invisible life going on inside us. We are accustomed to living on the outer edge of ourselves, on the surface, never under the skin, while deep down inside us there is an area neglected and ignored because we have no inkling of its existence. Our education in the name of logic has accustomed us to believe, more or less consciously, that the way to express ourselves is in the language of words; anything non-verbal seems marginal, elusive, or at least of secondary importance. We make use of gestures and movement with children 'because they like it' (and sometimes 'because that keeps them quiet') and at best interpret this manner of acting according to our adult way of thinking.

What if non-verbal expression is itself a language, even a basic language, enabling us to say what words cannot express and which can never be conveyed because there are feelings and perceptions which cannot be chained in a set form of words? Is the human being really, as we sometimes say, a 'thinking animal' or must we not end up by using apparent contradictions? 'Thought-emotion' or even 'soul-body' in order to rediscover the unity of each person?

Psychological research has brought us back to a vision which is that of the Bible. We only have to think of the language of the Psalms and of classical theology where the human being is considered as a whole so that he or she can be seen under various aspects without being divided into parts.

The Dance Eucharist for Creation

Greeting/Processional Dance

An Act of Penitence

Leader Creator God
breathing your own life into our being,
you gave us the gift of life:
you placed us on this earth
with its minerals and waters,
flowers and fruits,
living creatures of grace and beauty!
You gave us the care of the earth.
Today you call us:
'Where are you; what have you done?'

  Silence

  We hide in utter shame, for we are naked.
We violate the earth and we plunder it;
We refuse to share the earth's resources;
We seek to own what is not ours, but yours.

All Forgive us, Creator God,
and reconcile us to your creation.

Leader O God of Love
You gave us the gift of people –
of cultures, races and colours,
to love, to care for, to share our lives with.
Today you ask us:
'Where is your brother, your sister?'

  Silence

  We hide ourselves in shame and fear.
Poverty, hunger, hatred and war rule the earth;
the refugees, the oppressed and voiceless
cry out to you.

All   Forgive us, O God of Love, and reconcile us
to yourself and to one another.
Teach us, O Creator God of Love,
that the earth and all its fullness is
yours, the world and those who dwell in it.
Call us yet again to safeguard the gift of Life.

Dance Kyrie Eleison

Prayer

We give you thanks, most gracious God,
for the beauty of the earth and sea;
for the richness of mountains, plains, and rivers;
for the songs of birds and the loveliness of flowers.
We praise you for these good gifts,
and pray that we may safeguard them for our posterity.
Grant that we may grow in our grateful
enjoyment of your abundant creation;
to the honour and glory of your Name,
now and for ever. **Amen.**

Reading (*the Gospel is enough*)

Meditation/Silent Prayer

Dance/Sign of Peace

Eucharistic Prayer (*use the Gallican Preface and Eucharistic Prayer on page 233*)

Our Father

Communion

Silence

Final Prayer

O God, our God: You have brought all
spiritual and rational powers into being
for the sake of obeying your will.
We beseech you to accept the hymns,
which we, in unison with all your creatures,
sing to your glory as best we can.
Reward us with the overflowing graces
of your bounty, for every creature in heaven,

on earth, and below the earth bows down before you
and every creature sings of your ineffable glory.
You are the only true and all merciful God,
and all the powers of heaven praise you;
and we glorify you, Father, Son and Holy Spirit,
now and ever, and forever.

Recessional Dance (Tripudium to Pachelbel's *Canon*)

Or:

Come to the Hills

1 Come to the hills to the land where fancy is free
   And stand where the peaks meet the sky and the rocks meet the sea.
   Where the rivers run clear and the bracken is gold in the sun.
   And the cares of tomorrow must wait til this day is done.

2 Come to the hills to the land where life is a song.
   And sing while the birds fill the air with their joy all day long.
   Where the trees sway in motion and even the wind blows in tune
   And the cares of tomorrow must wait til this day is done.

3 Come to the hills to the land where legend remains
   Where stories of old fill the heart, and may yet come again,
   where the past has been lost, And the future has yet to be won.
   And the cares of tomorrow must wait til this day is done.

Gaelic song

DANCES FOR WORSHIP

Recessional dance 'Come to the Hills'

This dance is choreographed by the author. The original Gaelic song is entitled *Buach Aill An Eirne*. It is a call to contemplate the beauty of God's creation, the elements, the landscape and the creatures and to enter fully into the present, reminded by the words of the song, that 'the cares of tomorrow must wait til this day is done'.

The dance

Hold hands in a circle facing the centre. The steps follow the song's relaxed pace.

1 Walk forward on L foot, then R, then L, raising arms (hands still joined).
2 Step back on R foot, then L, lowering arms.
3 Breaking hands, turn clockwise to the R on the spot, stepping R, L, R as you turn (keep the same pace with these steps) and sweeping arms round the body to signify flowing air. End the turn facing to the R.
  Re-join hands in circle.
4 Step back on L with a swaying motion (don't forget this step) then walk forward R, L, R.
5 Turn to face centre and step in on L foot to begin dance as 1. This occurs without a pause in mid-verse but at the end of a verse there is a longer pause before beginning again.

I am the
        light of the cosmos,
                            who Dances
        flickering Down through heaD,

BReatheD,
            flowing in
        myriaD colours to the heart.

healing,
            the WORlD
        through the laying on of hanDs.

BRenDanus scotus

Healing by the Laying On of Hands

THE MINISTRY OF HEALING

When we have the intention to heal in the name of Jesus Christ, the Light of the World, then it is the Christ who heals. The laying on of hands focuses our intention to heal in the name of Christ and this action is, as it were, a conduit of God's grace to the recipient.

Through prayer, whether spoken aloud or in silence, the healer becomes a healing presence in relation to the person in need of healing. All personal barriers disappear and the act of healing takes on the element of a sacrament. The whole process is an archetypal symbol, where all is brought together in the One; a mystical moment when all barriers and resistance fall away and healing is known and effected.

Bishop Morris Maddocks defined Christian healing as 'Jesus Christ meeting you at your point of need'. It is Christ who heals and saves, not the person laying on hands. However, the facility is a gift given to the one exercising a healing ministry (cf. St Paul, 1 Corinthians 12). This gift is given each time God acts through his chosen servant obedient to his will. It is important to remember that it is through the authority of Christ that Christian healing takes place, rather than some esoteric atunement or ritual. There are useful techniques and prayers, which are of help and noted later. However, silent prayer and minimal touch may be equally effective. A pure heart and right intention as a channel of grace under obedience to the Word is imperative. The actual laying on of hands in the ministry of healing is only a part of the whole process.

The gift of healing is a natural gift, given to us that we may glorify God through his son Jesus Christ our Lord. Gifts are not given us for self-glorification. Natural gifts are given us by God that we may offer them to him through the healing of creation. They are not given us as a means to dominate or seek power over our neighbour.

It has been said that 'healing is to meditation what fruit is to jam'. The deeper our prayer the greater our sensitivity to the inner needs of others. Waiting upon the Holy Spirit in stillness and silence is a sure way to fill up inner strength and docility to the will of God who heals the sick through our laying on of hands. In many ways the ministry of healing proceeds from the inner silence of the minister of healing. It may be non-verbal and not expressed by any action. It is 'Christ in me relating to Christ in you'. It is first and foremost about Christ and follows the pattern set by Jesus Christ's own ministry. It relates to the whole work of Christ in body, mind and spirit, designed to bring that person to the wholeness, which is God's will for us all. The whole process or sacrament of healing is not therefore necessarily about a physical cure so much as the salvation of the whole person. This includes body and mind as well as the healing of the soul. There is a 'click-on' effect, as it were, a 'divine osteopathy'. Jesus Christ heals us; it is his will that we be made whole in every dimension of our being.

The predisposition and spiritual condition of the recipient is an important factor in the ministry of healing. We tend to set up barriers of our own to the process of being healed. There is very often a definite purpose in healing. People who have experienced healing often become a witness to Christ in his mission through his body the Church. It is not always apparent why some people are healed and others are not. However, we may not be healed or cured in the way we want but there is a knock-on effect as mentioned earlier which brings about healing in another part of our being, which may be in greater need of healing than the immediate intention-seeking cure. It could be that a relationship is reconciled which leads to better health as a result of unblocked negative feelings, which undermine well being. There is a traditional teaching on the four-fold need for good relationships with God, with our neighbour (that is, with everyone we meet), with ourselves and with creation. If we have a good conscience relating to all four then we are a happy person and well on the way to good health!

Healing is most easily effected when we offer ourselves up freely to God's care so that his will be done, not ours. We must trust in him with total commitment and not look back. As the *Cloud of Unknowing* states, 'Lift up thine heart, with a blind stirring of love' and all shall be well. As Jean-Pierre de Caussade taught in his book *Abandonment to Divine Providence*: 'A contrite and submissive heart opens the way to pleasing God'. An ecstasy of perfect love pervades the fulfilment of his will by those who surrender to it, and this surrender practised each moment embodies every kind of virtue and excellence. It is not for us to determine what manner of submission we owe to God, but only humbly submit to and be ready to accept everything that comes to us. The rest is up to him.

Living in God in this way, the heart is dead to all else and all else is dead to it. For it is God alone who gives life to all things, who quickens the soul in the creature and the creature in the soul. God's word is that life. With it the heart and the creature are one. Without it they are strangers. Without the virtue of the divine will all creation is reduced to nothing; with it, it is brought into the realm of his kingdom where every moment is complete contentment in God alone, and a total surrender of all creatures to his order. *It is the sacrament of the present moment.*

The Anointing of the Sick

The Prayer of Faith

Are any among you suffering? They should pray. Are any cheerful? They should sing songs of praise. Are any among you sick? They should call the elders of the church and have them pray over them, anointing them with oil in the name of the Lord. The prayer of faith will save the sick, and the Lord will raise them up; and anyone who has committed sins will be forgiven. Therefore confess your sins to one another and pray for one another, so that you may be healed. The prayer of the righteous is powerful and effective.

James 5.13–16

In the early centuries of Christianity it was customary for people to have oil blessed by a bishop or priest; which they took home and used for anointing the sick whenever the need arose. The oil was for the ministry of healing the sick. Lay people as well as clergy shared the task of anointing. It was not until the late Middle Ages that the rite of anointing became the prerogative of the clergy only.

Therefore, when we heal in the name of Christ, we not only affect the recipient but the whole created order as well, for 'we know that the whole creation has been groaning in labour pains until now; and not only creation, but we ourselves, who have the first fruits of the Spirit, groan inwardly while we wait for adoption, the redemption of our bodies' (Romans 8.22, NRSV).

We cannot treat the physical and the spiritual separately; the sacrament of reconciliation (confession) and sacrament of anointing the sick are interrelated by the very fact that a human being cannot be compartmentalized. The ministry of healing is not a practice reserved for the use of the clergy only. It is for all who pray and receive the gift of healing. However, it is through the body of Christ, the Church, that we continue Christ's healing mission. All and everything that the Church does which is 'beautiful, pure and lovely' is done in one way or another for the continuation of Christ's work of salvation, here on earth, and for the building up and healing of creation.

The sacraments are the channels and symbols of the healing love of Christ. *Symbola* means to draw together into one; *Diabola* means to split apart. A symbol effects what it symbolizes, that is it draws together and is a focus of the healing energy of the Cosmic Christ, the Holy Spirit.

The whole process then evolved into 'the last rites' when anointing and confession of sins became known as extreme unction. In the Roman Catholic Church the Second Vatican Council (1962–5) returned to the early understanding of the sacrament and changed the name to the sacrament of anointing of the sick. The Anglican Church reflects this change in its current rites. For example in the Church in Wales the following prayers are used as an indication:

For the blessing of oil (always olive oil)

Heavenly Father, giver of health and salvation,
send your Holy Spirit on this oil
that, as your holy apostles anointed many that were sick and healed
them, so those who in faith and repentance
receive this holy unction
may be made whole and, if it be your will, restored to health,
in the name of Jesus Christ, our Saviour and Redeemer. Amen.

The priest shall lay his hands on the head of the sick person and say:

N., in the name of God, Father, Son and Holy Spirit, may you be
released from your suffering and may your health be restored
according to his holy will.

or

N., in the name of God the Father, may you be released from your suffering and
may your health be restored according to his holy will.
In the name of Jesus Christ, may you be filled with new life.
In the name of God the Holy Spirit, may you receive inward health and the peace
that passes all understanding.

The priest then anoints the sick person, tracing the sign of the cross on his/her forehead, saying:

As we anoint you outwardly with this holy oil,
so may our heavenly Father anoint you inwardly
with the gift of the Holy Spirit
that you may receive the healing of all your infirmities
of body, mind, and spirit.
May the merciful Father comfort you,

give you confidence in his mercy
and keep you always in peace and safety,
through Jesus Christ our Lord. Amen.

N., we entrust you to God's most gracious mercy and protection.
May the Lord bless you and guard you;
may the Lord make his face to shine on you and be gracious to you;
may the Lord look kindly on you and give you peace. Amen.

PRAYER FOR INNER HEALING

1 The first step is to ask, with as much faith as you have, that the Lord heal you interiorly:

> Lord, you have told us to ask and we will receive, to seek and we will find, to knock and you will open the door to us. I trust in your personal love for me and in the healing power of your compassion.

2 The second step is repentance, a turning to the Lord for forgiveness. Coming into the light of his love and understanding, I am free to see myself as I really am and to become more aware of the sin, the disorder, and the hurts and the wounds inside me. I am free, in the Lord's love, to see better my need for forgiveness and for inner healing.

> Lord, I am sorry for all my sins, and I trust in your mercy. With your help, I renounce my sins and any sinful patterns in my life; I renounce everything that in any way opposes you. I accept with all my heart your forgiving love. And I ask you for the grace to be aware of the disorder in my inner self, to experience my own inner disorder with my wounds and hurts and sinfulness.
>
> Guide me in this prayer; show me what to pray for and how to pray. Bring to mind whatever pain or hurts you want me to ask you to heal.

3 Now, see what problem or painful experience comes to mind, and pray for healing regarding that problem or that memory. (If more than one thing comes to mind, take them one at a time.) It might be a failure or a broken friendship or the loss of a person you love. It could be something in childhood, such as a less than perfect relationship with your father or mother. It could be present anger or depression or some undesirable behaviour pattern.

Pray in your own words, lifting up the hurt or the painful memory or the problem to the Lord. Pray simply, like a child.

4 Forgive everyone involved, praying for them by name and telling the Lord that, with his help, you forgive each one. Imagine the person to be forgiven and, in your imagination, put your arms around the person and say, 'I forgive you.' Then see the Lord in your imagination, his arms outstretched to embrace you

both, and – with one arm around the person you have forgiven – walk with that person into the Lord's arms and let him forgive you both and reconcile you to each other and to himself.

5 Picture in your imagination the situation the problem goes back to, or the place of the hurtful memory. Picture the Lord in that place and situation, filling it with his healing love, being with you there. And ask him to heal you, again praying simply and in your own words.[12]

CHRIST THE LIGHT

You wrap yourself with light as with a cloak.

Psalm 104.2

Light in Christian spirituality is a sign of God's active presence and power. It represents in the Hebrew and Christian Scriptures life, healing, truth, grace, holiness, wisdom and prophecy. It stands for the deepest relationship between God and humanity. It is the essential manifestation of God's active presence in the world. Light symbolism permeates the prayer of the Church. The morning and evening prayer of the Church are rooted in the symbolism of light and darkness.

The passage through darkness to light is central to the theme of Advent and Christmas and is the constant unifying movement. During the Lent-Easter season, with its central symbolic progression through death to life, the light/darkness contrast continues as a secondary motif. Darkness here is manifested as evil, sin, and death. Light overcomes darkness in Christ's victory over death through his glorious resurrection. At the Easter Vigil as at baptism and the Presentation of the Lord, the faithful are presented with lit candles, symbolic of new life and the light of Christ.

Light is central too, to the inner mystery of healing through the channelling of the energy of white light into the body, that is, through harnessing the higher vibrations. It is a gift given to those called to this particular form of healing ministry and manifests a combination of nature and grace. It is in many ways a focus of what is happening within the whole of creation. The created order is sounding at every moment like 'shook foil'. It is full of energy vibrating at various levels of existence. The uncreated energy of God is within all matter by the fact of his Incarnation in Christ. In his essence God is absolute transcendence. But for humankind he is not known as purely transcendent. He is also imminent. He 'comes forth' to us in his uncreated energies. As related to us through matter, God is *grace*. He is working equally in nature as well as above nature. The whole of the created order is filled with the love of God in his activating energies, that is, the Cosmic Christ. We are called to contemplate God as love in all things and love him in return by loving, sharing, being beautiful and pure and healing in his name. God has created the whole world in order that he may share himself through his gifts with humankind.

Lord of Creation

Although our nature is unfinished we have nevertheless been gifted by God with spiritual faculties to communicate God's love and knowledge and to heal in his name. We are made 'according to the image and likeness' (Genesis 1.26) of God. We can freely receive grace from God and share in his nature by participating in his 'going-forth', which, to use Pseudo-Dionysus's term, is simply grace in the primal sense (cf. Ephesians 1.4–7). God, therefore, is grace as he goes out of himself in his uncreated energies to share his very own life with us.

We can truly experience God and know him through co-operating with his loving energies to be loving energies towards others. Through experiencing his love for us in contemplation we are then able to mediate that love to others in the ministry of healing. God's creative presence shines as light through the contemplative healer, that is one who 'con-temples' the light of Christ through becoming a vessel of his healing energy.

We have been told by Christ to 'walk in the light' and by St Paul to 'put on the whole armour of light'. These commands are symbolic and they are also a means of healing. What we are we radiate, for better or for worse. We are to become channels of light radiating forth that which we receive in contemplative prayer. A channel of light must also be a channel for healing, both of oneself and others.

A channel of light may be experienced by visualization:

On an in-breath visualize and draw down a shaft of light through the centre of the cranium to the heart-centre. Then, on an out-breath visualize the light passing through the hands gently laid on the head of a recipient. The ability to do this exercise is of incalculable value for light-energy can be transferred and it affects the health of the recipient. To absorb light and radiate it can lead to a higher quality of health and spiritual development.

Light is an energy that increases the ability of the brain to function more efficiently. Lack of natural light is known to lead to poor health and the condition known as SAD syndrome.

The more we are open to the healing light of Christ, that is the power of the Holy Spirit whose uncreated presence is within all created being, the more effective his healing energy will be with consequent rejuvenation and good health. Surely, the ministry of healing affects the whole of life. It is essentially holistic and addresses all levels and elements of a person's life: air (breath), earth (food), water (feelings), fire (light) and spiritual life. To 'be well' rather than just to 'get well' is the ultimate goal. The ministry of healing relates to body, mind and spirit. When the body is unwell it is possibly a symptom of something else happening at a deeper level. We might therefore ask ourselves what we should be paying attention to in our lives. 'What do I need to change in my life to really heal?'

The more practised we are in deep contemplative prayer and in purity of life, the more effective will be our spiritual care of others. The act of healing is to transmit the healing energy of grace gratuitously given by God through his Son Jesus the Christ. It is Christ who heals and we are his chosen vessels or channels of love. We have evolved from the primordial energies of light and sound. 'In the beginning was the Word.' Out of no-thing, all things came into being. We ourselves are an expression of this energy – light, colour and sound. Colour and sound are vibration and affect all other vibrations. In the beginning was the Word, that is sound, which is vibration. Colour is scientifically known too to be vibration. Sound evolved into colour and this affects all other vibrations, which is the essence of matter. The human body is energy/vibration. It is also form and space; the form is filled with space. It is extremely important that our bodies receive the right nutrients to be properly nourished. However we are also deeply affected and nourished by light. The more open we are at all levels of our being to receive light vibrations, the more likely we are to live balanced and spiritually healthy lives.

Remember that light is energy that is also found vibrating in each colour. Light, colour and sound are vibrations of energy, which can manifest itself to those sensitive enough to tune in to it through the practice of healing meditation. After all, we are made up of these energies and therefore influenced by them for good or evil. All forms of energy affect us.

Healing through the practice of light meditation is an integrative blend of visualization, silent prayer and intuition informed by rational and scientific knowledge. Light, using the whole colour spectrum, can be used in the ministry of healing and in self-therapy. This is not as 'far-fetched' as those not used to this form of healing may think – after all, at the deepest levels of microcosmic reality, the atom consists mostly of empty space. At this level all matter is a form of frozen light energy. The word 'quantum' is a term in physics meaning 'an invisible unit of energy' such as found in photons (which are a quantum of electromagnetic energy, that is light).

Light nurtures and is an agent for healing. However, I am not advocating the supposed effects of various colours in 'colour therapy' here. Nevertheless colour is therapeutic and has a role to play in healing. When light is visualized as flowing down from above the healer's head, down through his/her body and through the hands to the recipient, various colours may be experienced by both the practitioner and the patient.

Ultimately, it is the one light who heals for 'this is the message we have heard from him and proclaim to you, that God is light and in him there is no darkness. If we say that we have fellowship with him while we are walking in darkness, we lie and do not do what is true; but if we walk in the light as he himself is in the light, we have fellowship with one another' (1 John 1.5). We are called to be light bearers for the greater glory of the one Light of the World and the building up of his kingdom.

'Be still and know that I am the Light within you.'

An excellent repetitive prayer for concentrating, that is con-centring, the healing love of Christ is the phrase I AM THE LIGHT OF THE WORLD. An exercise in the technique in light originally taught by Olive Pixley and given to me by Mollie Nettleton of the Omega Order is as follows:

When you wake in the morning, lying relaxed in bed, visualize or think a radiant horizontal figure of light at your feet, the soles of whose feet are touching yours. Immediately after this, send your vision upwards to a point of light in infinity: your contact with the light of God the Father. Once you have visualized the light and made your contact there is no need to dwell on it but you can refocus at any time during the day to be revitalized and inspired. The next need is for protection from the many energies on a horizontal level which will impinge on you during the day. This protection can be received by visualizing a circle of light, flashing from the crown of your head to the right, touching the crown of the head of the figure of light and back to your own head, thus completing the circle of protective light.

The next step is the starting up of life and activity. As with a newborn baby this is done by breathing, but in this case by breathing consciously and by visualization of your breath. Physical breathing is largely unconscious but conscious breathing brings to life a rhythmical contact with the light at your feet and the point of light in infinity. As you inhale, visualize breath as seen on a cold day, coming from the solar plexus down to the figure of light at your feet; as you exhale again visualize breath coming from the solar plexus and rising to contact the point of light in infinity. Six breaths only, before you get up, are needed to assure your contact, but the conscious breathing can be used at any time of the day or night as need arises, whether it is to restore equilibrium, a call for help and inspiration, the revitalizing of a tired body, or as an aid to sleep.

Jesus said, 'I am the Light of the world.'

CHRIST the LIGHT

ILLUMINE and guide me!
christ be the light
before and behind me!
CHRIST be the LIGHT
above and below me!
christ be the light
on my left and my right!
christ be the light
all round about me!

O LIGHT of light
you illumine my heart
with your love and your joy,
may that light be as a lamp
on my path that it may
guide me from darkness to light;
lead me from the unreal to
the real;
deliver me from death to
IMMORTALITY.

BRENDANUS SCOTUS

Light of Splendour

A light of utmost splendour
Glows on the eyes of my soul.
Therein have I seen the inexpressible ordering
Of all things, and recognized God's unspeakable glory –
That incomprehensible wonder –
The tender caress between God and the soul,
The sufficiency in the Highest,
Discipline in understanding,
Realization with withdrawal,
According to the power of the senses,
The unmingled joy of union,
The living love of Eternity
As it now is and evermore shall be.

Mechthild of Magdeburg (trans. anon.)

Further reading

A *Time to Heal* (a report for the House of Bishops on the Healing Ministry. An excellent text book, gives a framework for the development of the healing ministry in the twenty-first Century), Church House Publishing: London, 2000.

A *Time to Heal Handbook: The Development of Good Practice in the Healing Ministry,* Church House Publishing: London, 2000.

Maddocks, M., *The Christian Healing Ministry* (an eloquent defence of healing in an orthodox Christian context beginning with the teaching of Jesus, then outlining the ministry of healing in the Church both in New Testament times and today), SPCK: London, 1981.

Maddocks, M., *Twenty Questions About Healing* (some of the most frequently asked questions about healing), SPCK: London, 1988.

Mac Nutt, F., *Healing* (the first comprehensive Catholic book on healing ministry in the RC Church), Ave Maria Press: Notre Dame, Indiana, 1974.

Heron, B., *Praying for Healing: The Challenge* (exploration of the ministry of healing and especially the place of prayer in it), New Life Publishing: Luton, 1989.

Cowie, I., *Jesus' Healing Works and Ours* (in a very direct and informative way, Ian Cowie carefully dissects the actions and words of Jesus in each healing incident and draws conclusions which are often at odds with current perceptions and interpretations. The first book to cover every single healing miracle of the

New Testament, including those of the apostles), Wild Goose Publications: Glasgow, 2000.

Cowie, I., *Prayers and Ideas for Healing Services* (a helpful analysis of various Church traditions and suggested prayers. A structured and inspiring presentation drawing on the Celtic Christian mentoring of the faith), Wild Goose Publications: Glasgow, 1995.

Tuckwell, G. and Flagg, D., *A Question of Healing* (the reflections of a doctor and a priest, organized around a series of questions, to which Gareth Tuckwell and David Flagg respond, the book addresses a number of key issues including 'pills of prayer', healing miracles, handling grief, alternative therapies, M.E., eating disorders and living with suffering. Their advice is practical, biblical and thoughtfully balanced), Eagle: Guilford, Surrey, 2000.

Sayre-Adams, J. and Wright, S. G., *Therapeutic Touch* (reviews the background and up-to-date research and clear guidance for the practice of Therapeutic Touch), Churchill Livingstone: Edinburgh & London, 2001.

Sayre-Adams, J. and Wright, S. G., *Sacred Space: Right Relationships and Spirituality in Healthcare* (this book is about pathways towards right relationships for individuals, groups and organizations; restoring wholeness, healing and caring), Churchill Livingstone: Edinburgh & London, 1999.

the more i REFLECT
upon the profound laws of EVOLUTION,
the more i am convinced that the
universal christ
would be unable to appear at the END of TIME
at the world's summit,
unless
he had previously inserted himself
into the course of the world's movement
BY way of BIRTH
in the form of an element.

teilhard de chardin [13]

Lord of the Elements Workshop

Preliminary Walking Meditation

Grant me, Christ, to walk to you,
with you let me be
who are not frail nor fickle
nor feeble-willed like me

Irish, eighth century

Walk around freely – breathe from the heart area – place your hand on your heart and feel your breath.

Then walk forward. You are a pilgrim seeking God, walking towards the One you love and who is calling you to him.

STOP: With deep breath, breathing out to the plants . . . to the earth . . . to all that is created.

ELOHIM . . . YAHWEH . . .

And so we walk with confidence; breathe in through the nose and feel the solidity of the earth beneath our feet.

Walking with confidence we bring everything into focus, our feet firmly on the ground, not going out for a walk but journeying on.

The attention settles at the centre of things, and the leaving and arriving release their customary hold on our goal-orientated mind, this is no ordinary journey.

We still the mind and open the heart to land and sea.

(The yielding, balance and serenity of this experience is embodied in the group's interaction.)

King of the earth, King of the sea,
King of heaven, of the angel's King,
King of the City, my treasureling.

From the Gaelic

Pilgrimage is once again a central theme in the life of many Christians. However, it is usually embarked upon with a particular destination in mind. The whole of life is a journey and there is also a certain restlessness of the heart for the true home of the spirit. Outwardly we may be seeking God who is the ultimate object of our search, but inwardly it is he who is leading our search for him. A sign of this is that certain nostalgic yearning for our true spiritual home, a sadness (the *penthos* of the Greeks and the *hiraeth* of the Welsh) or nameless woe, which will not rest until it rests in the heart of God. Saint Columba, who himself suffered deeply in exile from his native Ireland, taught his disciples that there were three types of traveller: those who leave home with uncleansed spirit and whose journey is purely physical without spiritual merit; those under authority to an institution and so only free to travel in spirit; and finally those who leave their native land entirely, body and spirit to suffer separation in exile.

This exile where the journey is more important than the arrival has been described as the white martyrdom of exile. The 'white martyr' is not asked to give his life through the spilling of blood; but to let go of the attachments, comforts and securities that go hand in hand with everyday home life. This suggests the typical restlessness of the Celtic saint, constantly moving from place to place in the knowledge that he had no abiding city. He did not plan his journey, or work out his route in advance, in fact, he did not even know his ultimate destination; his whole reason was to live the spiritual life of exile. He set out in pilgrimage for the Lord of the Elements, sometimes even entrusting himself to the ocean without oars or rudder, like those Irishmen who came to land on the coast of Cornwall in 891, 'Who had stolen away', says the Saxon chronicler, 'because they wished for the love of God to be on pilgrimage, they cared not whither.' This type of pilgrimage necessarily implied a journey overseas as a pilgrim for Christ's sake, as was the case for Columba. There were different types and levels of pilgrimage in the Celtic kingdoms and Britain during this period in history.

The essential truth concerning the whole theme of pilgrimage is the search for God. There is the outer journey, the reflection of the inner journey. The difference between the pilgrim and the tourist is that the former is seeking an experience of God. However, the paradox is that if we set out in search of God we shall not find him. It is God who comes to us: 'You would not seek me if you had not already found me.'

This retreat workshop is a physical/spiritual exercise to bring body, mind and spirit into oneness through seeking the presence of God within. It is both an inner journey and an outer journey inspired by the Celtic pilgrim's search for the Lord of the Elements. We shall explore the four elements 'within' and 'without' our-selves. Themes will be meditation, dance, walking-prayer and chant, culminating in a liturgy or an agape put together by the group relating to the elements, earth, air, fire and water, the components of our physical world, the four elements that may also be used to describe aspects of our personalities: earthy, airy, fiery, watery. We instinctively internalize our external reality in an attempt to make sense of life and our place in the universe. By exploring the elemental forces within ourselves we may become aware of the healing adjustments necessary to discover the Lord of the Elements, the God within.

By practising embodied prayer we may connect our inner being with the Spirit of creation. Silently walking the landscape as 'peregrinators' or pilgrims on hallowed ground we enter into our inner world, our own 'inscape', where the imagination can wander, reflect and then be silent. The path may lead us to a holy well, our baptismal font and the entrance to the 'other world' of our own inner being.

Sacred dance, like walking-prayer, can symbolize the journey of spirit along a path or inner maze that will lead to transformation and final union with the divine at the still centre. Myths in several cultures speak of the creation of the world as the dance of God. By rediscovering ancient dance-forms, in a circle or a processional line, we too may 'dance the world into being' thus renewing our own creativity.

Within me – the continuum of time and space.
Moves freely with no limitation.
I praise the highest of the high and the deepest of the deep.
My voice is the song of the earth,
My dance is the movement of the stars.
My voice is the song of the earth
My dance is the movement of the stars.

Prayer of Azariah

Blessed are you, O Lord, God of our
ancestors,
and to be praised and highly
exalted for ever;
And blessed is your glorious, holy
name,
and to be highly praised and
highly exalted for ever.
Blessed are you in the temple of
your holy glory,
and to be extolled and highly
glorified for ever.
Blessed are you who look into the
depths from your throne on
the cherubim,
and to be praised and highly
exalted for ever.
Blessed are you on the throne of your
kingdom,
and to be extolled and highly
exalted for ever.
Blessed are you in the firmament of
heaven,
and to be sung and glorified for
ever.

vv.29–34[14]

Introductory Exercises

Greetings exercise

> There's a time when what you're creating and the
> environment you're creating it in come together.
>
> *Grace Hartigan*

We begin the workshop with a greetings exercise. It is a good way to introduce people to one another as well as to 'ground them' in preparation for what is to follow.

Form a circle and hold hands and lightly close the eyes – pray for light, love and grace – leaving behind negative thoughts, worries, insecurities, etc. Imagine a light high up in the universe and on an in-breath bring the light down through the centre of the cranium down, down into the centre of the heart.

On the out-breath send light from the heart through the right hand to the person on your right and receive light from the person on your left.

Carry on doing this exercise until the group's circle of light is fully realized. Finally, breathe the light into the centre of the circle and say together:

> God is light.
> In him
> is no darkness
> at all.
>
> *1 John 1.5*

This prayer phrase may be said rhythmically together on the in- and out-breath.

Name Game

1 Each person (still in the circle mode) introduces themselves by name.
2 When this is completed each person may then introduce the name of the person on their right until everybody in the circle has been named.

Breathing Exercise

Take three deep breathes (breathe in and out slowly)
Three 'light' breaths
Three 'short' breaths
Three 'heavy' breaths
Three breaths for Joy
Three breaths for Love
Three breaths for Peace

Finally – inhale for the count of seven . . . and hold the count of one. Exhale for the count of seven, and hold for the count of one.

Said or chanted:

> Christ be with me
> Christ be within me,
> Christ be before me,
> Christ be behind me,
> Christ on my left hand
> Christ on my right hand,
> Christ above me,
> Christ be below me,
> Christ round about me.
> (*final line sung twice*)

Hands and arms may be used to indicate the directions during the chant.

Either during or after the chant the following invocation may be said, facing the appropriate direction:

> We welcome all the plants
> To the south – we trust.
> We welcome all the animals
> To the north – we know.
> We welcome our Mother Earth

Lord of Creation

To the west – we feel.
We welcome our Brother Sun
To the east – we see.
In the centre we welcome all the humans
And walk in time with them –
In the Name of the Holy Spirit – we are.

There are four directions,
north, south, east and west,
and the direction we are
travelling is NOW.

The above prayer exercise gives us an awareness of the inherent creative power of God present and coming forth from the mouth of the Almighty Creator as he speaks his Word. That Word, spoken in the wind, the sun, moon, stars, mountains, lakes, oceans, goes forth and shall not return empty (Isaiah 55.11). Truly, not only 'by the word of the Lord the heavens were made' (Psalms 33.6), but the whole created world has been created in God's Word (Colossians 1.16). Nothing exists or moves to perfection except by God's creative power immanently present in all things. 'In him we live and move and have our being' (Acts 17.28).

The very sad fact is that many people do not see God or sense his presence through creation. We see the view and point out the flowers, the rivers, the trees and yet fail to see the wondrous face of God shining forth through it all. We have been given the tremendous gift of faith, yet we enjoy the artefact without an intuition, even, of the Artificer. We have been given the responsibility, not only to believe in this omnipresence but also to see him there by faith and point out this presence to others and yet we fail because of our blindness to the light of his presence: 'I am God . . . the Holy One present among you' (Hosea 11.9).

We could easily be accused for:

My watchmen are blind,
all of them unaware;
they are all dumb dogs,
they cannot bark,
dreaming as they lie there
loving their sleep.

Isaiah 56.10

Yes, we can see the view and point out the beauty without seeing or sounding out the inner presence of God shining through.

'My Beloved is the mountains, the solitary wooded valleys, strange islands . . .
silent music'

St John of the Cross

God's loving presence is there at all times at all levels of being.

> Only a fool would fail
> to praise God in his might,
> when the tiny mindless birds
> praise Him in their flight.

Irish, eighth century

We fail to see him. And yet we are 'invaded' constantly by God's energizing love
in each event. Yet most of us are asleep to that presence. Jesus the Christ is still
shouting out to us: 'Why are you sleeping? Wake up!' (Luke 22.46).

External holy space begins when we call upon the energies of creation.

South	Fire, energy, heat, life, will
North	Earth, body, sustenance, nature
East	Air, mind, intuition, wind, breath
West	Water, emotions, feelings, the unconscious, fertility

The centre of the circle is the point of transformation. We visualize the Lord
Christ at the centre; he is the Cosmic Christ, King of the Elements, the Holy
Spirit.

In almost all cultures breath is synonymous with life, in both the concrete and
the spiritual sense; with breath further life is granted. It is possible that the
custom of kissing another's hand is in order to transport my breath in this form
as a life-wish blessing to the recipient and therefore to participate in the breath of
God as a blessing. In similar manner we venerate a sacred object by kissing, for
example an icon or medal or crucifix.

We relate the Presence of God especially through the use of breath.

GREETINGS DANCE: *ENAS MYTHOS*

From the Greek island of Kos, this is one of the most ancient surviving European dances and may have been a dance used by the Knights Templar. It is suitable for meeting or leave-taking. The same steps could be danced however to other appropriate music. The easily learned steps allow dancers to greet each other across the circle by glancing, smiling or nodding – within reason!

The dance

Standing in a circle facing the centre, each dancer crosses their R arm over their L, then everyone's hands are joined as in *Auld Lang Syne*. If there are too few people to do this comfortably, just join hands in a circle. The latter feel more relaxed but the former naturally creates a closer link between dancers.

1 Step forward with L foot.
2 Bring R foot to close beside L and in closing slightly bend or 'bounce' the knees twice.
3 Step back with R foot.
4 Bring L to close and bounce knees twice.
5 Still facing centre, step sideways with R foot to the R.
6 Bring L to close and bounce knees twice.

Prayer of Azariah

Bless the Lord, all you works of the
Lord;
sing praise to him and highly exalt
him for ever.
Bless the Lord, you heavens;
sing praise to him and highly exalt
him for ever.
Bless the Lord, you angels of the
Lord;

sing praise to him and highly exalt
him for ever.
Bless the Lord, all you waters above
the heavens;
sing praise to him and highly exalt
him for ever.
Bless the Lord, all you powers of
the Lord;
sing praise to him and highly exalt
him for ever.
Bless the Lord, sun and moon;
sing praise to him and highly exalt
him for ever.
Bless the Lord, stars of heaven;
sing praise to him and highly exalt
him for ever.

. . .

Let the earth bless the Lord:
let it sing praise to him and highly
exalt him for ever.
Bless the Lord, mountains and hills;
sing praise to him and highly exalt
him for ever.
Bless the Lord, all that grows in the
ground;
sing praise to him and highly exalt
him for ever.
Bless the Lord, seas and rivers;
sing praise to him and highly exalt
him for ever.
Bless the Lord, you springs;
sing praise to him and highly exalt
him for ever.
Bless the Lord, you whales and all
that swim in the waters;
sing praise to him and highly exalt
him for ever.
Bless the Lord, all birds of the air;
sing praise to him and highly exalt
him for ever.

Lord of Creation

Bless the Lord, all wild animals and
cattle;
sing praise to him and highly exalt
him for ever.

vv. 35–41, 52–59

The Earth sees herself through our eyes
dances our senses
to each new day's surprise.
The rainbow of existence
says stay
stay you
stay delicately conscious,
mindfully awake,
for life is
life is like she is.
Never empty never full
but never too much
never too much beauty
never too much love
never too much life
to discover . . .

the **earth** is at the same time **mother,**
she is mother of all that is **natural,**
mother of all that is **human.**
she is the **mother** of all,
for **contained** in her
are the **seeds** of all.

the **earth** of **humankind**
contains all **moistness,**
all **verdancy,**
all **germinating power.**

it is in so many ways **fruitful.**
all **creation** come from it.
yet it **forms** not only the basic
raw material for humankind,
but also the **substance**
of the **incarnation** of
god's son.
abbess hildegard of bingen [15]

EARTH

These are they whom the Lord hath sent to walk to and fro through the earth.

Zechariah 1.10

Walking meditation on the elements – befriending creation

Participants gather with enough personal space for free movement.

Appropriate soft background music may be played.

The leader of this walking meditation may use the following script for 'voice over' during the exercise:

Leader (voice over):

The breath is the normal breath, that is breathe in through the nose and out through the nose. Visualize the breath coming up through the earth and then up through the feet and through the body permeating the bones and ligaments.

Begin a slow meditative walk and as you walk feel the earth beneath you; become aware of a certain 'springiness' as you walk the earth. Feel the support of the earth through the bones of the feet, legs, across the hips and up to the shoulders and head.

Your spine goes right up to the middle of the head. This is where the cranium rests on the body, that is on the spinal column.

Now gently breathe in through the nose and out through the mouth.

As you continue your meditative walk feel the support of the earth, not pulling yourself away from the earth. Each step is an experience of being supported by the earth all the way up to the head.

Experience the vibration of the footsteps and breathe up through the body with the sense of breathing in the energy of the earth and purifying one's being.

This is a walk of support empowering us to go into new situations where we need support and where we are not necessarily sure of what we are getting ourselves into.

It's a grounded, everyday supportive walk with the earth giving us a sense of confidence.

We are all affected by the elements whether we know it or not in the various situations of our lives. By making sure of our steps we become more centred and experience support from Mother Earth. If our steps are tentative and fearful then we may experience the flip-side effect of being at the mercy of earth and its darkness.

Talk

When we use 'visualization' we use pictures and make use of the creative, subjective side of our brain, the right hemisphere. This has a powerful effect on the unconscious mind.

Orthodox and alternative practitioners are well aware of the use of visualization and imaging in self-healing. It is suggested that imagery can stimulate the auto-immune system and begin the healing process. Sometimes, however, the opposite effect is encountered as, for example when a hay-fever sufferer is affected by artificial flowers which are believed to be real.

Imagery should be used confidently and regularly. The most effective images are those constructed intuitively. For example, the imaging of a golden light flooding the body with warm healing rays. The more vivid, the better.

The use of the imagination as an aid to meditation is one method among many in the search for the 'still centre'. Further examples of this method will be found on pages 124ff.

Tree of meditations meditation

> For ye shall go out with joy, and be led forth in peace:
> The mountains and the hills shall break forth before you
> into singing, and all the trees of the field shall clap their hands.

> *Isaiah 55.12*

Form a circle and join hands.

Leader (voice over):

Breathe deeply into your belly. Stand in a relaxed manner with feet firmly planted on the earth.

Straighten your spine and release the tension in your shoulders.

Lord of Creation

Now imagine that your spine is the trunk of a tree with roots that go down deep into the centre of the earth. Breathe down into these roots and let all the tensions within you flow down with your breath dissolving into the earth.

Feel the way the roots connect under the earth and how we are made of matter. The earth is the body of our ancestors. It made our grandmother's flesh, our grandfather's bones.

The earth sustained the generations that gave birth to us. As we draw on their power, the power of the earth, as we feel it rise through the roots in our feet and through the base of our spines let us bear in our memory our ancestors – those who came before us, who inspired us.

Feel the energy of the earth rising into our bellies as we draw it up with our breath, feel it rise into our hearts and spread out from our hearts up through our shoulders and down through our hands.

Feel it move around the circle through our hands – feel how it connects us through our breath. As we breathe together – breathing in, breathing out – we link ourselves together.

Feel the power rising up through our throats and out through the top of our heads like branches that sweep up and return to touch the earth again; creating a circle, making a circuit.

The branches are our children and grandchildren, the generations that come after us. Feel them intertwining above our heads in the knowledge that they are not separate from us.

Through the branches of the trees, through the leaves, we feel the sun shining down upon us, the wind moving and the moon and the stars shining down. We can draw in the power of that light, draw it in as a leaf draws in sunlight and feel it spread down through all the twigs and branches, down through the trunk, down through the roots, until we are filled with light and as the light reaches the roots, we feel them push deeper and deeper into the earth.

And as we relax, we feel the connection, the ground beneath our feet and know that we cannot lose that ground.

> the sense of the Earth
> opening and exploding upwards into God;
> and the sense of God taking root
> and finding nourishment downwards into Earth.
>
> *Teilhard de Chardin*[16]

Blessed are those who trust in the Lord
whose trust is the Lord.
They shall be like a tree planted by water,
sending out its roots by the stream.
It shall not fear when the heat comes
and its leaves shall stay green;
in the year of drought it is
not anxious,
and it does not cease to bear fruit!

Jeremiah 17.7–8

While preparing for prayer to begin

A time to align oneself to the love of God within and beyond, to become aware of those praying around:

A time to relax and become still . . .

Stretch . . . shake . . . settle . . .

Sit with back straight up and down and with both feet on the ground . . .

Breathe out gently and a long way and then simply let the air in . . .

Relax into any aches and pains . . .

No strain . . . relax . . . let be . . .

Bring a word to mind . . . peace, healing, spirit . . .

Bring a picture to mind . . . running water . . . wide ocean . . . caring hands . . .

Abide in the Presence . . .

Living, loving God, our Father and Mother, the source of life and health, of strength and peace:

Show us the way, the truth and the life: take from us all that hinders the flow of your spirit,

with hands of compassion wash away
(our sin and) our fear,

our resentment and our hardness of heart,
enable us to become centred and still,

aware of your Presence, here, now,
to heal, (to redeem), to transform . . .

We pray in the Spirit of the Christ
Our (Saviour and) Healer . . .

Prayer of Azariah

Bless the Lord, all people on earth;
sing praise to him and highly exalt
him for ever.
Bless the Lord, O Israel;
sing praise to him and highly exalt
him for ever.
Bless the Lord, you priests of the
Lord;
sing praise to him and highly exalt
him for ever.
Bless the Lord, you servants of the
Lord;
sing praise to him and highly exalt
him for ever.
Bless the Lord, spirits and souls of
the righteous;
sing praise to him and highly exalt
him for ever.
Bless the Lord, you who are holy and
humble in heart;
sing praise to him and highly exalt
him for ever.

vv. 60–65

Earth meditation

Lord, grant me by your grace
A quiet end, an easy mind,
And light my pathway with your face
When my dead flesh is left behind.

Adapted from Ancient Irish

Face north. Ground and centre by feeling your feet on the earth/floor – take a breath – be in the present moment. Feel your bones, your skeleton, the solidity of your body.

Be aware of your flesh; all that can be touched and felt. Feel the pull of gravity, your own weight; your attraction to the earth, your mother from whence you came. You are a natural feature, a human being.

Merge with all that comes from the earth: grass, trees, grains, fruits, flowers, beasts, metals and precious stones.

Return to compost, to mud, to dust.

Ashes to ashes . . . Adam! [*adam* means dust/clay/earth.]

'And over' the grave we make our song. Alleluia, Alleluia, Alleluia!

Footsteps of Love

I am walking on the earth;
the earth is my mother.
Wherever I walk, I will be home.

I am walking with the people who love me;
their love surrounds me.
Wherever I walk I will be loved.

I am walking on the circle of the Creator;
Creator above, Creator below.
Wherever I walk I am with the Creator.

I am walking upon the earth with people who love me;
We are walking on the circle of the Creator.
I will always be home.
I will always be loved.
I will always be with the Creator.

Ancient prayer (adapted)

Plant meditation

A Philosopher:	'How do you manage without the consolation of books?'
Anthony the Great:	'My book is the nature of created things, and it is there whenever I want to read the words of God.'

First use the basic relaxation technique (page 26).

Leader (voice over):

Picture a sea of bluebells seeming to flow over the woods, weaves of sapphire light and amethyst shade fill the whole scene with beauty.

Above, the sky mirrors the lovely colour and the warmth, sweetness and fragrance bring athrill that is almost unbearable in its poignant joy.

Through the hanging leaves which sway and quiver in the breeze, the clear and unbroken blue sky is caught and held like a radiant gleam of pure colour in a cathedral window.

The whole vision is a cosmic prayer – an offering of loving worship.

Let the image of a plant come into your mind . . .

any kind of plant that is seeking to grow.

Observe the plant carefully . . .

Now draw close to the plant . . .

and in your mind, become the plant.

Experience being the plant . . .

Experience the kind of soil you are in . . . and how it contains and holds you.

Experience also how the soil restricts you . . .

Experience the kind of garden you are in . . .

Experience your roots . . .

And whether they are strong

And firmly anchored in the soil . . .

Are they intertwined with other roots?

Experience any other plants encroaching on you . . .

And taking moisture or nourishment from you.

Lord of the Elements Workshop

Do you need to extend your roots or put down new roots?

Experience your stem and leaf structure above the ground.

Experience the vitality growing in you and how it is expressed.

Be aware of any weakness in your own structure

That limits your growth . . .

Is there any sickness?

Are there parts that are overgrown or leggy?

Are there any dead parts . . .

or parts that are stunted . . .

maybe with mould or some kind of parasite?

Are there parts that need pruning?

There are also predators of different kinds which may menace or threaten you . . .

Experience who they are . . . and what you do in reaction to them.

Experience your reaction to all these challenges . . .

that come from outside you, as well as from within yourself.

Silence.

Reading

A man had a fig tree planted in his vineyard; and he came looking for fruit on it and found none. So he said to the gardener, 'See here! For three years I have come looking for fruit on the fig tree, and still I have found none. Cut it down! Why should it be wasting soil?' He replied, 'Sir, let it be alone for one more year, until I dig round it and put manure on it. If it bears fruit next year, well and good; but if not you can cut it down!'

Luke 13.6–9

the SPIRIT glides over the WATER
immersion is the RETURN to the
formless, the dissolution of form,
the plunging into night,
the BIRTH of the new BUD,
therefore also creative.

DEPTH is more GODLIKE than height
sinking is more HOLY than climbing.
the CREATOR GOD, a great underground river
awaits our SINKING more than our CLIMBING.

the reason we can TRUST the sinking is
that, at the very depths, at the bottom
my GROUND and GOD'S are the same.
we need to RETURN to our origins,
the darkness of the WOMB,
deep contentment, then
healing.

WATER

Letting go meditation

(Suitable meditative music)

God is a great underground river
that no one can dam up
and no one can stop

Meister Eckhart (1260–1329)[17]

Leader (voice over):

We have started with a sense of being supported by Mother Earth.

Now we are to experience a sense of release through the body's meditation on the element of water.

We associate this with our breathing in through the nose and out through the mouth. Breathing water into ourselves as we breathe in through the nose and with pursed lips and refined breath we breathe out through the mouth in a shower over us.

This meditative movement is connected with the muscles and connective tissue which includes the digestive organs, the facia, the diaphragm and all those areas of our body with more fluidity.

As people get older, their muscle and connective tissue has less moisture and so they tend to shrivel-up somewhat, thus there is less flexibility.

Begin to walk freely wherever you want to go. Breathing in through the nose and out through the mouth – letting go.

What and where are the areas of less flexibility in my body?

Work for more fluidity of movement in free-form walking – with a flowing, waving motion of hands and arms and then spinning and spiralling as you walk, helping many areas of your body to wake up and let go; breathing a purifying and clarifying water element through the use of breath.

This style of walking-meditation is good for inner cleansing, flushing-out the mental and physical blocks created by tension.

> Your way was in the sea, and your paths in the great waters,
> Yet your footsteps were not seen
>
> *Psalm 77*

We may walk this exercise in a centred or un-centred way doing 'water-spins', that is spinning to the left or to the right as we go.

Water awareness helps us to be more fluent and flexible.

Water is a feminine symbol.

'In the beginning was the feminine' – God does not stop creating.

> The Lord says: I will guide them to streams of water by a level path where they will not stumble, for I am a Father to my people.
>
> *Jeremiah 31.7–9*

Prayer of Azariah

Bless the Lord, all rain and
dew;
sing praise to him and highly exalt
him for ever.
Bless the Lord, all you winds and
sing praise to him and highly exalt
him for ever.
Bless the Lord, fire and heat;
sing praise to him and highly exalt
him for ever.
Bless the Lord, winter cold
And summer heat;
sing praise to him and highly exalt
him for ever.
Bless the Lord, dews and falling
snow;
sing praise to him and highly exalt
him for ever.

Bless the Lord, nights and days;
sing praise to him and highly exalt
him for ever.
Bless the Lord, light and darkness;
sing praise to him and highly exalt
him for ever.
Bless the Lord, ice and cold;
sing praise to him and highly exalt
him for ever.
Bless the Lord, frosts and snows;
sing praise to him and highly exalt
him for ever.
Bless the Lord, lightenings and
clouds;
sing praise to him and highly exalt
him for ever.

vv. 42–51

Water meditations

I

Being in the darkness of pain and sorrow experiencing the muddy depths.

Surfacing.

Surrendering.

Visualize a pool, well or spring – face inwards.

All move forwards, drawn to the central focal point, arms outstretched downwards, palms down.

Feel the weight of darkness – be with our pain in the weedy, muddy depths which are also divine depths. Slowly raise the arms, feeling the weight of water.

At shoulder level we reach the surface, and we meet each other.

Arms continue upwards and backwards, then bend over backwards, then bend over backwards to allow water to drop . . . splash back in a gesture of surrender.

Return, bringing heavenly light down into the depths.

Lord of Creation

2

In a pool.

Move forward, arms and body bent down; in a crouching movement.

Move upwards with the arms moving up as if through the weight of the water.

You have a reluctance to leave the dark, cool depths, but are drawn upwards by light.

Arms straight ahead at the surface . . . then continue upwards, bringing the peace and healing wholeness of the depths as an offering to the world. As the arms come down we meet each other and share peace and love and strength.

As a follow-up to the above body-meditation, the group may move to these verses as they wish:

> The flowing of the water
> in the ever-living fountain.

> The rising and the setting
> of the sun upon his way.

> The wide encircling of my own horizon.

> The heavens above.

> The earth beneath my feet.

> The roots, the rise
> to stems, leaves, flower
> and the falling of the seed.

3

Face west.

Ground and centre (as before).

Feel the liquidity of your body (we are made up of a very high percentage of water).

Feel the liquid tides within each cell of your body.

Find the calm pools of tranquillity within you, the rivers of feeling, the tides of power.

Sink deep into the well of the inner mind, below consciousness, deep down within the soul into the deepest point at which you meet the waters of your baptism. 'I am the Alpha and the Omega – the beginning and the end.

Floating meditation

Music

Lie down on a rug (or yoga or prayer mat) – close eyes.

Just let go of your muscles, your body, your bones, your thoughts, emotions.

Float on the surface of the sea, float . . . float . . .

Every time you become aware of something . . .

Let it go from your mind and body as you breathe out . . .

Leave weight behind, become light, become empty, become nothing . . .

> If you would float on the ocean of truth you must reduce yourself to a zero.
>
> *Gandhi*

Let go, let be, breathe deeply, trust the empty spaces and the silences. Of sinking therefore, not of climbing

We sink into depth and in this depth, we find God, who dwells especially in the depths and in the dark.

Yield to darkness and coolness, like the sinking of the sun and the cooling of the day.

Let go by breathing deeply in and out, by entering the inner music of the body, its breath, the tympanum of the beating of the heart or lung.

Here, we experience little trace of will-power.

The waters are cooler and darker the more deeply we sink.

Experience the emptying of yourself and the resulting receptivity.

> Everything that is receptive must be empty
>
> *Eckhart*[18]

Embrace 'nothingness'.

Trusting.

> All creatures
> have been drawn from nothingness
> And this is why
> their origin is nothingness
>
> *Eckhart*[19]

Our falls into nothingness must be trusted . . . we can learn to let ourselves fall, sink – as the seed falls to sprout eventually into new life. Creation, re-creation needs nothingness.

Sinking meditation

Now be aware of your body once again and feel as though you are sinking, sinking slowly through the depths of the sea. Breathing is no problem, breathe easily. You are at home here. Surrender to the darkness, the coolness, trust the empty space. Sink, dissolve into the divine depths.

At the bottom, my ground and God's are the same.

Return to the darkness of the womb.

Sink into the sea-bed.

Feel cherished, nurtured, deeply contented.

Connect with the source of peace and love.

You have returned home.

I once had a dream.
I dreamt that I, even though a man, was pregnant,
Pregnant and full with Nothingness
A woman who is with child.
And that out of this Nothingness
God was born

Eckhart[20]

Birthing

from all eternity
god lies on a maternity bed
giving birth.
the essence of god is birthing

meister eckhart [21]

Beach meditation

1 Breathing exercise (cf. page 88).

2 Use Basic Relaxation Technique (cf. page 26).

3 Sit comfortably or sit in lotus position, that is cross-legged, or use a prayer stool.

4 Or, if wished, lie on your back on a mat or futon.

Soft music may be played

Close your eyes and imagine you are lying alone on the beach . . . on a sunny afternoon. The air is wonderfully clear and you are sheltered by rocks . . . take a deep breath and let your body sink into the warm sand . . . allow the muscles of your face to relax.

Relax your neck . . . relax your shoulders and your chest . . . relax your back . . . relax your arms and feel your hands grow limp. Relax your stomach, relax your abdomen. Relax your legs and feel your feet go limp.

Listen to the sound of the sea . . . feel the power of the water . . . sense the compassion stirring within you . . . Feel all your tension flowing outward into the water, and allow the sea to fill you with her healing.

Take a deep breath and imagine your whole being filled with blue light . . . keep breathing slowly and deeply . . . imagine yourself surrounded by a bubble of blue healing light . . . feel yourself floating in this bubble . . . weightless, no fear, no anxiety . . . sense the blue light all around you . . . experience the opening of trust . . . now allow your body to begin to open . . . allow your pelvic area to relax . . . (pause).

Imagine blue light flowing through you into the area of your womb . . . Feel the cleansing power of this light . . . and allow your tensions, anxieties and worries to dissolve into the healing blue light as your body heals itself.

Lord of Creation

When you are ready, place your right hand over the heart centre in the middle of your chest.

Place your left hand over the area of your womb . . .

Sense the connection between the two . . . feel the energy flowing between them . . .

Pray in the silence for inner healing . . . see yourself doing this . . . Imagine your heart and womb filled with light, radiating love . . .

Now, imagine that it is evening on the beach, the waves are lapping gently on the sand and there is a full moon above you.

Experience its energy and draw down this moonlight into you – draw down the moon.

Experience the beauty of your soul and the interconnection between you and all created beings. Flow out from the very centre of your being into creation . . . allow creation to enter into you to penetrate deep within you.

In your inner solitude experience the presence of God. Be open to that presence.

Discover that you and God are one.

(long pause)

Now imagine yourself standing on the beach holding hands with everyone you love . . . .

Imagine this circle expanding until it includes all created beings. Imagine there is only one heart in the universe, and you are a part of it . . . Experience the flow of love between you and all that is . . . Feel yourself growing more and more powerful.

Now imagine yourself dancing on the beach, surrounded by love . . . . safe and protected.

See yourself opening without fear to all the elements.

Open yourself to the earth . . .

Open yourself to the sea . . .

Open yourself to the moon . . .

Open yourself to your own spirit . . .

(Long pause)

When you are ready, slowly come back and gently open your eyes.

The blessing of water

There is an old saying that the devil hates holy water! It evidently reminds him of holy baptism and the Christian promise to fight against evil. The practising Christian, on the other hand, should love holy water, since by the means of it he or she began the new life in Christ, and became a member of his mystical body, the Church. In addition to its use as a reminder of baptism and remission of sin, holy water is a sacramental that conveys a blessing through the intercession of the Church. Thus, when water is blessed, a blessing is invoked upon all who use it and upon all objects on which it may be sprinkled.

Rite for the blessing of water

Dear friends,
This water will be used
to remind us of our baptism.
Let us ask God to bless it
and keep us faithful
to the Spirit he has given us.
God, our Father,
your gift of water
brings life and freshness to the earth;
it washes away our sins
and brings us eternal life.
We ask you now
to bless † this water
and to give us your protection on this day
which you have made your own.
Renew the living spring of your life within us
and protect us in spirit and body,
that we may be free from sin
and come into your presence
to receive your gift of salvation.[22]

The priest/minister sprinkles himself (herself) and the assembled people.

Meet for Father, Son and Spirit,
the Triune of power.

Lord of Creation

A small drop of water
to encompass my beloved,
meet for Father, Son and Spirit,
the Triune of power.

A small drop of water
to fill thee with each grace,
meet for Father, Son and Spirit,
the Triune of power.

Carmina Gadelica III, 21[23]

You are our breath. You are the flight
  of our longing to the depths of heaven.
You are the water, which flees from
  the wilderness of our anxiety and fear.
You are the salt, which purifies.
You are the piercing wind of our pomposity.
You are the traveller who knocks.
You are the prince who dwells within us.

Waldo Williams[24]

Song of purification: immersion

Our Mother, who created us from a single drop of blood from her holy womb,
Our Mother who gave us this design of body,
these protected parts, this internal architecture,
Our Mother who enabled us to cunningly feed and nourish, to the cavern of life,
We act with your strength, and in your dignity,
each of us different in her faith, her colouring and her shape,
each of us alike in our structure.
Oh, Mother, rejoice with us in this meeting of your daughters!
We bless each woman as she enters the water.
We say that water is what all women share,
water of amniotic fluid, water of rivers where clothes were washed,
water of cleaning and cooking
We say, at the edge of the pool:
We are part of the body of women, of earth and water.
May we survive at sea, on land, in shallow straits or over our heads.
May we rescue one another in deep water.

E. M. Broner

Lord of the Elements Workshop

the creative operation of god
does not simply mould us like soft clay.
it is a FIRE that
animates all it touches,
a spirit that gives life.
so it is in LIVING
that we should give ourselves
to that CREATIVE action,
imitate it, and
identify with it.
teilhard de chardin[25]

FIRE

Fire has the qualities of illumination, purification and renewal. It also has an element of fruitfulness but it may purge, consume and annihilate everything; this quality is signified by purgatory and hell-fire.

In the Christian liturgy we have the 'Easter-fire' and the Easter candle at the Easter Vigil.

Yahweh, the God of the Israelites, made fire the symbol of his theophany, for example in the burning bush and in the pillar of fire which went on ahead in the night through the desert.

In common with Prometheus, the Greek fire-bringer, Christ was seen as a fire-bringer. In both cases death and becoming is a form of baptism by fire, seen as a rebirth into new life.

Fire and flames are symbolic of both martyrdom and religious fervour. Flames of fire have traditionally been ascribed as an attribute of St Anthony of Padua, the patron saint of protection against fire. St Laurence, too, is connected with this element and is often depicted wearing a burning tunic, in reference to his torture on a gridiron. Fire and flames may appear as signs of fervour of such saints as St Anthony Abbot and St Agnes. It is even personified as a monster vomiting flames; or by a salamander, which, according to legend, can live in fire without being burned. In paintings of Pentecost, flames on the heads of the apostles signify the presence of the Holy Spirit. It is interesting to note that hell-fire and the fire of heaven are not two different forces, but only opposite manifestations of the same energy.

Fire is the brother of wind, they get on well together! Fire contains within itself both the demonic and the divine, hell and heaven, death and life, opposition, contradiction and oneness. This contradiction and oneness is especially evident in the relationship between fire and the element water, manifested as agents of the rites of purification and cleansing. Ritual washing plays a central role in many religions (even today in Islam), the spiritual bathing in holy rivers, for example the Euphrates and the Ganges. This ritual cleansing means the bringing of enlightenment, becoming illuminated. Also fire has a purifying action, so that the flame becomes the image of cleansing and cleanliness; cremation cleanses from earthly taint. Cleanliness too is a symbol of healing, fresh, new, undamaged life. Cleanliness is therefore always a form of beginning. We even know it in our everyday life; to feel new-born after a bath, therefore purified through the element of water.

It is interesting to note that in the liturgy of the new fire at the Easter Vigil the Easter candle lit anew is immersed three times in the water of the font.

Fire, too, has a part to play in the philosophical thinking on truth. This is reflected not so much in the collection of knowledge, as in the notion that 'pure' thought contains fire *vis-à-vis* being 'on fire', or to be ablaze with something. To be aglow, to be inflamed, to deliver a fiery speech . . . it's only a 'straw fire'; fire has become associated with forward thinking, as with the Greek Prometheus' way of inner, active thinking.

> Lord Jesus Christ
> the world's true sun,
> ever rising, never setting,
> whose life-giving warmth
> engenders, preserves, nourishes
> and gladdens all things
> in heaven and on earth:
> shine in my soul, I pray,
> scatter the night of sin,
> and the clouds of error.
> Blaze within me,
> That I may go my way without stumbling
> Taking no part in the shameful
> Deeds of those who wander
> In the dark,
> But all my life long
> Walking as one native to the light.
> Amen.

> *Desiderius Erasmus, 1467–1536*

Fire meditations

I

Befriending our Divinity

Music: Stravinsky's *Fire Bird Suite*

Blazing Spirit, FIRE, personal, supersubstantial, the consummation of a union so immeasurably more lovely and more desirable than that destructive fusion of which all the pantheists dream: be pleased yet once again to come down and breathe a soul into the newly formed, fragile film of matter with which this day the world is to be freshly clothed.

Teilhard de Chardin, Hymn of the Universe[26]

Leader (voice over):
We now have the element of fire.

Breathe through the mouth and out through the nose. Here we are aware of the diaphragm, which should be loosened up by the water element walk and movement. We are aware also of the heart and the pulsing of the blood from the heart around the body.

Breath in and out from the heart centre – experience a sense of the blood pulsing.

We now breathe with refined breath and deepen the sense of pulsing in the fire-walk.

As we walk with an ever-deepening awareness of the pulsing of blood within us we become aware of our pulse-beat, that is fire-in-the-blood, an experience of 'pulsing towards' our goal with the breath in touch with the heartbeat and so we become engaged and enthused.

The stylized form of this walk is to jump up and strike hands with the arm up and the opposite leg up. Try to breathe in on the 'up' and out on the 'down'. Continue doing this for a while.

> Whoever would enter Paradise
> must go through fire and water,
> whether he be Peter, to whom
> the keys of heaven were entrusted,
> or Paul, a chosen vessel of God,
> or John, to whom all the secrets
> of God were revealed.
>
> St Augustine

2

Face south. Ground and centre. Be conscious of the electric spark within each nerve cell as pulses jump from synapse to synapse (the places where the nerve cells join). Be aware of the combustion within each cell as food burns to release energy.

> If the Fire has come down into the heart of the world it is, in the last resort, to lay hold on me and to absorb me.
>
> Teilhard de Chardin[27]

Let your own fire become one with the Light of Christ – the spark within you. 'Oh Light of Christ – Inflame me!'

Dance

'God has given me the power' – Mechthilde of Magdeburg's Dance, or another suitable dance, for example, Shepherd's Dance; Oneg Shabbat.

Talk: suffering

In one way or another we have all suffered pain either in the body or in the mind, usually in both body and mind. Pain has the effect of emptying us and if we allow it to, it can enable us to benefit, for the resultant void can be entered into through prayer, and healing brought about. By entering into the source of our pain the cause is resolved by a process of spiritual exercise (*ascesis*) so that an inner transformation takes place for the healing of the whole person. The whole of creation benefits from the fire of suffering for all being is interconnected.

> When Christ was in pain we were in pain. All creatures of God's creation that can suffer pain suffered with him. The sky and the earth failed at the time of Christ's dying because he too was part of nature.

Julian of Norwich

Through entering into our pain and grasping it we are brought up into the whole process of the incarnate and suffering God in Christ.

An excellent description of how we could learn from pain even as it grasps us is to be found in *Original Blessing* by Matthew Fox[28]. This book is a primer in creation spirituality. Fox quotes the Japanese poet Kenji Miyazawa, who has given a powerful image of dealing with pain, when he said that we must embrace pain and burn its fuel for our journey. The image that comes to Matthew Fox's mind is that we pick up our pain as we would a bundle of sticks for a fireplace; we necessarily embrace these sticks as we move across the room to the fireplace, then we thrust them into the fire, getting rid of them; they are a symbol of sacrifice and we are warmed by them and energized. Matthew Fox suggests that 'this is the manner in which we can and indeed must deal with our pain. First comes the embrace, the allowing of pain to be pain; next comes the journey with the pain; then the letting go, into a cauldron where the pain's energy will serve us. And finally comes the benefit we do indeed derive from having burned this fuel.'

As a result of having suffered mental or physical pain we are more able to understand other people's pain. We learn compassion for others and become

Lord of Creation

more sensitive to the good, the pure and the lovely in life. It also gives us a deeper appreciation of beauty.

Meditation on being with pain

Use the basic relaxation technique (page 26).

Be aware of any thought or physical sensation which is painful to you . . . One is enough . . .

Concentrate on this sensation for a while and allow yourself to stay with the discomfort . . .

Be aware of how your mind or body seeks how to close off or deny the experience.

Feel the pain, explore it and experience how you feel both the pain itself and the resistance of your whole self against the pain.

The pain and the resistance to the pain are both present . . . and yet separate from one another.

Be aware of how you may attempt to deny the presence of the pain . . . try not to attempt to push away the pain but remain with it and be as gentle as you can with it . . .

In the same spirit of gentleness, let go, let it be and be aware that the struggle of resisting the pain may be more painful than the pain itself . . .

Experience your deep sense of relief and how much more open you feel, for in resisting the pain you may have increased it through the tension, dis-ease and struggle . . .

Keep relaxing your grip-on-the-pain and any fear that has gathered around the sensation or thought . . .

Allow your tension, stress and fear to fade away through your ceasing to resist the experience . . . soften up, dissolve the fear and open up to the process of letting-go . . .

Be aware of any unpleasant fears, thoughts, sensations or emotions that surface . . . note them and . . . let them go.

All of these experiences are part of the process of being human. They are thoughts, sensations, experiences and reactions . . . that is all . . . nothing more than that.

And so we clear away these resistances and thoughts and enter into the very centre of our being into being-with-God, the very ground of our eternal life.

Open, released, centred . . . in the heart of God, in the heart of Christ.

God be with thee in every pass,
Jesus be with thee on every hill,
Spirit be with thee in every stream,
headland and ridge and moor.
Each sea and land, each path and meadow,
each lying down each rising up
each step of the journey thou goest.

Gaelic Traditional[29]

That first burst of Fire
from which we came
Love was its name and that
sacred Fire still burns
to create its magic in our hearts.

Someday, after we have
mastered the winds, the waves,
The tides and gravity,
we shall harness for God
the energy of love.

Then for the second time
in the history of the world,
Man will have discovered
Fire.

Teilhard de Chardin[30]

Rite for the blessing of fire

The blessing of fire is in accord with the reference in the Gospels to baptism by fire. It is mentioned that Jesus baptized with fire and the Spirit. Fire has a far greater purifying effect than earth or water. It is radical in its effect because it burns and disintegrates everything that is subject to decay although the one thing that it cannot reach is the Spirit, because the Spirit is not subject to change and decay. We can see ourselves therefore to be in a continual state of consumption – our bodies, our minds, our thoughts. We are a living holocaust as a result of this burning process. The light of our consciousness arises out of this burning process and shines forth when the impurities have been burned. As a consequence of this burning process we become radiant.

To perform this rite for the blessing of fire we need a bowl or cauldron (an excellent resource is the base of a fondue burner); some incense, candles, pen and paper, and holy water.

Leader: Dear friends in Christ
             we have come together
             to pray to be released
             from whatever may be
             on our conscience or is
             troubling us, whether in mind
             or in body.
             We ask forgiveness for what
             we have failed to do or that
             we ought to have done.
             We are sorry and truly repent.
             For the sake of Jesus Christ who
             died for us, may we be forgiven
             for all that is past and may
             we walk in his way
             as children of light.   Amen.

Let us pray:

             Lord God
             we share in the light of your glory
             through your son, the Light of the World.
             Make this fire holy and
             inflame us with new hope.
             May it be a symbol of the
             disintegration of our impurities
             and the purification of our minds
             that one day we may come to
             the feast of eternal light.
             We ask this through Christ our Lord.

We now write on a piece of paper whatever it is that we wish to release and, in turn, place the paper in the fire bowl. When this has been performed a dance of peaceful joy may be in order.

It is important to note that deep within ourselves a fertile void has been created through the releasing of inner pain. A 'grounding' exercise may be in order to root ourselves.

Take a few deep breaths, relaxing your body.

Allow tensions and negative emotions to escape with your exhaled breath.

Imagine yourself green and growing.

Feel roots growing down from your feet into the earth, down to its core.

Draw energy up from the earth through your root system into your feet, legs, torso, arms and head.

Feel it shoot out through the top of your head like branches soaking in the light of the sun.

Watch as the branches grow back down towards the earth, creating a closed circuit and returning to its source, from whence it came.

> Being is God's circle
> and in this circle all creatures exist.
> Everything that is in God is God.
>
> *Eckhart*[31]

Prayer of Azariah

Bless the Lord, Hananiah, Azariah,
And Mishael;
sing praise to him and highly exalt
him for ever.
For he has rescued us from Hades
and saved us from the power
of death,
and delivered us from the midst
of the burning fiery
furnace;
from the midst of the fire he has
delivered us.
Give thanks to the Lord, for he is
Good.
For his mercy endures for ever.
All who worship the Lord, bless the
God of gods,
sing praise to him and give thanks
to him,
for his mercy endures for ever.

vv. 66–68

OUR *WAY* IS NOT SOFT GRASS,
IT'S A *MOUNTAIN PATH*
WITH LOTS OF ROCKS.
BUT IT GOES *UPWARDS*,
FORWARD, TOWARD THE
SUN.

anon.

Cave of the Heart

Meditation

Close your eyes, lightly . . .

Wriggle your toes and gently put them to sleep . . .

Waggle your knees and gently put them to sleep . . .

Move your hips and gently put them to sleep . . .

Rotate your shoulders and gently put them to sleep . . .

Shake your head and let it rest at ease . . .

Nod your head up and down very slowly and balance it gently . . . gently

Keep your eyes lightly closed and your head inclined slightly downwards,

your spine erect and your whole body like a puppet-on-a-string.

Now imagine away up above you in the cosmos a bright globe of light – a very bright light . . .

and I want you to draw down a ray of that light on an in-breath, down through the crown of your head, down, down the spine . . . into your heart.

The ray of light floods your heart
and then you breathe out that light
on an out-breath.
(Keep inhaling and exhaling in this manner several times)

What I want you to do next is to imagine that your spine is the shaft of an elevator.

On an in-breath, breathe down the shaft until your breath stops at the ground floor.

Open the door of the elevator and step through into a cave-like room.

The heart-cave.

Lord of Creation

Hanging on the walls of the cave are sconces, rush torches, spluttering and giving off a dim light.

On the wall of the cave opposite you is a door with a large brass door handle.

Walk over and turn the handle
– opening the door. Step through.

You are standing on a mountain path which runs past the cave door, below you is a valley of green fields.

To the right the path leads upwards circling the mountain, spiralling upwards towards the summit.

You begin to walk the footpath and look back down into the valley below, aware all the time of moving upwards.

Now focus your gaze on the summit of the mountain as you climb.
Far ahead of you see the peak of the mountain.
Experience as you climb higher the vision becoming clearer and become aware of the figure of a person standing ahead of you.

As you draw nearer witness the beauty of this figure.

It is Jesus Christ.
Transfigured in radiant light before you is the resurrected Christ.
As you draw nearer you feel the impulse to kneel before him.

Aware of the tremendous love, power, joy and compassion that he is radiating to all the world.

For a few moments, remain in the light of his presence in worship . . .

Now I want to ask you – in your imagination – to rise from your knees, to stand and step forward, taking the place of that tremendous figure . . .

Experience being absorbed into his person, into his transfiguring light so that you become one with him. No separation. Totally oned.

Experience turning around and radiating his light to all the world.

Full of this Presence you begin to walk back down and around the mountain on the footpath you used before. As you descend be aware that you are full of radiant light.

Once again arrive at the door in the side of the mountain. On opening the door you return to the heart-cave, dimly lit by spluttering sconces.

Ahead of you is the elevator door, which you open.

Lord of the Elements Workshop   125

Step into the elevator, close the door behind you and on inhalation of the light and the breath return to the place where you are sitting now.

Come out slowly . . . very slowly . . . take three deep breaths. When you let out the air from your third breath softly, open your eyes.

(Give people plenty of time to do this)

Prayer

O God, your light never fades,
within our hearts
it strengthens us inwardly
by the brightness of your presence;
may darkness find no entrance in us.
We pray this through Jesus Christ our Lord. Amen.

the WIND BLOWS where it
WILLS, you hear the
SOUND of it, but you do not know
where it COMES from or
where it is going.
so it is with everyone
who is BORN from
the spirit.

JOHN 3.8 REB

AIR

Fiery Spirit,
fount of courage,
life within life,
of all that has being!

O sacred breath, O blazing love
O savor in the breast and balm
flooding the heart with
the fragrance of good,
O limpid mirror of God
who leads wanderers
home and hunts out the lost,

O current of power permeating all
in the heights upon the earth and
in all deeps:
you bind and gather
all people together.

Out of you clouds
come streaming, winds
take wing from you, dashing
rain against stone;
and ever-fresh springs
well from you, washing
the evergreen globe.
O teacher to those who know,
a joy to the wise
is the breath of Sophia.
Praise then be yours!
you are the song of praise,
the delight of life,
a hope and a potent honour
granting garlands of light.

Anon

Air signifies nothingness, emptiness, swift passing, impermanence, the divine breath and life itself. It may manifest itself as wind. The Lord God reveals himself in the wind and 'blows where he will' or shows himself as the wind-storm at Whitsuntide.

It has been an ancient tradition that the four directions correspond with the four main winds:

(Colder) North and East Winds
(Warmer) South and West Winds

Air meditations

1

We now deal with the outermost layer of our being.

Be aware of the breath. With refined breath, breathe in and out through the pores of the skin. We bathe our body with our breath.

'Breath-bathing' (as against sun-bathing).

We have moved through different layers of body awareness. Now we have an awareness of the skin. We are to experience light and air and 'freedom walking'. Walking as if on a spring, that is on air. We walk about in a light, reflective manner flowing with the wind, airily and spiritually buoyant, mounting up every now and again as if taking wing.

We now spiral in the air, like a feather on the wind – and yet, in control . . . space . . . Bathing in air.

2

Face east.

Ground and centre, that is feel your feet on the floor, watch the ebb and flow of your breath; see it as a support, moving into a force of transcendence within yourself. Feel it as the breath of the Holy Spirit and take in the incarnated grace and energy of the Cosmic Christ. Become aware of and experience your inner space, your spacefulness being filled with divine experience, by the eternal now – the beautiful presence of the Lord Christ. Become one with the Lord. All who are in Christ, St Paul declared, are a 'new creation' (2 Corinthians 15.17).

Be aware of the beauty of the earth, the heavens, the seas and rivers, the plains and mountains and all that are living and dying within it.

Let your breath merge with the winds, the clouds, the great currents that sweep up over land and ocean with the turning of the earth.

O Holy Spirit, inspire me!

3

Music: *Jonathan Livingston Seagull*[32]

Air is not an easy element to come to grips with, unlike the other elements whose essential nature is clear, AIR is much less tangible. We cannot see it although we may feel it in the gentle breeze as well as in the full-blown gale. It provides us with oxygen and is intimately connected with the function of communication, which it represents. Sound waves are communicated by it and our sense of smell is dependent upon it. Without its filtering effect the sun's radiation would kill us as it moves to and fro across the surface of the earth. It connects land to land and person to person. Remember these things as you undertake this journey of the air and try to come to a deeper understanding of its nature both within the words and within yourself.

Use the first part of the cave of the heart meditational exercise (see page 124), until you arrive near the top of the mountain where you come to a small grassy plateau, warmed by the sun. You lie down with the sun shining down on you and a gentle breeze caressing your skin.

Open your senses up, feeling the soft grass under your hands, the warmth of the sun and the air moving all around you. You begin to daydream . . . and imagine yourself rising up, floating upon the air, lifting, wheeling and turning, just like the birds, free and untrammelled by the confines of a physical body . . .

You soar upward away from the hillside and see the land spread out below you as you dip-and-soar – and turn – feeling the wind against your body, insubstantial though it is in this state.

You find that almost with the speed of thought you can be where you wish to be . . . so diving, darting across the land, seeing it from high up you begin to investigate this element of air, sensing the different temperatures that exist at different heights . . .

Soaring upwards you find a passing cloud and rest upon it a while . . . Its fluffy formation cradling you gently, giving you support . . . and then leaving it, once more allow yourself to drift downwards, slowly seeing in the distance again the smoky haze from some factory.

You move swiftly towards it and as you get closer you realize how tainted the air is becoming with the smoke and the chemicals pouring into the atmosphere. And how it blocks out the sunlight and turns the land beneath into a hazy relief.

Turning again you leave it behind coming lower, you look at the grassy fields and the corn growing, the cattle feeding quietly, the farmhouses scattered here and there. Traffic meandering through the roads that twist and turn through the countryside. And then soaring upwards again you move higher and higher into the mountains, the air becoming chillier and stronger as you rise towards the peaks and yet at the same time the air is sharper, fresher in some manner, more rare too.

And the sun's rays beat down even stronger at this height now that there is less atmosphere to filter them. In the distance you can see clouds massing over the mountain range and you know at the very least that rain is on the way. And you head towards it flying through the air. As you come closer you can see the deep rain clouds dark and grey against the back-drop of the sky. (And) the wind now grows stronger and even the birds do not come this high . . .

You sense the wind gaining strength driving the clouds before it. But you continue to head for it knowing that no harm can come to you in this state. That you can experience this element of air in yet another of its guises.

The storm is growing closer now and the wind rises moaning fitfully through the mountain peaks, driving before it a flurry of dust. Here and there fly leaves from trees torn from their branches and swept up into the ever-growing strength of the air.

Clouds now are sweeping down from the mountain-tops towards the land below. And in their midst you see the lightning flashes and hear the rumble of thunder and you begin to appreciate the awesome power that can exist within the atmosphere.

For a while you revel in that power darting in and out among the clouds . . . but you also realize that in other circumstances such power can be destructive. However, at this time all is well, and the storm plays out its part amidst the mountain peaks. The rain falling into high lakes . . . running into the streams, to run down through the mountains and the hillsides, to form rivers, which flow onwards towards the sea. Water which once was in the ocean is drawn up by the heat of the sun into the atmosphere and carried many, many miles inland only once more to be released on the land below to find its way back to the ocean from whence it started its journey . . .

You begin to appreciate how important the atmosphere is to the whole planet, and its nature of communication . . . as it takes one thing and another; one part of the globe to another.

Now it is time to return lower down the mountains to the hillside and so swooping and turning following the currents of the air like a glider you spiral down the mountains, down the high hills to the grassy plateau below, coming to rest once more upon that grassy plain . . . The trees around you, the grass beneath your hands and body and the sun's warming rays still coming down. You get up and begin to walk back, clambering down the side of the hill toward that rocky ledge and the door back into your own world . . . The wind down here has come back to being a gentle breeze once more . . . softly wafting, the sounds and smells from the land beneath and all around you . . .

And you walk back along the rocky ledge feeling exhilarated from your journey in the sky and with a new-found understanding of the nature of air.

There ahead of you is the door – the open door through which you passed in order to return back into the inner chamber . . . and you turn to watch the door as it slowly swings to closing quietly but firmly . . . and shutting out the inner worlds once more.

Stand within that inner chamber – softly lit by the rush torches still flaring in their sconces and, as you do so, the grey walls around you begin to fade away becoming as misty and unreal as the element of air that you have just been experiencing. And as they fade away you begin to rise up once more in the planes of consciousness returning to your normal state of awareness and reality.

(Rising) Become more and more aware and conscious of the room from which we started our journey.

And at the count of 5, 4, 3, 2, 1 you stretch open your eyes and become fully aware of this room in which we sit, returning to full normal consciousness.

Take a few moments to rest quietly remembering your journey (you may write up notes on it while it is still fresh in your mind).

Lord of Creation

Dance of the Elements

Air: *Veni Sancte Spiritus*

This dance was inspired by the Taizé chant *Veni Sancte Spiritus* (Come Holy Spirit). It reflects a human yearning to experience 'spirit' (the Holy Spirit) within matter. The dancer reaches 'heavenward' in supplication, asking to act as a conductor of Holy Spirit to the earth. She then draws spiritualized matter upwards through the body to meet the 'gleam of love streaming down from heaven'. Now the human spirit can radiate compassion, touching others at the heart level reflected by the arms outstretched horizontally from the vertical figure – we meet each other in the form of the cross.

The dance

Standing in a circle, hands held.

1 As the music begins, all sway gently from left to right.
2 When the violin begins (this is soft), slowly move forward on R foot, gradually raising the arms until reaching right up (2 chants).
3 In the centre sway gently, arms still reaching up (1 chant).
4 Slowly walk backwards out of the centre, sweeping arms right down to brush fingertips on floor (2 chants).
5 Gradually stand up (2 chants).
6 Repeat 1–5.
7 Stand, hands in an 'inverted' prayer position (i.e. pointing downwards, fingertips touching). When the solo voice begins, gently bring your hands (still in the same position) upwards. At heart level turn your hands round into a normal prayer position. Continue to raise your arms, opening the hands and turning them outwards above the head. Describe a wide arc as arms descend outwards allowing your hands to touch those on each side at heart level. Bring your arms down into 'inverted' prayer position.
8 Wait for the voice again and repeat 7.
9 Repeat 1–8., but this time at the end of 7, bring the hands round to cross over your heart, hold there for a moment then drop hands to join with others in the circle and gently sway until the music ends.

Choreographed by Julie Trier

AGAPÉ, 'FOR THE LORD OF THE ELEMENTS'

An agapé is an ancient form of table fellowship or 'love feast'. When people gather together as the community of the body of Christ, the Church, the Lord of Creation is present, as effectively as he is as the risen Christ present in the Eucharist. In the agapé his presence is manifest within the gathered community and the Word.

At the centre of the liturgy or public Christian worship is the Holy Eucharist in balance with the Church community and the Word. In this dynamic there is a bringing together of the wholeness of God – symbolized in the consecrated loaf, which is also a symbol of the people of God, and the consecrated wine, symbol of the life of God. All of this signifies the offering of the Son to the Father in his once and for all sacrificial offering on the cross and in which we participate in the Holy Eucharist.

The agapé in a non-eucharistic manner is a meal which could be described as a table-liturgy that uses food and drink and the fruits of the earth to signify love bonded together through the blessing and sharing of food. The agapé is an ideal way in meal form for bringing together the various 'elements' explored through the prayer of body, mind and spirit in the worship of the Lord of the Elements.

Lord, the lover of life, you feed the birds of the skies and array the lilies of the field. We bless you for all your creatures and for the food we are about to receive.

From a form of grace before meals proposed by the bishops of the
Catholic Church in the USA

Lord of Creation

CONCLUSION TO THE
LORD OF THE ELEMENTS

Do a meditation walk bringing the four elements together. First the earth walk, a grounded walk on an earth supportive to the bones and ligaments. Here we experience a sense of self-esteem. It is good to be walking here on the earth, pressing down on the firm ground of our being. We experience good contact with Mother Earth.

We then move into the phase of the element of water where we experience 'letting-go' and enjoyment of the sensation of being cleansed, refreshed and absolved. Keep moving with a flowing movement and experience swimming in a somewhat buoyant manner.

When ready, change into the element of fire and become aware of the pulsing from the heart. Fired-up, purposefully walk as if toward your goal.

We are nearly there when we are 'fanned' by the wind and experience the freedom of air and so we 'float' as if a feather on the wind.

We spiral and circle around – bones, muscles, diaphragm, blood and skin. Earth, water, fire and air. The layers of oneself, contacted, purified, encouraged and clarified.

We have walked the earth by the earthwalk, a walk of confidence where we breathe in through the nose and out through the nose and feel the earth through bones and ligaments. We stand, then we walk.

In the water meditation we breathe in through the nose and out through the mouth and move in a left-to-right flowing motion as well as sinking and rising.

The firewalk is a walk where we breathe in through the mouth and out through the nose with the option of a 'sparky' movement 'clapping' up to the right, while hopping on the right foot.

Airwalking is done through breathing with a 'refined' breath in and out through the skin . . . 'breath-bathing'. Arms up to shoulder height in the front going up-and-down, spiralling, circling, etc.

Each person has an affinity to a different element and a foreign reaction to another. It is interesting where one needs to explore in the areas of awareness.

This meditational exercise affects the whole person, through the body to the emotions and passions to the spirit. By seeking the Lord Christ, King of the elements, through the physical, emotional, mental and spiritual areas of our composite being, we are brought up into one by the indwelling Cosmic Christ, the Holy Spirit incarnated within all creation. We have entered into the kingdom of God.

> The creation waits with eager longing for the revealing of the children of God; for the creation was subjected to futility, not of its own will but by the will of him who subjected it in hope; because the creation itself will be set free from its bondage to decay and obtain the glorious liberty of the children of God.
>
> *Romans 8.19–23*

To enter into the kingdom of God is to experience the unitary consciousness of body, mind and spirit. It is to experience the Creator who is beyond time and space from ones experience within creation. It is to go beyond time and space as God is beyond time and space and to experience the unity of the whole creation. Subject and object disappear. If God is in us and the whole of creation is in God, then the whole of creation must also be in us. There is no coming in or going out. God is our Mother. Every creature is a word of God, is a book of God. We can see God in all things for he is within all things. As Eckhart said: 'God is at home. It is us who have gone for a walk!'

When God pronounced that his creation was good, it was not only that his hand had fashioned every creature; it was that his breath had brought every creature to life. The presence of God's spirit in all living beings is what makes them beautiful; and if we look with God's eyes, nothing on earth is ugly.

Pelagius

God created all things in such a way that they are not outside himself, as ignorant people falsely imagine.
Rather,
All creatures flow outward, but nonetheless remain within God.
God created all things this way:
    Not that they might stand outside of God,
    nor alongside God,
    nor beyond God,
but that they might
    come into God
    and receive God
    and dwell in God.
For this reason everything that is bathed in God, is enveloped by God, who is round about us all enveloping us!

Eckhart[33]

Lord of Creation

the eight materials of man

from the **EARTH**, the flesh;
from the **WATER**, the **BLOOD**;
from the **AIR**, the **BREATH**;
from the **hardness**, the **BONES**;
from the **salt**, the feeling;
from the **SUN**, that is, **FIRE**, his **motion**;
from the **TRUTH**, his **understanding**;
from the **holy spirit**, that is, **god**,
his **SOUL** or **life**.

ancient welsh text

Agapé for Earth, Water, Fire and Air

Chant: 'Within our darkest night' (Taizé)

In the darkness the leader says:
In the beginning, darkness covered the face of the deep.
Then the rushing breath of life hovered over the waters.

Pause

Let us breathe together.
(Pause)

Let us catch our breaths from the need to make, to do.
(Pause)

Let us be conscious of the breath of life.
(Pause)

We breathe out what the trees breathe in.
(Pause)

We breathe in what the trees breathe out.
(Pause)

Together we breathe each other into life.
(Pause)

Blessed is the One within many.
(Pause)

Blessed are the many who make one.

Meditation: Breathe the light within (*see Greetings exercise, page 87*).

First Speaker (*says after the hand bell is rung*)
And the darkness gave birth to light.

(*Light the Candles*)

Psalm 63

O, God, you are my God, I seek you,
my soul thirsts for you;
my flesh faints for you,
as in a dry and weary land
where there is no water.

Because your steadfast love is better than life,
my lips will praise you.
So I will bless you as long as I live;
I will lift up my hands and call on your name.

For you have been my help,
and in the shadow of your wings I sing for joy.
My soul clings to you;
your right hand upholds me.

Verses 1, 3, 4, 7–8

Prayer

God of truth,
I ask that I may receive,
so that my joy may be full.
Meanwhile, let my mind meditate on it,
let my tongue speak of it,
let my heart love it,
let my mouth preach it,
let my soul hunger for it
and my whole being desire it,
until I enter into the joy of my Lord,
who is God one and triune, blessed forever.
Amen.

Second Speaker
Why is this meal different from all other meals?

Lord of Creation

Leader says

At all other meals we eat one kind of bread;
today (or tonight) we eat from grains and breads
and fruits of many colours.

On all other days (nights) we see light in whiteness;
today (tonight) we see in lights of many colours.

On all other days (nights) we breath however we like;
today (tonight) we pray by pausing to breathe together.

Third Speaker responds

Our foods come from the Earth; we come from many parts of this land.

The water unites us.
The lights are fire; what burns in our hearts is varied.
The air unites us.

Reader

A Story of Creation

Once upon a time,
in the beginning,
a labour of love was undertaken.

It started with a sign,
to show that something was about to happen.
Light came forth from the deep darkness,
bright, clear and unmistakable.

And it was very good.

At the second time,
the waters were broken.
At first, they gushed,
then they dried to a trickle,
and a space was created.
It was exactly the right size.
By now, creation was well under way.

And it was very good.

At the third time,
a cradle was made ready.
It was comfortable and beautiful and waiting.

Agapé for Earth, Water, Fire and Air

And food was prepared,
issuing warmly and sweetly
and in precisely the right measure
from the being of the labourer.

And it was very good.

At the fourth time,
rhythm was established.
Ebbing and flowing, contracting and expanding,
pain and joy, sun and moon,
beginning and ending.
The labour of love progressed.

And it was very good.

At the fifth time,
there was ceaseless activity:
fluttering like the wings of the dove,
humming like the murmur of the dragonfly,
swimming like the darting golden fish,
wriggling like the lithe serpent,
surging like a mighty lion.

And it was very good.

At the sixth time,
there was a momentary, endless hesitation.
Then a child was born.
And the child looked just like the one who had given it life.
The child, too, was born with the power to create,
and to make decisions,
and to love.

The labourer looked at all that had been accomplished,
and rejoiced,
for it was very good.

At the seventh time,
the labour was finished.

The task was complete.
and the labourer rested,
for she was very, very tired.

Kathy Galloway[34]

Lord of Creation

Fourth Speaker (pointing to the bowl of water)
This water, how do we gather it?

Fifth Speaker
We gather the rains and the Ocean.

For this water is the water of drowning
and this water is the water of birthing,
and this water is the water of life:
Let us drink
(*The bowl of water is passed round for all to drink in turn*)

(*When all have drunk*)

All say together
Blessed is the One within many.
Blessed are the many who make One.

Leader
We are of the earth
who spring from the earth.
We are of the earth
who live on earth
and from it.
We are of the earth
and the earth feeds us.
We are from the earth
and we feed the earth.

(*Someone passes the platter of breads, grains and fruits, and each person takes some of each.*)

Reader
Many of the colours of our fruitful earth
nourish the many colours
of our fruitful earth dwellers.

All together
Blessed is the One within the many.
Blessed are the many who make one.

Agapé for Earth, Water, Fire and Air

Come with me, my love, come away
for the long wet months are past,
the rains have fed the earth
and left it bright with blossoms.

Birds wing in the low sky
dove and songbird singing
in the open air above.

Earth nourishing tree and vine,
green fig and tender grape,
green and tender fragrance
Come with me, my love, come away
finding our doorways
piled with fruits,
the best of the new-picked
and the long-stored, my love,
I will give you all I have saved for you.

All say
Blessed is the One within the many.
Blessed are the many who make one.

Prayer

God our Lover
You draw us to search for you;
You give us clues to your presence
in creation;
earth, water; fire and air;
we find you in each other's faces,
in the challenge and the intimacy
of human love.
Yet always you elude our grasp;
familiar and yet always strange,
you both comfort and disturb our lives.
We surrender all our images of you,
and offer ourselves to your darkness;
that you may enable us to become your likeness
more than we can imagine or conceive. Amen.

Liturgical dance or chant

at
tara

at tara today in this fateful hour
i place all heaven with its power,
and the sun with its brightness,
and the snow with its whiteness,
and fire with all the strength it hath,
and lightening with its rapid wrath,
and the winds with their swiftness along the path,
and the sea with its deepness,
and the rocks with their steepness,
and the earth with its starkness:
and all these i place
by god's almighty help and grace,
between myself and the powers of darkness.

saint patrick

Sacred Landscape and Pilgrimage

Man is the sole inhabitant of a border country, where matter marches with spirit.

David Jones, Welsh artist d. 1974

King of the mysteries

My dear King, my own King,
Without pride. Without sin,
You created the whole world,
eternal, victorious King.

King of the mysteries,
You existed before the elements,
before the waters covered the ocean floor
beautiful King,
You are without beginning and without end.

King, you created the land out of shapeless mass,
You carved the mountains and chiselled the valleys,
And covered the earth with trees and grass.

King, you measured each object
And each span within the universe:
The heights of the mountains
And the depths of the oceans;
The distance from the sun to the moon,
And from star to star.

And you created men and women
To be your stewards of the earth
Always praising you for your boundless love.

Saltair Na Rann[35]

Question:	What is best in this world?
Answer:	To do the will of our Maker.
Question:	What is his will?
Answer:	That we should live according to the laws of his creation.
Question:	How do we know those laws?
Answer:	By study – studying the Scriptures with devotion.
Question:	What tool has our Maker provided for this study?
Answer:	The intellect, which can probe everything.
Question:	And what is the fruit of study?
Answer:	To perceive the eternal Word of God reflected in every plant and insect, every bud and animal, and every man and woman.

St Ninian, Apostle of the Picts c. 432

You are worthy, O Lord
our God, to receive Glory
and honour and power,
because you created all
things; by your will
they were created and
have their being!

Revelation 4.11 (REB)

Outside time the consciousness of God exists.

In the consciousness is a thought of such intensity that within it all and everything conceivable and inconceivable, imaginable and unimaginable possible and impossible is contained.

That thought is uttered and from the vibrations of that sound from the resonance of that Word,

From what scientists call 'The Big Bang', the multitudinous forms of being are spreading in ever increasing circles.

Our being is the expression of God's thought: we contain the love of God and God contains us as we evolved on earth through shell creature – fish form, reptile, bird and mammal – we are learning step-by-step what that containment means.

The circles are still widening – still evolving the Mighty Concept – the Magnificent Idea.

Lord of Creation

Six days, seven, a million years, a thousand million . . . the count is nothing, the Being – All.

Praise Be to our God and the Word that resonates in our hearts still.

May we not separate ourselves in arrogance from the great work for we know the Sound of the Word but not its meaning.

Brendanus Scotus

WE ARE STAR DUST

Generations of stars that lived and died in our galaxy before the sun was formed created an inheritance of heavy elements that was bequeathed to us. The carbon atoms in the ink of every book, the oxygen you are breathing now, the calcium in your bones and the iron in your blood are all products of stars. This grand idea, that we are literally made of star stuff, is embodied in the popular song 'Woodstock' by Joni Mitchell. She sings: 'We are star dust, billion-year-old carbon'.[36]

The death of stars is part of the origin of life. Humankind came from outer space, created from the heart of a star. In fact, as noted we are recycled star dust, although greater than the sum of our particles. The constantly creating divine movement of God is within all moving things of the universe and we are an integral part of the dance of the whole cosmic order.

The Trinitarian dance is present within the whole sweep of creation at the still point of being. We could say therefore that the cosmos is an instrument of the ever-birthing God whose rhythm is conducted by the Cosmic Christ, the Holy Spirit. As Meister Eckhart said: 'God is creating the entire universe fully and totally in this present now.' The voice of the Cosmic Christ calls to us through the hidden beauty present in creation.

> The whole landscape flushes on a second at a sound
>
> *Gerard Manley Hopkins*[37]

Everything in creation is vibration and therefore in movement, making sound. This celestial sound is of very low frequency, below what the human ear can hear. These sound waves shaped the universe out of the 'hot soup' of electrons, protons, light and matter. Modern astronomical sciences have discovered that light and matter were coupled in the very early period of the universe's history before matter re-combined. Sound wave fluctuation and density are the seeds of matter, which has repercussions throughout the universe.

The sun, too, resonates with different frequencies. It is like a large musical instrument or gong, which gives off sound when struck. By actually observing these resonant frequencies within the sun, scientists are able to map them out and tell how the sound speed varies through different parts of the sun. It is a

Lord of Creation

way of probing the inside heart of a star, which otherwise we would not be able to do.

Black holes in space hum at variable pitches. They 'suck in' matter and are part of the celestial harmony or music of the spheres. They give out a low-frequency sound wave – b flat –, which can be gauged because of the spaces between the concentric ripples or sound waves caused in the inter-cluster atmosphere.

This sound we hear is not God, yet, it points to God and is created by God. Therefore, at the level of the Spirit, every sound that we hear in nature proceeds from the Creator and is his voice calling to us; every step we take, is a movement into the deeper presence of God. Through God becoming matter in Christ, by virtue of the Incarnation, all being at every moment is invaded by the Cosmic Christ.

The landscape is the gift of God. It is a holy gift, it is sacred. True contemplative prayer is the realization that the power of creation, the uncreated energy within creation flows in our hearts. It is to feel the Divine Presence coming through this sacred landscape, which draws us closer to God the more aware we are that the landscape in our heart is a reflection of the beauty of the Divine.

We, who are made in the 'image and likeness of God' (Genesis 1.26), are called to contemplate God as love, shining out in all creation, and to love and serve him in return through the care and stewardship of all that he has made. At every moment God is sounding a melody of love, going forth through the matter of creation. We are to choose which part to play through service and adoration of him that he may be glorified throughout the entire universe.

While it is true that God is transcendent and above all human thought and understanding, nevertheless, we may come to know him through the experience of love. Through co-operating with his holy will, through purification of our hearts of all self-centredness and self-seeking, God who is always present to us reveals himself in a new way of knowing.

Primarily he reveals himself through grace, which is God 'going forth' out of himself through his uncreated energies in order to share his own life with us. Although we cannot know him as he knows himself in his Godhead, yet in his energies he can be experienced.

God is in relationship with us at many different levels and his energies are really God in his reaching out to us in our hearts through baptism in Christ, as well as in our human relationships and in the energizing loving presence of God in nature.

To the contemplative, God is in all things and the energies of God flow out from the three persons within the Trinity. This is the essential experience for the contemplative in the landscape for everything is seen as being 'full of grace' at every given moment. We can therefore understand that the whole of creation is 'charged with the grandeur of God'. The love of God is the most powerful and still the most unknown energy of the world, as Gerard Manley Hopkins has beautifully described in the need for humankind to 'behold' the presence of God in nature:

> And the azurous hills are his world-wielding shoulder
> Majestic – as a stallion stalwart, very-violet-sweet! –
> These things, these things were here and but the beholder
> Wanting; which two when they once meet,
> The heart rears wings bold and bolder
> And hurls for him, O half hurls earth for him off under his feet.[38]

When we walk the landscape and make a conscious effort to experience the presence of God in creation, we are enabled to sense his energies and see the beauty of nature as a constantly recurring 'event'. God is 'coming forth' (Latin, *evenire* – to come out) at every given moment and the contemplative is able to witness, through the eyes of faith, God's loving, dynamic, energetic presence at the heart of matter. The divine Creator is pouring himself out to us by his divine energies – sharing his life, love and joy. Every step we take is a movement into the deeper presence of God; and so we make our breath rhythmic, taking consciously slow, meditative steps, aware that as we walk we are treading the footsteps of love on holy ground. This 'faithful' contemplative walk is to practise the presence of God and to be aware of the divine presence everywhere.

As our bodies are temples of the Holy Spirit (1 Corinthians 6.19) we are enabled to see how meaningless it is to treat them as rubbish bins. Made in the image and likeness of God our bodies too are sacred. They are not sinful or evil but open to the activity of God's grace at all levels of being, that is mind, spirit and body: one being, not separated into compartments, but a total whole, that is holistic incarnational entity.

The way we treat our bodies affects the way we treat our spiritual, moral and intellectual life. Therefore the foodstuff we feed on, the way we clothe ourselves, our sexual behaviour and manner of speech, etc. all reflect what we really are. 'By their fruits ye shall know them'! Thus it is important to note how we use our bodies in prayer. Our spiritual life is not something detached from physical or social life but intimately entwined with them. Our spiritual life should affect the attitude we adopt toward the environment as well: do we look after it as stewards or do we treat it as rapists? Are we aware of liminality, that is, the closeness of the 'other world' present to us in, through, and beyond our work-a-day, every-day experience? For this is reality . . .

To understand the world
knowledge is not enough,
you must
   see it,
     touch it
       live in its presence
       and drink the vital heat
       of existence in the very heart
       of reality.[39]

This sense of reality is the realization of a sense of the earth 'opening and exploding upwards into God and the sense of God taking root and finding nourishment downwards into Earth'.[40] It is to be aware of God's personal loving involvement – evolvement in all things and through all things. Imbued with this reality we should only want to serve his creatures, love his creation and adore his glorious presence shining through the entire universe.

The landscape of my heart should be a reflection of the beauty of God.

Since God is nigh unto all who call upon
Him, we are under no obligation to cross
The sea. The Kingdom of heaven can be
Reached from every land

                    Abbess Samanthann (Early Irish)

As you stroll along in walking meditation, feel yourself in rhythm with all that is natural in creation – the winds, the rain, the sun, the earth and the colour and sound of all that is going on around you.

- pay attention with gratitude in the knowledge that it is God's gift to you
- smile with interior happiness and peace
- let the rhythm of your psalm, phrase or prayer sentence or word and the rhythm of your breath merge in a way that feels natural
- with every step you take, know that they are the footsteps of love and that you are walking on holy ground
- bless the earth with your feet as you go
- know that you walk towards the One Light who said . . .
- I AM THE LIGHT OF THE WORLD

Further reading

Sheldrake, P., *Living Between Worlds: Place and Journey in Celtic Spirituality* (Among other insights into place and journey in the experience of the Celts, this book looks beyond 'Celtic mists and golden sunsets' to consider 'place' or 'space' in the Celtic mind: how and why particular places in the landscape were chosen for Christian communities. Highly recommended.), DLT: London, 1995.

Pennick, N., *Celtic Sacred Landscapes* (From the original Celtic site of the castle at Tintagel, passing through the sacred forest of Brocéliande in Brittany on to the monastery of Scellig Mhichil off the coast of Ireland, we are taken on an exhilarating tour of the Celtic holy places of Europe.), Thames & Hudson: London, 1996.

Rees, E., *Celtic Saints in their Landscape* (an armchair tour of the sites where some 50 Celtic saints worked and prayed across Ireland, Scotland, Wales, Northumbria and Cornwall), Sutton Publishing: Gloucestershire, 2001.

PILGRIMAGE:
THE JOURNEY OF FAITH

It was St Augustine who said:

> People travel to wonder
> at the height of the mountains,
> at the huge waves of the sea,
> at the long courses of rivers,
> at the vast compass of the ocean,
> at the circular motion of the stars,
> and they pass themselves by without wondering.[41]

Today many people, particularly the young, are experiencing a desire to go on a journey. They do not want to travel as a curious tourist but as a pilgrim. The difference between a tourist and a pilgrim is that a pilgrim seeks an experience of God. The beauties of nature or of a holy place may provoke thoughts that tend towards prayer in anyone, but the difficulty for many – for pilgrims and particularly for tourists – is how to make the transition real.

The idea of a pilgrim's manual, a companion to prayer, which can always be 'at hand', is an ancient one. What could be more natural when hearing the larks singing, watching the sun's rays emerging through the mist over the sea, or visiting some holy well or place, than to have thoughts that turn to prayer and to feel the need for a suitable method of liturgy or worship to collect prayer together, thus enabling the practice of the presence of God individually or in a group?

All pilgrims might be defined as persons who undertake journeys for a religious purpose, a quest with a religious purpose, a quest with a hidden spiritual meaning. There is a sublime analogy between such definite journeys and an individual's journey through life. To travel is as natural to the human being as it is to swallows or salmon. The search for inner life is mirrored in the outer journey to an event or holy place. 'Seek ye my face, thy face Lord, I will seek' (Psalm 29.9).

Pilgrimage is the emblem of our life, the symbol of our being, but life is not hurrying on, it is standing aside to witness the eternity within. The physical art of going on pilgrimage, holiday or honeymoon therefore reflects the hidden, deeper meaning of the need to journey.

Pilgrimage in all its aspects is a deep and intensely rewarding means of healing affecting all levels of being. In Christian terms this is to experience salvation. The word 'salvation' comes from the Latin root *salvare* – to heal, or to make whole. Salve and heal have the same meaning. We seek salvation when we search wholeness or personal integration, and so people find the need to search for reconciliation and healing. It is therefore possible to experience through the act of pilgrimage a sacramental encounter with the incarnate God present both within the traveller and the planet on which he walks.

It is a question of spiritual integration with the Creator God. The desire to seek, find and experience the risen Christ both within and without produces a thirst and a longing to see the face of God. It may be likened to a nameless woe, *penthos* to the Greeks, or *hiraeth*, that untranslatable Welsh word which names a deep spirit of longing.

> Let me drink forever deeply
> of salvation's mighty flood,
> till I thirst no more for ever
> after any earthly good.
>
> *Ann Griffiths*[42]

In the Welsh hymn-writer Ann Griffiths' letters and hymns there is a deep spirit of longing for heaven and to see the face of God. There is even a sense of alienation from what she felt was her true destination, the kingdom of heaven. She felt, too, a sense of belonging, belonging to heaven, her true homeland. In this she experienced the essence of the true pilgrim whose emotional landscape is sculpted within, creating a tension of existence between the 'now' and the promise of the future, a sweet sadness, yet a foretaste of the transcendent joy promised at the end of our earthly journey.

> There is not on earth an object
> that can bring comfort to me;
> my sole pleasure, my sole comfort
> is thy glorious face to see.
>
> *Ann Griffiths*[43]

It is in this spirit of quest, of pilgrimage that we too, when travelling the spiritual life, may walk toward the One. It is the desire to seek and to find the One and it is the will to pray in so doing, which is the essence of the spiritual walk.

'Walking prayer' has a goal both physical and mental in God. In our mind's eye we journey towards someone we love and this constant state of expectancy

Lord of Creation

raises our spirits and lessens much mental stress or fatigue. We walk toward the Divine Lover and constantly repeat 'Lord Jesus Christ, Son of God, have mercy on me a sinner' and combine the sentence with our breath in rhythm with the movements of our body. This ejaculatory prayer becomes automatic as it beats to the basic rhythm of the body at the same time 'anointing' creation with its silent utterance. Through the practice of constant prayer and the forward impulsion of the body we are taken up, as it were, into the heart of the Creator.

> Stepping along the paths of the gospel, singing psalms every hour;
> An end of talking and long stories, constant bending of the knees.
> My Creator to frequent me, my Lord, my King,
> My spirit to seek him in the eternal kingdom
> Where he is!

Old Irish poem

The Celtic saints in their search for God were imbued with the reality of the continuing presence of God. They were 'grace-filled' through the practice of constant prayer, open-hearted hospitality to God, to his presence in the little everyday moments of their lives. Today, pilgrims seek the nectar of spiritual and physical enlightenment at the very same places where dwelled the holy ones long ago. As with the early followers of the saints, the modern pilgrim seeks spiritual nectar or grace when visiting a holy place. They are spiritual bees in search of the word . . .

> Weaving a psalm
> to the unutterable Word
> which dwells in the dewdrop and
> the rock . . .

as the Welsh poet Rhydwen Williams said.

The Presence of God, the Cosmic Christ, has made this the canvas of these places so that the visitor may, as George Herbert wrote: 'look on glass and on it may stay his eye, or, if he pleaseth, through it pass, and then the heaven espy!'

The pilgrim is on holy ground, perhaps at first only dimly aware of the immanent Presence of God. Celtic holy ground, such places as Iona, Lindisfarne, St David's, Glendalough, Crough Patrick, Whithorn or Bodmin are attractive to people very close to nature. These places are both mystical and very down to earth, reflecting the saints who dwelt in their sacral environment and for whom their every well-spring, wood and stone took on a mystical significance. No doubt, this tradition of creation spirituality proceeded from the pagan past, but that had been transformed, its numinous properties spiritualized by Christian prayer. The Scottish Gaelic language has a phrase, 'Are you going to church?' which when literally translated says, 'Are you going to the stones?' The awareness of the whole world as incarnational was linked with a tremendous 'spirit of place'. Most of the Celtic holy places locate for us this long and deep, spiritual and cultural tradition.

The divine life is the pervading presence of the Holy Spirit, the Cosmic Christ in everything that has being. It is the same life that wells up within us, in the innermost recesses of our heart, as we become open to the presence of God not only within ourselves, but perceived and sensed in the unfolding of creation. It is 'thin', the divine veil between human being, creation, and the God of Being, who is present in the core of the whole matter and spirit. He is our ceaseless call and longing. He is the sounding wave, the voice of the sea.

> That I may see its heavy waves
> over the glitter ocean
> as they change a melody to their Father
> on their eternal course.
>
> *Early Irish nature poem*

To enter beyond this 'thin veil' is to enter into a felt experience of the kingdom of God, both created and uncreated. It is to go beyond time and space. As we experience the drawing of the veil, subject–object distinction disappears. God is within us and the whole of God's creation is in God; the whole of creation is in us too. He is the pulsing life of all, the ceaseless call and longing, the unquenchable thirst, the One Thing That Matters.

> It swims with the seal in his laughter.
> The sacrament of being you share with me!
>
> *Ray Howard Jones*

I am talking about an experience where there is only the divine NOW. We are all eternally created in the uncreated womb of our Mother God. In God, we already possess and enjoy the things-to-come, for all things are already present in the eternity of God.

In holy places, the veil is thin. The 'thin place' is an archetypal symbol, the parting of the veil on holy ground, breaking through time and space into the imminent Presence of the King of creation, the Cosmic Christ.

Lord of Creation

Pilgrim God

Pilgrim God, bless us with courage,
　　where our way is fraught with danger.
Bless us with good companions,
　　where the way demands a common cause.
Bless us with humour, for we
　　cannot travel lightly when weighed
　　down with over-much solemnity.
Bless us with humility to learn
　　from those around us.
Bless us with decisiveness, when we have
　　to move quickly.
Bless our lazy moments, when we need to
　　stretch our limbs for the journey.
Bless us, lead us, love us and bring
　　us home, bearing the gospel of life.[44]

The Itinerary

The blessing of those beginning a journey

Sentence

Blessed are those who observe the
instructions of the Lord, who seek him
with all their hearts, and, doing no
evil, who walk in his ways.

Psalm 119.2

Confession and forgiveness

Have mercy on me, God, in your kindness.
In your compassion blot out my offence.
O wash me more and more from my guilt
and cleanse me from my sin.

My offences truly I know them;
my sin is always before me.
Against you, you alone, have I sinned,
what is evil in your sight I have done.

A pure heart create for me, O God,
put a steadfast spirit within me.
Do not cast me away from your presence,
nor deprive me of your Holy Spirit.

O rescue me, God, my helper,
and my tongue shall sing out your goodness.
O Lord, open my lips
and my mouth shall declare your praise.

Psalm 51.1–4, 10, 11, 14, 15

Lord of Creation

Now my heart submits to you, imploring your great goodness.
I have sinned, Lord, I have sinned,
and I acknowledge my transgressions.
I beg and beseech you spare me, Lord, spare me;
destroy me not with my transgressions on my head,
Do not condemn me to the depths of the earth,
for you, Lord, are the God of the penitent.
You will show your goodness towards me,
for, unworthy as I am, you will save me
Father, Son and Holy Spirit. Amen.

Blessed are you, Lord God, Our Father.
You deliver us from every evil,
You grant us peace in our day and protect us from all anxiety.
I proclaim Jesus Christ the way to the Father.
May he bless me on my journey and
    bring me in union with him in heaven.
May the same Jesus Christ nourish me in
    his truth and inspire me to persevere to the end.
May the life of Christ within me from
    baptism sustain and deepen my love of the Father.

Guide me/us in your truth and teach me/us, Lord, for
you are the God who saves me/us.

Psalm 25.5

O thou full of compassion,
I commit and commend myself unto thee,
    in whom I am
    and live,
    and know.
Be thou the goal of my pilgrimage,
    and my rest by the way.

Let my soul take refuge
    from the crowding turmoil
    of worldly thoughts
    beneath the shadow of thy wings;
let my heart, this sea of restless waves,
    find peace in thee, O God.

Sacred Landscape and Pilgrimage   161

Thou bounteous giver of all good gifts,
  give to him who is weary refreshing food,
gather our distracted thoughts and powers
    into harmony again;
    and set the prisoner free.

See, he stands at thy door and knocks;
    be it opened to him,
    that he may enter with a free step
    and be quickened by thee.

For thou art the well-spring of life,
    the light of eternal brightness,
    wherein the just live
    who love thee.
Be it unto me/us according to thy word.

St Augustine[45]

Heavenly Father, protector of all who trust in you, you led your people in safety through the desert and brought them to a land of plenty. Guide me as I begin my journey today. Fill me with your spirit of love. Preserve me from all harm and bring me safely to my destination. I ask this through Christ our Lord.

or

Father, you have called us to a pilgrimage of faith. The light of your truth summons us, and the call of faith is a constant challenge on our journey. We give thanks for the desire to seek you: we give thanks for voices from the past that offer guidance, for signposts pointing to the next stage, for companions who share the journey, for footsteps in the sand of pilgrims before us, for the conviction that unseen but not unknown, you are with us. Father, keep us faithful to the vision, and steadfast on our pilgrimage so that the distant goal may become a reality, and faith at last lead to sight.

  And the blessing of Almighty God, the
  Father, the Son and the Holy Spirit,
  come down upon me/us and remain with
  me/us for ever and ever. Amen.

Lord of Creation

Pilgrim Prayer

Dear God
Be with me
as I walk your paths,
in places I sometimes
do not want to go.
Be with me
as I say goodbye
to those I want
to stay with.
Be with me
as I leave the gift
so newly given and
hardly seen.
Be with me, Lord
as I try, sometimes sadly,
to walk
your way.[46]

THE STATIONS

Build cairns to mark your way, set up signposts;
make sure of the road, the path which you will tread.

Jeremiah 31.21

When on pilgrimage every now and then we stop at a 'station', a word which simply means 'I stand'. A 'station', as on railways, is just a stopping place, whether one stops for tea or for thought; often we want to sit down and meditate when on pilgrimage. To have a book to be a companion to prayer is a natural desire for the sojourner and it is difficult to conceive of a Christian pilgrim without a Bible (or at least a Psalter) in hand, indeed, it is the perfect tool to deepen the traveller's awareness of God.

However, a Bible, which is a collection of books in one volume, is not an easy library to delve into when one wants just the right sentence or phrase to feed the mind and heart at a particular moment. That is why the devotional manual became so popular with pilgrims in ancient times. The travelling Celts particularly used handbooks of prayer, which contained collects, hymns, versicles, and responses to accompany the singing of the Psalms and the reading of the Gospels on the course of their journey.

The ideal prayers for a station consist of a sentence, a Psalm chosen for suitability whether to reflect the mood of the pilgrim or the environment, and a collect to gather the whole exercise together with a centring prayer to use as a repetitive rhythmic prayer when journeying along.

Remember, though, that the real journey in life is interior.

Pilgrim, take care your journey's not in vain,
a hazard without profit, without gain,
the King you seek you'll find in Rome, it's true
but only if he travels on the way with you.

Medieval Irish lyric

Lord of Creation

Station 1

Sentence

Grant me, I beseech thee, O merciful
God, prudently to study, rightly
to understand, and perfectly to fulfil
that which is pleasing to thee, to
the praise and glory of thy name.

St Thomas Aquinas

Read Psalm 23

Collect

I am praying and appealing to God,
The Son of Mary and the Spirit of truth,
to aid me in distress of sea and of land:
May the Three succour me, may the
      Three shield me,
May the Three watch me by day and
      by night.

Carmina Gadelica III 173[47]

Centring prayer:

Lord Jesus Christ, Son of God,
have mercy on me, a sinner.

Station 2

Sentence

The woods are lovely, dark, and deep,
But I have promises to keep,
And miles to go before I sleep,
And miles to go before I sleep.

Robert Frost[48]

Read Psalm 16

Collect

O Lord, be with me at every
change and turn of the way as I
seek you down the pathway of my
life. Help me to keep the promises
I have made, through Jesus Christ our
Lord. Amen.

Centring Prayer

O God come to my aid,
O Lord make hast to help me

Station 3

Sentence

Dear, chaste Christ,
Who can see into every heart and read every mind,
Take hold of my thoughts.
Bring my thoughts back to me
And clasp me to yourself.

Irish, eighth century

Read Psalm 34

Collect

Grant Lord, that I may not
for one moment, admit willingly
into my soul any thought contrary
to thy love.

E. B. Pusey (1800–82)

Centring Prayer

All shall be well, and all shall be well
and all manner of things shall be well.

Julian of Norwich

Lord of Creation

Station 4

Sentence

There is no place where
God is not.
Wherever I go, there God is.
Now and always he upholds me
with his power,
and keeps me safe in his love.

Read Psalm 139

Collect

Let the heavens and the earth
praise him, the glorious, and every
creature which is in heaven and
on earth and under the earth, in the
seas and all that are in them.
Let us praise and exalt him above
all forever.

St Francis

Centring Prayer

Bless O God the earth beneath
my feet.

Station 5

Sentence

Help, me to hear and
understand how in the beginning you
created heaven and earth.

St Augustine

Read Psalm 104

Collect

Now we must praise the author of the heavenly Kingdom, the
Creator's power and counsel, the deeds of the Father of glory;
now he, the eternal God, was the author of all the marvels –
He, who first gave to the sons of men the heaven for a roof,
and then, almighty Guardian of mankind, created the earth.

Caedmon

Centring Prayer

The earth is the mother of all,
for contained in her are the seeds of all.

Hildegard of Bingen

Station 6

Sentence

More things are learnt in
the woods than from books.
Animals, trees and rocks teach you
things not to be heard elsewhere.

St Bernard

Read Psalm 148

Collect

For those, O Lord, the humble beasts
that bear with us the burden and the
heat of the day, and offer their guileless
lives for the well-being of their countries;
we supplicate thy tenderness of heart,
for thou hast promised to save both man
and beast, and great is thy loving kindness,
O Master, saviour of the world.[49]

Centring Prayer

Blessed art thou, O Lord our God, King of the Universe,
who hast such as these in thy world.

Hebrew Prayer Book

Station 7

Sentence

There is only one life and that is God's life,
which he gives us from moment to moment,
drawing us to himself with every breath
we take.[50]

Read Psalm 121

Collect

Here is my heart, O God,
here it is with all its secrets;
look into my thoughts,
O my hope,
and take away all my wrong feelings:
Let my eyes ever be on you
and release my feet from the snare.

St Augustine, Confessions *IV, 6*

Centring Prayer

O God make speed to save me,
O Lord make haste to help me.

Station 8

Sentence

Our earthly condition is essentially that of wayfarers, of incompleteness moving
towards fulfilment and therefore of struggle.

Yves Congar

Read Psalm 73

Collect

O God, thou art my God alone;
early to thee my soul shall cry,
a pilgrim in a land unknown,
a thirsty land whose springs are dry.

Sacred Landscape and Pilgrimage

Yet through this rough and thorny maze
I follow close to thee, my God;
Thy hand unseen upholds my ways,
I safely tread where thou hast trod.

James Montgomery (1822)

Centring Prayer

I love thee, O Lord my strength.

Psalm 18.1

Station 9

Sentence

God is Christ-like and in Christ we see the image of God.
    Lord Jesus Christ
    Son of God
    Have mercy on me
    A sinner.

Read Psalm 84

Collect

O Father, give the spirit power to climb
To the fountain of all light, and be purified.
Break through the mists of earth, the weight of the clod,
Shine forth in splendour, Thou that art calm weather,
and quiet resting place for faithful souls.
To see thee is the end and the beginning,
Thou carriest us, and thou dost go before,
Thou art the journey, and the journey's end.

Boethius

Centring Prayer

Blessed are those who find their strength in you,
whose hearts are set on pilgrimage.

Lord of Creation

Station 10

Sentence

To believe in him is to go to him by loving him.

William of St Thierry

Insomuch as love grows in you so in you beauty grows. For love is the beauty of the soul.

St Augustine

Read Psalm 149 and 150

Collect

O Gracious and Holy Father, give us
Wisdom to perceive thee,
Diligence to seek thee,
Patience to wait for thee,
Eyes to behold thee,
A heart to meditate upon thee,
and a life to proclaim thee;
through the power of the Spirit of
Jesus Christ our Lord. Amen.

St Benedict

Centring Prayer

The person who loves God is with
God to the extent that he loves.

St Bernard

Holy sprinkling at a river or a holy well

Sentence

God is a great underground river
that no one can dam up
and no one can stop.

Eckhart[51]

Let us commend ourselves and each other to the grace and power of Jesus Christ,
that the Lord may ease our suffering and grant us health and salvation.

(The sign of the cross with water is made on the forehead)

A small drop of water
To thy forehead, beloved,
Meet for the Father, Son and Spirit,
The Triune of power.

A small drop of water
To encompass my beloved,
Meet for Father, Son and Spirit.
The Triune of power.

A small drop of water
To fill thee with each grace,
Meet for Father, Son and Spirit.
The Triune of power.

Carmina Gadelica III, 22

Read Psalm 40

Collect

Lord in your mercy give us living water, always
springing up as a fountain of healing: free us,
body, mind and spirit from every danger and
admit us to your presence in purity of heart.
Grant this through Christ our Lord. Amen.

Centring Prayer

Out of the depths I cry to you, O Lord;
O Lord, hear my voice.

Psalm 130.1

Pilgrim's Rest

In thy name O Jesu who wast crucified
I lie down to rest;
Watch thou me in sleep remote,
Hold thou me in thy one hand.
Watch thou me in sleep remote,
Hold me in thy one hand.

Bless me, O my Christ,
Be thou my shield protecting me,
Aid my steps in the pitful swamp,
Lead thou me to life eternal;
Aid my steps in the pitful swamp,
Lead thou me to the life eternal.

Keep thou me in the presence of God,
O good and gracious Son of the Virgin,
And fervently I pray thy strong protection
From my lying down at dusk to my rising at day;
And fervently I pray thy strong protection
From my lying down at dusk to my rising at day.

Gaelic Prayer

Arrival

Sentence

God has given me the power to change my ways.

Mechtild of Magdeburg

Meditation

Bring us, O Lord God,
at our last awakening into the house and gate of heaven,
to enter into that gate and dwell in that house,
where there shall be no darkness nor dazzling,
but one equal light;
no noise or silence,
but one equal music;
no fears nor hopes,
but one equal possession;
no ends nor beginnings,
but one equal eternity;
in the habitations of thy majesty and thy glory,
world without end.

John Donne

Read Psalm 122

Collect

May he support us all the day long, till the shades lengthen, and the evening comes, and the busy world is hushed, and the fever of life is over, and the work is done! Then in his mercy may he give us a safe lodging, and a holy rest, and peace at the last.

John Henry Newman

End Prayer

I find thee enthroned in my heart, my Lord Jesus.
It is enough.
I know that thou art enthroned in heaven.
My heart and heaven are one.

from the Gaelic

Further reading

Sumption, J., *Pilgrimage* (Brings alive the traditions of pilgrimage prevalent in Europe from the beginning of Christianity to the end of the fifteenth century. A wonderful image of medieval religion.), Faber & Faber: London, 1975.

Robinson, M., *Sacred Places, Pilgrim-paths: An Anthology of Pilgrimage* (A super anthology reflecting the experience of pilgrims throughout the ages.), Fount (Harper/Collins): London, 1998.

Davies, J. G., *Pilgrimage Yesterday and Today* (An excellent book of general interest in pilgrimage, which should encourage today's pilgrims assisting them to make an enriching experience even more profound.), SCM Press: London, 1988.

Coleman, S. and Elsner, J., *Pilgrimage Past and Present in the World Religions* (This book brings together all major religious traditions from Classical Greece to the Present. It looks at the different practices of the different faiths, and asks how they may be meaningfully compared. Of great interest to anyone interested in anthropology, history of art and travel.), British Museum Press: London, 1995.

Harrison, P., *Pilgrimage in Ireland: The Monuments of the People* (An in-depth survey of the landscape of Ireland with a radical hypothesis: that a great many of the monuments of Ireland can be explained in terms of ecclesiastical pilgrimage. Highly recommended.), Barrie & Jenkins: London, 1991.

a person without a
soul friend
is like a body
without a head.

BRIGID OF KILDARE

Prayer and Spirituality

Soul Friend

He is pure gold, he is a heaven round a sun,
He is a vessel of silver with wine,
He is an angel, he is wisdom of saints,
Whoever doth the King's will . . .

He is a sweet branch with its blossom,
He is a vessel full of honey,
He is a precious stone with its goodness,
Whoso doth the will of the Son of God of heaven . . .

Whoso doth the will of the Son of God of heaven
Is a brilliant sun round which is summer,
Is an image of God of heaven,
        is a vessel glassen, pure.

He is a race-horse over a smooth plain
The man that strives for great God's kingdom,
He is a chariot that is driven under a king,
        That bears off prizes in the east.

He is a sun that warms holy heaven,
A man for whom the great King is thankful:
He is a temple prosperous, noble,
He is a holy shrine which gold bedecks.

He is an altar whereon wine is shed,
Round which is sung a multitude of melodies;
He is a cleansed chalice with liquor [therein],
He is white-bronze, he is gold.

Life of St Molin[52]

Soul Friendship

In the society in which we live, a great deal of help is given to us to grow physically and intellectually. Not much help is given to us to grow spiritually.

It is a wonderful experience to become familiar with the workings of our spiritual life so that we are no longer blown about by the winds of fads and fancies, trends or whatever is in fashion. It is so easy to become attracted to a pick and mix of Eastern and Western religions or pantheistic New Age spiritualities and a relativist insistence that your God is as good as mine and so it is very helpful to have a friend or spiritual mentor who will be a wise companion on the spiritual journey. With such a soul friend we learn the stability rooted in Christ who is at the centre of our being. Growth needs planting and rooting and it also needs cultivation. A soul friend helps us to persevere in the practice of the spiritual life and to remain in the rootedness of Christ in our centre.

The term 'soul friend' is Irish in origin and is derived from the Gaelic word *anam*, which means soul and *cara*, which is the word for friend. Essentially it is about being present to a friend who is seeking God, is actually serious about it and needs to sound out and share their thoughts and aspirations with an empathic mentor. It can be seen at its most simple level as a conversation between two people on the ways of prayer and the journey of faith. It is helping a person get in touch with the raw material of life and seeing how it relates to their experience of Christ present within all things. The process may happen in a small co-spiritual direction group but generally it is in the context of a one-to-one relationship in which a competent soul friend or companion, that is *com-panis*, fellow 'bread-breaker', helps another Christian to grow in the spiritual life by means of personal encounters that have the directee's spiritual growth as their explicit object. Therefore the aim of the exercise is not so much about 'direction' as giving counsel in an atmosphere of shared experience concerning the mysterious presence of God.

The result of spiritual direction is that it gives us confidence, for if we know the way, then we are likely to proceed more effectively towards maturity in Christ.

The *raison d'être* of the spiritual journey is growing in holiness, which is essential to the right 'heart-set', which must be at the centre of our life. It is about relationship with God, relationship with others and with oneself. The spiritual life is about growth in holiness or it is nothing. To know God, to love him, is the one thing that matters. It is the response of our hearts 'being set on fire with the love of God'. It is the task, not of denying our personalities and what has been given us by God, but looking to ourselves, to see those things which might either be exaggerated or underdeveloped, so that we can find ourselves and deepen ourselves in the service of God. Within this is the vital need to come to terms with one's own woundedness. We are, all, walking wounded, and it is out of this that we have anything to give.

The task of the soul friend is to mirror for the person seeking help that which is apparent to him/her, and to enable the seeker to see what is happening in his/her spiritual life. It is very important that the spiritual director is a good listener and in touch with their own dark side. Not allowing their own agenda to intrude on the relationship and yet having a good grasp of modern theology and some knowledge of the history of spirituality. Although in some ways it is easier if we are ahead of the directee, nevertheless, we must remember that the true spiritual director is the Holy Spirit and that God's ways are not necessarily our ways. All of us who seek to give this sort of help know how often we are surprised by what we find ourselves saying or discerning, as the Spirit moves in us.

Rule of life

It is primarily the task of the soul friend/director to help the person to formulate and keep a rule of life. Hopefully, over a period of time help will be given to the directee to make changes in their rule and evaluate its appropriateness in changed circumstances. The rule consists of the particular areas outlined below. Its intention is to help in preserving stability. It is not an expression of a target strived after so much as a minimum which the person can without enormous difficulty reach, so as to keep them in the right direction when under stress or arid or bored. It is also the discipline which sets us free on a daily basis in good times as well as bad. It is a pattern or outline of what the directee plans and intends to do on a daily, weekly, monthly and yearly basis. Many people, when trying to draw up a rule for the first time, tend to be wildly optimistic about what they can set themselves and achieve, and some caution is usually necessary.

A rule is very important to the spiritual life. All those serious about the practice of the spiritual life should keep a rule and all rules are of the same basic nature, applying themselves to the areas listed below. The details are specifically drawn up with and by the individual concerned.

Centring Christ

The areas covered by the rule may consist of PRAYER, WORK and STUDY:

1 The Holy Eucharist
2 Penitence/reconciliation
3 Personal prayer/meditation
4 Liturgy/public worship
5 Retreat
6 Study/*lectio divina*
7 Simplicity
8 Work
9 Obedience
10 Recreation
11 Family duties
12 Self-discipline
13 Creation/environment

Broad goals of the soul friend

1 To help a person discover God's will for him/her and to grow in that will.
2 To be an objective adviser and resource person in matters of personal prayer life, spiritual discipline and the living of a godly life.

Dos and don'ts (in no particular order)

1 The person you direct may have quite a *different form of spirituality from your own*. He/she may differ in background, training, churchmanship, and personality type.
2 There is no need for the director also to be the confessor.
3 What is told you in direction must, of course, be held in *complete confidence*.
4 Ask for honesty and *be honest* in return.
5 You *don't have to be a mystic* yourself, even if the person you are directing is. You *don't have to be as 'advanced'* as they are.
6 So do *discourage any dependency* on yourself, and beware of any tendency in yourself to collude with the *desire for dependency*. It may have to start that way, but *don't allow it to remain so*. Instead, keep the dependence on God. However, there is another side to this coin. This *is* a mutual relationship and, if you are meeting their needs, they also are meeting yours. It is a general

point in counselling that you must be aware of your own needs before you can attend to those of your client. Again, this is about *self-knowledge.*

7   There are many *variations of practice and belief* in Christianity, therefore your task is to allow the person you are directing to follow his/her *own way* as led by God. The important thing is for them to be helped to decide what they think God's will is, *not* for you *to force* a particular interpretation upon them. Understanding that will help you to have fewer problems with your own prejudices or beliefs (of which you need to become increasingly aware).

8   If you feel you cannot work with a person because of *important or basic differences* then *you must say so* and suggest that they find someone else.

9   The person you are directing should at least be willing to try out your suggestions. If they *constantly ignore your advice*, again you should ask them to look for someone else.

10   If you don't think that *prayer* in any of its manifold forms and styles is of paramount importance as an expression of a relationship with God *don't* take on this task.

11   Be sensitive as to when to advise and when to listen. *Listening* is the most important part of this ministry and is likely to take up most of the time.

12   During the initial stages of your relationship it might be helpful for you to meet with the person directed quarterly. Some people settle for only twice or three times a year as a norm, but it is necessary to allow for crises or upheaval when an unplanned session might be necessary. *Don't meet too often* or spend too long on it. Usually an hour is enough.

13   Try to be as *objective* as you can. There is a narrow line to steer over being *professional* and businesslike (which helps the person to be so also) and also *warm*, which helps the person to open up. However, love contains both of these elements.

14   At the beginning ask the directee to give you a brief *profile* and history of him/herself. Knowledge of background is a great help. Educational background needs to be known, too. A housewife might be a theology graduate. A dentist might have tested his/her vocation in a community. It is useful to know what spiritual classics have been read, if any, or what books, preachers, retreat conductors, etc. have most impressed the person.

15   It is also very necessary to know something about the *state of life* that a person is in. One of the great dangers that Western Christendom has been in for the last four hundred years, has been that of setting standards of spirituality that come out of a monastic background, assuming that they are equally appropriate for people living lives in a secular world. It is *important to know* whether people have demanding work schedules and little or no free time; whether they are married and have small children or elderly parents at home; whether they live fairly static lives or travel all over the world. All that

is going to affect the sort of spirituality they develop, for all that is part of their journey with God.

16 The relationship with God is indeed at the centre of the whole exercise and *thanksgiving* needs to be at the centre of that relationship. If they are not used to reflecting on their lives it is something we can help them to seek, to see the hand of God and give him thanks for what he has already done with them.

17 Another area is the use of *silence*. We should be helping people see the significance of a regular use of silence, even if it has to be very short. There is also the need for *quiet days* and also for *retreats*. You may, however, need to recognize that many people find silence frightening.

18 Our relationship with other people is also part of our relationship with God, for it is with other people, for the most part, that we work it out. Here is need to be careful. It is fine to listen as people explain the intricacies so far as they feel able to. Make sure, though, that you *remain objective*. Not allowing them to be angry or express strong feelings of a negative kind can be counter-productive. If they feel 'X' is to blame, they must be given permission to say so and then walk forward from that. *Don't*, however, encourage your penitent to linger in blaming other people for situations. Help them to reflect on the role they should be taking in building peace and harmony.

19 Don't worry if people describe *experiences* you've never met before. Some people do have mystical experiences, visions and the like (some though can fabricate them to gain attention). Some people are called into a very deep, intense contemplative experience. Others lead their lives out at a mundane level – but God is in and with both. Some people are called by the charismatic movement and feel the presence of the Spirit, very closely, giving expression through the speaking of tongues or in other ways. Some have never had that experience and yet are equally full of the Spirit.

20 The best advice for the spiritual friend is to *keep his/her feet firmly on the floor*, one hand firmly in God's, with the other in his spiritual friend's – and 'let the Spirit do the walking and talking'.

Spiritual Direction

They fainted and were scattered abroad as sheep having no shepherd.

Matthew 9.36

This is a fair description of many people today. There is much fainting under the considerable pressures of modern life. Folk are scattered abroad in search of new and valid life-styles; the quest for meaning is on. As the familiar religious, political and social structures totter on every side, people instinctively look for some sort of direction. We are all suffering today from a certain disorientation. We need companions on the way.

'We don't have to apologize to God for being human.' It is our spiritual condition which determines our whole outlook on life. Once our spirits are in good working order, the rest of our lives will come into perspective.

Yes, but it is the duty of each Christian to discover in detail, in everyday practicalities, how Christ can be the way for him or her. A director can be a great help in the matter of reading the spiritual map. However, we have to do the driving ourselves.

Spiritual direction gives you freedom. Sometimes we tend to feel that being a good Christian should rid us of our difficulties and hang-ups. A glance at the lives of the saints will disabuse us on that score. The saints did not, on the whole, lose their hang-ups, they simply learned to hang something useful on them. With a little bit of help, we can do the same.

Don't drown your troubles; teach them to swim! For example:

obstinacy	can become perseverance.
critical spirit	can become discernment.
failures	can become prayer
self-centredness	can become God-centred

If we lose our lives: we shall find them again in him.

It is very exacting, that is why we need soul friendship if we are to carry our programme out. We need to learn – eventually – to do without our director. 'My eyes are ever looking unto the Lord.'

Elementary guidelines for directors

The three 'Rs':

1 Relevance
2 Respect
3 Relaxation

Relevance

- Christianity is only relevant insofar as it reflects the mind of Christ.
- We need to lead the pilgrim by the way God has chosen for him/her, *not* imposing our own way.
- Eyes must be fixed on Christ to give direction without turning round.
- The spiritual director must know Scripture and prayer. Godward, not manward.
- Be aware of our weakness.

Respect

- You must not be paternal/maternal.
- Souls may need to be referred elsewhere. 'The Spirit bloweth where he listeth.'
- Souls are delicate things and are not to be handled carelessly.

Relaxation

- We can relax because God is in charge. We often pay lip-service to this truth and then proceed to busy ourselves as if everything depended on us.
- 'Worry hinders charity in ourselves and others' (St Clare).
- To hinder charity is to hinder God.

We do our best, but don't confuse this with 'being a success'. It is plain from the Gospels that God is not interested in success. Blessings go to the unsuccessful; the beggars, the harlots, the lepers, the excommunicated. 'Being fruitful' is the aim.

A spiritual director is above all a person of the Beatitudes – a poor person who expects all from God's hand; who is meek towards God and fellow human beings; one who mourns for him in self and others; a merciful person who feels and shares a brother's or sister's pain; who hungers and thirsts for the coming of the Kingdom in people's hearts; who strives to keep his or her gaze fixed purely on God in order to learn the mind of Christ; and who longs to bring God's peace and order to the souls in his or her care.

A lofty ideal? Yes, and, humanly speaking, quite impossible. That is precisely why the spiritual director can and should relax, letting go his/her feeble strength, allowing Christ to do the sustaining. Paradoxically, the harder the going the more he/she can relax. The saint is hilarious when he or she is crushed with difficulties because the thing is so ludicrously impossible to anyone but God.

For the directee

What to expect from a spiritual director/soul friend

1. Spiritual Directors have been there on the Christian landscape all the way back through the centuries. Nowadays terms like 'direction' are often avoided since they seem to assume that our responsibility is removed. Perhaps it is best to see directors, then, as helping us to take our responsibilities more seriously. Another person, especially one with some expertise in counselling, can often help us see things that we miss ourselves. What should they help us see?

(a) They should help us see that our life is all of a piece. If there is something wrong with our family life, our work or our friendships, it will affect our spiritual growth.
(b) They need to help us to real growth and penitence. Often, if we practise sacramental confession they will be our confessor too.
(c) They will be ready to ask awkward questions, by looking at our rule of life to see that it is realistic, neither too strict nor too lax.
(d) They will understand us as persons. They need to be perceptive, show warmth and to see the specific needs and pressures of our own situation.
(e) They will be able to talk to us at the very deepest levels on all that matters, and if they feel unable to help us they will be honest enough to suggest we look for *another director*.

2. How to use a spiritual director
(a) Choose carefully. If you are a priest or training for full-time ministry you may wish to opt for a priest. As a lay person you may opt for either another lay person or a priest, or religious. Your choice should relate to how much you think the person will appreciate your circumstances.
(b) Be honest with your director from the start, even to the extent of admitting that the relationship does not work and that you may have to part company.

(c) In your honesty, move towards the position where you can discuss all aspects of your life with your director, so that true spiritual growth may follow.

(d) Be realistic about penitence and self-examination – this can be one of the most valuable ways in which a director may help you.

(e) See your director regularly so that you can keep an eye on yourself, but do not go so often that you become dependent on him or her.

(f) Be ready to review your rule of life, it may need to change. Help your director to ask penetrating questions – have you been on retreat, are you really praying, finding time for silence, etc.?

Some ideas to help in drawing up a rule of life

A. Introduction

The rule should involve the nine areas of spiritual life that follow. The first thing is to keep in mind that a rule should not contain promises that one would like to keep but which are beyond reach. The spiritual life may develop and require changes from time to time but should start with what you are doing already, or what you are sure you can keep, starting today.

We need a spiritual counsellor. It is a mistake to think that we can guide ourselves, however clever or well-intentioned we may be. We are often blind to our own spiritual health and need advice and encouragement from someone who knows something about spiritual counselling and to whom we can relate.

B. The rule should include:

1 *The Holy Eucharist* This should include Holy Communion on Sundays and greater festivals, and more frequently if this has been your custom.

2 *Penitence or self-examination* This means setting aside, preferably each week, time for self-examination, looking over the past week and seeing where we have failed in loving God and our neighbours. Friday is a good day for doing this. There are some who use sacramental confession and some who prefer to discuss problems with their spiritual counsellor.

3 *Personal prayer* This should not be less than 15 minutes a day and can include *lectio divina*/Bible reading with the aid of a commentary.

4 *Self-denial or self-discipline* For some the old rules of fasting as laid down by the Church may suit, others may prefer to do something that encourages self-control and at the same time effectively serves God and neighbour.

Lord of Creation

Some ideas:

(a) For those who are withdrawn – a definite undertaking to visit a sick or lively person regularly;
(b) For the busy or over-active, a rest rule – either for an earlier bedtime or a rest after lunch, not as a self-indulgence but as a time to recharge;
(c) An extra five minutes' prayer in church each week;
(d) Regular letter-writing, either to a neglected family or to someone who is lonely;
(e) Taking the daily paper, pick out some one item for concern. Study this paragraph or column carefully and make it a special subject for intercession during the following 24 hours;
(f) For those who have a tendency to be over-indulgent – to make a resolution to refrain the offering of a second helping.

5 *Retreat*   A retreat should be made annually. In exceptional circumstances a stated number of quiet days may be substituted, but this arrangement must be reviewed at regular intervals with the spiritual director. A retreat is probably the one time in the year when you can put on one side the daily chores and problems and be open to new insights and to perceive what God is trying to say to you. You will find that often you seem to grow more spiritual in that couple of days than in the whole year of church-going.

6 *Study*   There is no rule about what you should read. We should all try to improve our knowledge and so our devotion. The first priority should be Bible reading, study means keeping a book on the go and it is important to set aside half-an-hour or an hour each week – this should be put in the rule.

7 *Simplicity*   This rightly means that everything is supplied to us by God and we should treat everything as his, in other words, simplicity is part of respectfully using and sharing material things as well as the spiritual things in life. We express our love for God and our neighbour in the many ways in which we can demonstrate simplicity – for example, having lonely people in for a meal, taking someone elderly out for car rides, transport to church or hospital, putting people up, helping the young and the disadvantaged, prison visiting, helping at homes for the mentally handicapped, the elderly, the physically handicapped, the Samaritans, CAB and many more.

8 *Work and service*   Pilgrims should think about their work and the way they do it. 'Work' for most will mainly be their daily work but often can include other forms of service. For some, it will be service in connection with the Church. For others, it will be service in connection with secular or charitable organizations. Service has always been an important part of the Christian vocation. The form of your service should be discussed with your spiritual

director and if it is decided that this is best expressed by a statement such as 'through their daily work', this should be stated in the rule. For some busy people it may be something like visiting an elderly person regularly once every two weeks.

9 *Spiritual director*   The spiritual director or soul friend can be one of your own choosing, a person you can really talk to and be open with, and who will really understand. When you see your spiritual counsellor, take your rule along and talk about it – this gives you an opportunity to talk about other areas of your life that you may need to share with someone who is outside your ordinary life. Any psychiatrist will tell you that half our troubles come from 'bottling up' things inside which then get totally out of proportion. Your counsellor may be a local priest, a suitable lay person or brother/sister in a community.

Rule of life

A rule of life should be the minimum I know I can do for God. It is a framework only and should not be burdensome. It should be reviewed from time to time, for example, once a year or when circumstances of life change significantly. A rule of life may include details of frequency, quantity, place, and time.

1 The Eucharist . . . .

2 Daily Offices/prayer . . . .

3 Meditation . . . .

4 Intercession. . . . .

5 Bible study/*lectio devina*. . . . .

6 Confession or times of being open with the soul friend . . . .

7 Fasting . . . .

8 Giving. . . . .

9 . . . .

(I am grateful to the late Elizabeth Coulter, TSSF, an experienced soul friend to many, for her advice and help.)

That which tends to bring me to life	That which tends to deaden

Further reading

Ball, P., *Journey into Truth* (Spiritual direction in the Anglican tradition which points us back to the distinctive and continuous Anglican tradition, deserving consideration far beyond Anglican circles – an excellent book.), Mowbray: London, 1996.

Ball, P., *Introducing Spiritual Direction* (A clear and practical guide to what happens in spiritual direction.), SPCK: London, 2003.

Leech, K., *Soul Friend* (This essential book of spiritual direction draws on the teachings of the great spiritual guides to help those who are themselves seeking direction on the spiritual way, and who wish to know more about the Christian tradition of prayer.), Sheldon Press: London, 1977.

Leech, K., *True Prayer: An Introduction to Christian Spirituality* (This book is a companion volume to *Soul Friend* and is an introduction to the life of prayer and the Christian spiritual tradition.), Sheldon Press: London, 1980.

Hughes, G., *God of Surprises* (This is a guide book to the inner journey in which we are all engaged, with much to say to those seeking help to understand themselves, an excellent book of spiritual guidance.), Darton, Longman & Todd: London, 1985.

Hughes, G., *God in All Things* (A sequel to *God of Surprises*, the book of reflection on the inner journey; God, the ground of all things, is vibrant in every atom and creation itself is a manifestation of the reality of God: a must.), Hodder & Stoughton/DLT: London, 2003.

Rose, J., *Sharing Spaces* (A practical contribution to an under-explored area, looking at ways in which prayer can inform and nourish the counselling process, as well as ways in which the two areas can be difficult to integrate.), Darton, Longman & Todd: London, 1985.

Guenther, M., *Holy Listening: The Art of Spiritual Direction* (A good basic, very human reflection on spiritual direction using three images – hospitality, teaching and midwifery. Margaret Guenther helps us to see that spiritual life is grounded in ordinary everyday experiences, that it can reflect both laughter and tears, struggle and joy.), Darton, Longman & Todd: London, 1992.

Simpson, R., *Soul Friendship: Celtic Insights into Spiritual Mentoring* (A book using insights into the individuals' potential on their journey through life and the need for support at many different levels for example, soul-mates, spouses and prayer partners. It seeks to weave many strands of churchmanship into a modern Celtic-holistic spirituality.), Hodder & Stoughton: London, 1999.

THE JESUS PRAYER

Today many people are seeking God in the silence of their hearts. There is a hunger for the solitude of the wilderness and for places where they can rest away from everyday worries and anxieties of daily living. They suffer the exhaustion of busy-ness and haste and noise, which leaves them unfulfilled, stressed and lonely. However, they won't necessarily find God in the wilderness or even in 'holy' places. Deep within them, within us, in the very centre of the heart, is the presence of God in Jesus the Christ whom we received in baptism. There, in the heart, we can find him who is the essence of silence. How can we find him there? We can learn the way there through a way of prayer, which has come from the Christian East, called the Jesus Prayer.

It is a simple way of praying; deceptively so, considering the depth of spiritual insight that it can open. It is a 'phrase prayer': 'Lord Jesus Christ, Son of God, have mercy.' This prayer is simply repeated, over and over. It is used throughout the day, whenever we have time for it, whether in formal time of prayer or simply in odd moments of the day.

The Jesus Prayer has appeal for a number of reasons. Its very simplicity makes it attractive. It does not require elaborate preparation, and can be used at any time and in any place. It is not an intellectual way of prayer, nevertheless, it can be used by all whether academics or monks or cooks! Because it does not depend on the intellect it is especially effective when the mind is stressed, or when we are suffering in any way; when only the simplest of efforts to pray can be made. It is a wonderful prayer for 'pinning down' the intellect as it prevents our wandering thoughts and imaginations, the 'monkeys of the brain', from distraction. It gives us focus, so that with the rest of our minds we can be with God, who lives deep within each of us at the still, silent point of being.

Method

In order to use the Jesus Prayer most effectively, it is often helpful to adopt a technique for using it intensively during quiet prayer times, when we are free of distractions and can concentrate on our prayer. If this is done, the Jesus Prayer will establish itself within us, and develop a depth and receptivity that can be drawn upon when we need to use the prayer in a busier, more distracted atmosphere.

To do this, we need to make our bodies part of our prayer as well as our minds. Prayer is often thought of as a completely neutral process. But the body has a crucial part to play as well, and can either help us deeper into prayer, or distract us, until our attention is diverted away from seeking God. It is important that our bodies become our servants during prayer, and not the means by which we are carried away from God's presence.

To use the Jesus Prayer intensively, sit down. Sit still and upright. Close your eyes lightly. Sit relaxed but alert. Silently, interiorly begin to say the prayer. Listen to it as you say it, gently but continuously. Do not think or imagine anything spiritual or otherwise. If thoughts and images come, these are distractions at the time of meditation, so keep returning to simply saying the sentence.

Many people find it helpful to further co-ordinate body and prayer by saying half the prayer as they breathe in and half as they breathe out, bringing the prayer more deeply into the whole of their being. The prayer should be continued for as long as it can comfortably be maintained. This will often be only a short time at first, but proficiency does develop with time and the prayer becomes deeper and more sustained.

When you feel the time has come to end your prayer, it is best not to stop saying the phrase and immediately get up. Rather, first stop repeating the words of the prayer, sit quietly in the silence for a short time. Then deliberately but gently draw your mind back to the here and now of your surroundings. This will avoid any interior jarring or disturbance and will make a smooth transition between your prayer and the rest of your life.

In the recitation of the Jesus Prayer, most people begin by using the entire phase 'Lord Jesus Christ, Son of God, have mercy' but some use only a part of the phrase, and some only the word 'Jesus'. The longer form of the prayer is: 'Lord Jesus Christ, Son of God, have mercy on me, a sinner.' However, it is often true that as prayer deepens the phrase repeated tends to shorten, so that the prayer becomes more simple.

Regular use of a technique such as this establishes prayer within the 'heart', or depth, of a person, and for this reason the Jesus Prayer has often been called 'The Prayer of the Heart'. The interior use of this prayer can develop a reservoir of God's presence in us, which can be drawn on when such intensive use is not possible. In this way, the use of the prayer at other times during the day will be enriched and deepened.

Because it is so simple, the Jesus Prayer tends to have a simplifying effect on us. People who use it find their inner lives becoming more unified, their approach to God more direct. And they also discover that they are more at one, not only with God, but with themselves as well.

Distractions

The Jesus Prayer is not, of course, a 'quick remedy' for the distractions of thoughts and imaginations that plague the prayer of most people. Indeed, it sometimes seems that the use of the prayer makes us more aware of our distractions and our inner disunity than we were before. But the Jesus Prayer does contain a built-in remedy for these distractions. When we realize that we have become distracted by wandering thoughts or caught up in imagination, it is easy to gently bring our minds back to the content of the phrase we are repeating and to let our distractions float or 'wing' away.

Note then, these 'monkeys of the brain' and put them to the side; they are merely like clouds that temporarily obscure our view of the sky; then return to the constant interior recitation of the prayer. A gentle approach to distractions is usually more effective than a more determined use of will-power, and usually results in their being less troublesome to our prayer.

Constant prayer

When you have been using the Jesus Prayer for some time, you will begin to notice from time to time that you are praying without any remembrance of having started it consciously. Without having made any special effort you have begun to pray, and your awareness of prayer and God's presence becomes a more continuous experience. Deep within yourself, the prayer has established itself, and not only are you praying more frequently, you are using depths of yourself beyond the conscious. This is the beginning of the fulfilment of the injunction of the Apostle Paul in 1 Thessalonians 5.17 to 'pray without ceasing' and is a joyous proof that we can pray to God with our whole being, and not just with our conscious minds.

People unconscious on operating tables are sometimes found reciting the Jesus Prayer, I have known monks say it in their sleep and old men and women, sometimes far gone into senility, will retain this prayer when most of the rest of their conscious mind has deserted them. The Jesus Prayer, if used patiently and constantly, will lead us to a state where our whole being prays to God, and our union with God becomes not just a matter of the mind, but of our whole person. This is the fulfilment of prayer, and of Christianity, the union of a person with God.

REPETITIVE OR MANTRIC PRAYER

Theophan the Recluse said: 'The practice of the Jesus Prayer is simple. Stand before the Lord with the attention in the heart, and call to him "Lord Jesus Christ, Son of God, have mercy on me." The essential part of this is not in the words, but in the faith, contrition and self-surrender to the Lord. With these feelings one can stand before the Lord without any words, and it will still be prayer.'

There is a saying 'Man proposes, God disposes.' The most we can do in prayer is to place ourselves before God, attend to him with the mind in the heart and wait on his grace. It is important to remember that the Jesus Prayer is a phrase, or mantric or repetitive prayer. It is essentially an 'anchor phrase' to which we constantly return, and that is what mantric prayer is. It is this that enables the presence of God to be held perpetually in the heart. As the form of the words is repeated again and again (silently or aloud) the mind is drawn into them, so that they become rooted through constant remembrance of the Word. The prayer continues under its own inner energy and at its own level of being.

It is like riding a horse. At the early stages of learning how to ride we need to be conscious of how we use the various aids, that is the hands, seat, legs, heels and voice. After constant practice, self-discipline, and listening to instruction, we can forget about the conscious application of the aids and ride naturally. It is much the same with the exercise of prayer. On certain days everything goes well, but it will not always be the case. We need self-discipline, courage and faith to persevere. The main thing is to use your sentence, phrase or word to lead you into the silence. Let go, let be, in the presence, and when you become self-conscious or distracted, gently return to your phrase and repeat it.

It is essential to seek God's presence in the heart; that is why we meditate. Meister Eckhart (1260–1327), the great medieval spiritual teacher, said that we cannot know God unless we first know ourselves, and the only way we can begin to know ourselves is by returning to the heart. He said: 'The sublime and glorious reality which we call God is to be sought first and foremost in the human heart. If we do not find him there, we shall not find him anywhere else. If we do find him there, we can never lose him again; wherever we turn, we shall see his face.'

In saying the mantra it is well to remember that it is what happens at the level of the heart that is ultimately important. The heart is the engine, the fuel is love. Thomas Aquinas said: 'Where the mind leaves off, love goes on.'

Lord of Creation

Love is the whole aim,
Love is the completely
    transfiguring miracle,
Love is the one sole explanation.

Alternative mantras

The word 'mantra' is from the Sanskrit, meaning an instrument of thought
('man-think'). The word is now a universal religious term for a word or phrase
used in meditative prayer. Once a choice of mantra has been made, remain with
it, so that it may become rooted in the heart.

* I am that I am (Exodus 3.14).
* Be still and know that I am God (Psalms 46.10).
* Abide in me, and I in you (John 15.4).
* O God make speed to save us. O Lord make haste to help us.
* Into your hands I commend my spirit (Luke 23.46).
* Praise the Lord, my soul (Psalms 103.1).
* Maranatha (pronounce mah-rah-nah-thah), meaning: Come Lord, come (1
  Corinthians 16.22).
* Lord Jesus Christ, Son of God, have mercy on me, a sinner. (the Jesus Prayer).
* I am the Lord that healeth thee (Exodus 15.26).
* Lord, if you will, you can make me clean (Mark 11.30).
* Fear not, for I have redeemed you, I have called you by your name (Isaiah
  43.1).
* Hold thou me up and I shall be safe (Psalm 119.117).
* Jesus, God, for the sake of thy Blood, have pity on us (Irish Jesus Prayer).

One can recite the Jesus Prayer with the mind in the heart without movement
of the tongue. This is better than oral prayer. Use oral prayer as a support to
inner prayer. Sometimes it is required in order to strengthen inner prayer.

Theophan the Recluse

Further reading

Barrington-Ward, S., *The Jesus Prayer* (In this book we are taught how to use the
    Jesus Prayer and Bible passages crucial to the understanding of it are opened
    up.), Bible Reading Fellowship: Oxford, 1996.
Barrington-Ward, S. and Br Ramon, *Praying the Jesus Prayer Together* (Both Br

Ramon, the hermit, and Simon Barrington-Ward, the bishop, had been practising and teaching the Jesus Prayer for well over 20 years when they came together for a shared week of prayer at Glasshampton monastery. This book shares what they learned in an experience they described as a 'week of glory', yet also marked by the physical suffering of Br Ramon's illness.), B.R.F.: Oxford, 2001.

Bishop Kallistos of Diokleia, *The Power of the Name: The Jesus Prayer in Orthodox Spirituality*, Fairacres Publications No.43, 1985.

Sjögren, P.-O., *The Jesus Prayer*, SPCK: London, 1975.

The Way of a Pilgrim & The Pilgrim Continues his Way, translated by H. Bacovcin (This book was written by an unknown nineteenth-century Russian peasant and tells of his constant wrestling with the problem of 'how to pray without ceasing'. Through his journeys and travels, and under the tutelage of a spiritual father, he becomes gradually more open to the promptings of God. The reader is enriched as he shares these religious experiences in a most humble, simple and beautiful story. Forward by Walter J. Cizek, SJ.), *Spiritual Classics from Russia*, 1992.

the
name

i am with YOU, are
you seeking me?
i called upon your NAME,
O LORD, from the depths of
my heart;
and could not find you
in anything made.

when you really look for me,
let the name you LOVE be
what you do and you will see
me instantly -
in the tiniest point of light;
in the breath within the
BREATH who is JESUS.

BRENDANUS SCOTUS

THE PRAYER OF THE NAME

The most wondrous prayer in the whole world is the prayer of the Holy Name. It obtains for us countless graces, blessings of every kind and great happiness. It is the earliest of prayers to pray so that everyone without exception can use it and it is so certain that it never fails to produce wonderful effects. It consists simply in repeating frequently, with the use of the breath and with attention and devotion one word, JESUS. Nothing could be easier and yet many Christians know little of the infinite value and omnipotent power of the name of Jesus.

The Apostle Paul is the preacher of the Holy Name. With this name he worked all his wonders, converted Jews and Gentiles, confounded the pagan philosophers of Greece and Rome, cast down false gods and implanted the reign of Christ in their place. He tells us of the power of this name: 'In the name of Jesus every knee shall bend in Heaven, on Earth and under the Earth.' When we say Jesus we give immense joy to God and to all heaven, we obtain the fullness of grace and drive away evil. The Apostle tells us to do all we do in word and work in the name of Jesus. However, it is very important to know what we are actually saying when we pray the Word in this manner.

First of all, this one word, 'Jesus', is the shortest, the easiest, and the most powerful of prayers. Our Lord himself tells us that whatever we ask the Father in the name of Jesus we shall receive. Therefore when we say 'Jesus' we ask God for everything we need, and with unbounded confidence.

Second, each time we say 'Jesus' let us have the intention of offering to God the infinite merits of the passion and death of Jesus Christ because St Paul tells us that our Lord merited this name Jesus by his passion and death.

Third, each time we say 'Jesus' let us offer God our Father all the Holy Eucharists and prayers being said all over the world. We thus, with a 'lifting up of the heart with a blind stirring of love' share in the adoration and praise of God.

Fourth, each time we say 'Jesus' we pray as a member of the Mystical Body of Christ in union with all the angels and saints in heaven and on earth.

We can say the Prayer of the Name hundreds of times every day without difficulty. When we awake in the night it is the easiest of prayers to say and is the most wonderful method for slipping off to sleep again! The frequent repetition of the name of Jesus transforms lost moments into blessings and far from tiring us gives us a joy, a peace and a happiness beyond compare.

We may say the prayer when dressing. During our daily work we can continue the prayer. It is especially useful when caring, giving counsel or listening to others. This is what St Paul tells us to do: 'Whatever you do in word or work do all in the name of Jesus.'

If we are sick in bed we can say 'Jesus' thousands of times and Jesus will console us. When on earth he comforted the sorrowful, cured the sick, the blind and dumb. The Prayer of the Name of Jesus is a ministry of healing in itself. No effort is required; all we have to do is let this blessed name flow from our hearts and lips with devotion. If we pray it with care and attention, then we shall have an immense treasure in our hearts for time and eternity.

It is probably the easiest and best penance we can perform, for every time we are tempted, say the name, and the problem will become a mystery. Every time we say 'Jesus' we offer the passion and death of Jesus Christ for our sins!

Finally, pray the prayer on the in and out breath. Breathe in on 'Je' – pause – breathe out on 'sus'.

A blessing I wish you from ages unto ages.

The Jesus breath

Anthony called his two companions . . .
And said to them,
'Always breathe Christ'

> *Athanasius of Alexandra,* Life of Anthony

On a long in-breath, breathe in the presence of Jesus (his image, love, peace, light, person and spirit) into the head area. Rest with that presence and on an out-breath, breathe out your 'self'.

Again, on an in-breath repeat the above exercise, this time breathing the presence into the throat area. Rest lightly in the presence, then again on an out-breath, breathe out 'self' from the throat.

Repeat this simple body prayer exercise down through the areas of the heart, diaphragm, solar-plexus, genitals, limbs and feet.

This is an excellent exercise of preparation for recollection and contemplative prayer. It may also be applied to standing, sitting and walking meditation (see over).

A breathing exercise

Close your eyes. Gently.

1 Imagine a bright globe of light away above your head.
It is the light of Christ.
2 Activate this light on an in-breath and breathe the light down through the
centre of the cranium, to the centre of your heart.
3 On an out-breath breathe the light down to the molten centre of the earth.
4 Bring up the light from the centre of the earth through the feet, breast and head
to a high distant point.
5 'Fountain' the 'incarnated' light over your self and your surroundings on an
out-breath.

> You have three wings, the first
> unfurls aloft in the highest heights.
> The second dips its way dripping
> Sweat on the Earth . . .
> Over, under, and through all things
> Whirls the third.
>
> *Hildegard of Bingen*[53]

PRAYER BEADS

People throughout the ages have known what many of us are relearning – the things we touch and see and finger can bring the unseen near.

Anon.

I include the use of prayer beads in this book for the reason mentioned in the above quotation. I have always carried a set of prayer beads in my pocket. They play an indispensable part in my prayer life as they are an important means of grace, always there and always available. All of the great religions use beads as a means of sacramental prayer. They 'ground' prayer through the use of the body enabling a constant experience of the Divine. Whether in the pocket or around the neck they are close to us and therefore help us to stay closer to the Holy Spirit praying through us in our everyday lives; for Christ is already closer to us than we are to ourselves through our baptism. Praying the beads helps us to keep in touch with Christ as he calls out to the Father within our heart. As we breathe rhythmic prayer, he is the breath within our breath as we pray the word. This form of prayer has both spiritual and material elements to it. The beads have a sacramental character in that they combine matter and spirit and effect what they symbolize helping us to stay close to the Holy Spirit in everyday life. This practice therefore has a grounding effect, facilitating the sacrament of the present moment.

The repetitive prayer used when praying with rosaries acts as an anchor with which to focus the thoughts and still the mind, helping the person praying to remain at the still point where true prayer is to be found in the cell of the heart. All religious traditions hold that human beings are made in the image of the Divine. Religion is the means by which we link with the One Thing Necessary and the rosary helps us focus on this goal.

In the Christian tradition the most recognizable rosary is the Roman Catholic one: its provenance is generally thought to have been the revelation by the Blessed Virgin Mary of the rosary to St Dominic in the early thirteenth century. In Lourdes, France, and Fatima, Portugal, the Blessed Virgin Mary has again revealed the importance of praying the rosary. However, the tradition of praying with beads has roots in the prayer practices of the Desert Fathers and Mothers in the third century and it was well developed in the sixth century.

The word 'rosary' is thought to be derived from 'garland of roses' symbolizing the string of prayers. A *rosarium* is a rose garden indicating a place of contemplation. It may also denote an anthology of prayer or verse or any sort of prayer bead. Rosary beads were often made of crushed rose which, due to their high oil content, gave of a pleasant odour. The word 'bead' or 'bede' means prayer and is connected by association with the rosary, as each bead represents a prayer. The term 'bidding prayers' in the Eucharist means to bid prayer, that is to say prayer and to bid the beads is to say one's prayers. St Bede may have received his name due to his practice of constant prayer.

Prayer beads are portable, of easy access and use. We can tell our beads as we walk so that they become markers of the rhythm of prayer, a metronome beating the time as we bring into one the whole of us – body, mind and spirit. Bidding the beads helps concentration for they take care of our 'nerve endings' as it were, taking care of our need to be busy, while interiorly we are in the solitude of contemplative prayer. I can think of no better method of creating a temple for the Holy Spirit, a holy place, a temple for God within.

There are many methods or ways of praying with prayer beads or rosary. I shall limit the number to three due to the lack of space. However there are some excellent books available describing how to make and use prayer beads as well as giving information on the history of this form of devotion.

Using the Jesus Prayer

The Jesus Prayer (page 191) is a perfect prayer to use with the Orthodox prayer rope which is a knotted woollen prayer rope sometimes described as a *metanoia*, literally 'turning point' or 'change of mind'. In the Russian Orthodox Church it is called a *chotki*, and 33, 100 or even 300 knots are found. Orthodox bead-rosaries are not uncommon. They are usually made of wood and known as Jesus beads. I have a set of these fashioned in olive wood with a dove logo representing the Holy Spirit on the cross.

The Jesus Prayer

Lord Jesus Christ,
Son of God,
Have mercy on me,
A sinner

Method

On the in-breath at the first bead or knot, say 'Lord Jesus Christ'. Pray the words slowly, letting the words flow naturally with the breath.

On the out-breath, say 'Son of God'; on the next in-breath pray 'have mercy on me', and on an out-breath, say 'a sinner'.

It is important to be conscious of every word uttered. In this manner we pray before God with the mind in the heart.

Saying the Jesus Prayer regularly both morning and night is an effortless way of practising constant prayer. During the day at unguarded moments the prayer will 'bubble up' unaided like coffee in a percolator! With regular practice, increasing inwardness will be noted and the mind will repeat the prayer without any noticeable movement of lips or tongue. The prayer is a 'dominant prayer' as it quickly becomes the prayer we use for all contemplative moments. It can take over our whole personality as it identifies itself with the rhythm of the heart and the intake of the breath.

> What I do is pray
> How I pray is breathe.
>
> *Thomas Merton*

Anglican prayer beads

Anglican prayer beads, also known as the Anglican rosary, is a relatively new prayer form which is a blending of the Marian (Roman Catholic) rosary and the Orthodox Jesus Prayer rope. Many Anglicans use prayer ropes and beads. Since the 1970s, beads and invocatory prayer have been increasingly included as a support for meditation by contemplative prayer groups such as John Main's Christian meditation groups and the Centering Prayer movement.

The Anglican form of the rosary-style prayer method came out of a contemplative prayer group that met in the mid 1980s and was created by an Anglican priest. Comprised of 33 beads, the number of years Our Lord walked this earth, it is well grounded in incarnational theology and the symbolism contained in it points towards the Celtic view of the sanctity of all of God's creation.

The structure of Anglican prayer beads

Four groups of seven beads form the *weeks* and remind us of Creation, the temporal week, as well as the seasons of the Church year. The number seven also signifies wholeness or completion.

Four cruciform beads remind us that the cross is the central symbol of our Anglican Christian faith, as well as reminding us of the seasons of the temporal year and the four points on the compass, thus bringing us into the mindfulness of the created world.

Invitatory bead – just as the Daily Office of the Church begins with the invitatory, the bead just above the cross is an invitation to praise and worship God as well as an entry point into the circle of prayer of the rosary.

Trisagion and the Jesus Prayer

Cross	In the Name of God, Father, Son, and Holy Sprit. Amen.
Invitatory Bead	O God make speed to save me (us),
	O Lord make haste to help me (us).
	Glory to the Father, and to the Son, and to the Holy Spirit:
	As it was in the beginning, is now, and will be forever.
	Amen.
Cruciform Beads	Holy God,
	Holy and Mighty,
	Holy Immortal One,
	Have mercy upon me (us).
The Weeks	Lord Jesus Christ, Son of God,
	Have mercy on me, a sinner.

Or, if in a group setting:

Lord Jesus Christ, Son of God,
Have mercy upon us.

(Last time through)

Invitatory Bead	The Lord's Prayer
Crucifix	Let us bless the Lord (*or* I bless the Lord)
	Thanks be to God.

Lord of Creation

A Celtic prayer

Cross	In the Name of God, Father, Son, and Holy Spirit. Amen.
Invitatory Bead	O God make speed to save me (us). O Lord make haste to help me (us). Glory to the Father, and to the Son, and to the Holy Spirit: As it was in the beginning is now, and will be forever. Amen.
Cruciform Beads	Be the eye of God dwelling with me, The foot of Christ in guidance with me, The shower of the Spirit pouring on me, Richly and generously.
The Weeks *(Pray each* *phrase on* *a separate* *Bead)*	I bow before the Father who made me, I bow before the Son who saved me, I bow before the Spirit who guides me, In love and adoration. I praise the name of the one on high. I bow and adore thee, Sacred Three, The Ever One, the Trinity.
	(Last time through)
Invitatory Bead	The Lord's Prayer
Cross	Let us bless the Lord (*or* I bless the Lord) Thanks be to God.
	(Use a plural form in group settings)

Prayer of Julian of Norwich

Cross	In the Name of God, Father, Son, and Holy Spirit. Amen.
Invitatory Bead	O God make speed to save me (us). O Lord make haste to help me (us). Glory to the Father, and to the Son, and to the Holy Spirit As it was in the beginning is now, and will be forever. Amen.
Cruciform Beads	God of your goodness, give me yourself, For you are enough to me. And I can ask for nothing less that is to your glory. And if I ask for anything less, I shall still be in want, for only in you have I all.

The Weeks	All shall be well, and all shall be well, And all manner of thing shall be well.
	Or
	In his love he has done his works, and in His love he has made all things beneficial To us.
	(Last time through)
Invitatory Bead *Crucifix*	The Lord's Prayer Let us bless the Lord (*or* I bless the Lord) Thanks be to God.

A little office

Cross	In the Name of God, Father, Son, and Holy Spirit. Amen.
Invitatory Bead	O God make speed to save me (us). O Lord make haste to help me (us). Glory to the Father, and to the Son, and to the Holy Spirit: As it was in the beginning is now, and will be forever. Amen.
Cruciform Beads	Behold now, bless the Lord, all you Servants of the Lord. You that stand in The house of the Lord, lift up your hands in the holy place and bless the Lord.

The Weeks	I lift up my eyes to the hills;
	    from where is my help to come?
	My help comes from the Lord,
	    the maker of heaven and earth.

	(Last time through)
Invitatory Bead *Crucifix*	The Lord's Prayer Let us bless the Lord Thanks be to God.

(Feel free to use other verses from the Psalms to suit the time of day and season of the Church year this Little Office is said, or other prayers that are meaningful to you.)

Lord of Creation

The Marian or Catholic Rosary

The precursor of the present form of Roman Catholic rosary began to take shape as early as the sixth century. St Benedict, father of Western monasticism asked his monks to pray the 150 Psalms at least once a week. Although, no doubt, many monks were able to memorize the whole Psalter many more could not! Therefore the brethren were allowed to substitute 150 Paters ('Our Fathers'). The disciples of this method used beads to count the Paters, and so this string of 150 beads became known as a 'paternoster'.

Cistercian lay brothers used this form of devotion for centuries until Vatican II in the early 1960s, when they received their own office manual and eventually ceased to be 'lay' brothers, being finally admitted to the same status as the choir monks and given the same habit to wear. It is true to say that the brothers were often very holy men and inevitable 'prayer-engines' through the constant recitation of the rosary!

A regular Marian rosary comprises 150 Ave or Hail Mary beads, 15 Pater or Our Father beads, plus five beads that represent the entrance or introit beads such as the Glory Be.

As the full rosary set is rather lengthy to handle the more common five-decade (5 × 10 = 50 beads) is generally used.

Method

1 Kiss the crucifix and make the sign of the cross with it saying 'In the Name of the Father, and of the Son, and of the Holy Spirit. Amen.'
2 On the first bead following the crucifix pray the Our Father. On the following three beads say the Hail Mary:

> Hail Mary, full of grace,
>   the Lord is with thee.
> Blessed art thou among women,
>   and blessed is the fruit of thy womb, Jesus.
> Holy Mary, Mother of God,
> Pray for us sinners,
>   now and at the hour of our death.
> Amen.

3 On the final bead pray the Glory Be. This constitutes the introductory prayers.

The mysteries

The five decades (ten beads to a decade) on the rosary relate to three sets of five mysteries which are meditations or reflections on the life of Jesus Christ and his mother, the Virgin Mary. The art is to meditate on each mystery during the saying of the Our Fathers and Hail Marys.

The key prayers:

- The Our Father
- The Hail Mary
- The Apostles' Creed
- Hail, Holy Queen – said at the end before making the sign of the cross and kissing the crucifix.

The mysteries are:

- The Joyful Mysteries
- The Mysteries of Light
- The Sorrowful Mysteries
- The Glorious Mysteries

The Joyful Mysteries

1 **Annunciation**
'You are to conceive and bear a Son and you will call him Jesus' (Luke 1.31). Like Mary, let us always be open to the will of the Lord at all times.

2 **The Visitation**
'Why should I be honoured with a visit from the Mother of my Lord?' (Luke 1.43). Like Mary, let us also carry the gospel to the world.

3 **The birth of Jesus**
'Today, in the town of David a saviour has been born to you' (Luke 2.11). With Mary, let us make Christ present in the world.

4 **The presentation of Jesus in the temple**
'My eyes have seen your salvation, a light to enlighten the pagans' (Luke 2.30, 32). People of every nation, give thanks for the light you have received.

5 **The finding of Jesus in the temple**
'Three days later, Mary and Joseph found Jesus in the Temple' (Luke 2.46a). Like Mary, let us seek the Lord unceasingly.

The mysteries of light

1 **The baptism of the Lord in the Jordan**
'You are my Son, the Beloved: my favour rests on you' (Mark 1.11b). With Mary, let is realize fully that we are children of God.

2 **The wedding of Cana**
'Mary said to the servants: "Do whatever he tells you"' (John 2.5). Like Mary, let us do what the Lord tells us.

3 **Jesus proclaims the kingdom of God**
'Jesus said: Repent and believe in the Good News' (Mark 1.15). In Lourdes and elsewhere, Mary calls us to conversion. Let us listen to that call.

4 **The transfiguration**
'Lord, it is good for us to be here' (Matt. 17.4a). Like Mary, let us allow ourselves to be transfigured by the Holy Spirit.

5 **Jesus gives us the Eucharist**
Jesus says to us: 'Do this as a memorial of me' (Luke 22.19b). With Mary, let us be united in Christ's saving passion and resurrection.

The sorrowful mysteries

1 **The agony in the garden**
'Jesus said: "Father, let your will be done, not mine"' (Luke 22.42). With Mary, let us watch and pray in the midst of trials and temptation.

2 **The scourging at the pillar**
'After Pilate had ordered Jesus to be scourged, he handed him over to be crucified' (Mark 15.15).

3 **The crowning with thorns**
'The soldiers twisted some thorns into a crown and placed it on the head of Jesus' (John 19.2). With Mary, the mother of sorrows, let us seek humility.

4 **Jesus carries his cross**
'And carrying his own cross he went out of the city to the place of the Skull' (John 19.16–17). With Mary, let us pray for all who are crushed by life.

5 **Jesus dies on the cross**
'Jesus said "Father, into your hands I commit my spirit." Then he breathed his last' (Luke 23.46). United with Mary in suffering, let us pray for all who have died and for those who are in their last agony.

The glorious mysteries

1 **The resurrection of the Lord**
   'Why search among the dead for someone who is alive?' (Luke 24.6). With Mary, let us be witnesses of the resurrection.

2 **The ascension of the Lord into heaven**
   Jesus tells us: 'I will be with you always, until the end of the world' (Matthew 28.20b). Like Mary, let us be one with Christ who lives for ever.

3 **The descent of the Holy Spirit on the apostles**
   'Filled with the Holy Spirit, the apostles proclaimed the marvels of God' (Acts 2.11). With Mary, let us all proclaim the wonders of God in our own language.

4 **The assumption of Our Lady into heaven**
   'In heaven, I saw a woman with a crown of twelve stars on her head' (Revelation 12.1). With Mary, Bernadette and all the saints let us live in the hope of heaven.

5 **The coronation of Our Lady in heaven**
   'All nations will call me blessed' (Luke 1.48b).

Celtic prayer before the rosary

We humbly prostrate ourselves in the name of Jesus Christ,
Asking pardon and forgiveness for our sins.
We ask for your assistance and help to consider the welfare of our souls.
Do not give to us anything in this world
That would deprive us of the eternal glory of heaven;
But grant to us everything that will tend most to the peace and advantage of our souls;
Grant that we be seven times better a year hence in the sweet love of God.
And in the love of our neighbours;
Grant to us the final blessing and penance,
A Christian death, and a Christian bed in paradise. Amen.

Connacht[54]

Another prayer

Assembled together in Your name, O Lord,
We begin this prayer as Our Saviour, Jesus Christ,
Ordered for the peace of our souls.
We place ourselves in the presence of God
and we ask the help of the Holy Spirit.
O God, and O Holy Spirit, I pray you
come and take complete possession of my heart:
cleanse my conscience from every stain of sin:
and give me grace to be peaceful and charitable to my neighbour:
through Jesus Christ, Our Lord. Amen.

Seanfhocla Uladh[55]

After the rosary

O Lord, have mercy on us.
O Christ, have mercy on us,
O Queen of the bright light, have mercy on us.
Give mercy to us and grace, forgiveness and mercy to our souls.
Put nothing into our hearts that may deprive us of our share of the eternal glory
   of heaven.
Save us from the showers of calamity
And from the sicknesses of the year.
Preserve our property and our people,
Our health and our wealth,
In the love of God and of the neighbours. Amen.

Connacht[56]

Another prayer

I offer up a Pater and Ave to God to save me and all my people from every evil and every ill; from evil minds and evil hearts; from evil thoughts and evil deeds and evil company; from a violent and sudden death; from drowning, from wounding, from disease, from war, from plague, from worldly shame, from public scandal; from wrong of friends, from power of enemies, from mischief, from misfortune, from shame of scandal of Christ; but that we may be given the love of God and of the neighbours. Amen.
(Pater and Ave)

MacCrócaigh[57]

Further reading

Miller, John D., *Beads and Prayers: The Rosary in History and Devotion*, Burns and Oats. A Continuum imprint, London, 2001. A detailed and readable study of this ancient devotion to the Blesed Virgin Mary.

Wiley, Eleanor and Shannon, Maggie Oman, *How to Make and Use Prayer Beads*. Red Wheel, Boston, MA/York Beach. M.E. This book recounts the history and symbolism of prayer beads, teaches basic techniques for stringing beads.

Elliot, Kris and Seibt, Betty Kay, *Holding Your Prayers in Your Hands: Praying the Anglican Rosary*. 624 University, PMB/Penn 110, Denon, Tx 76201

Baumann, Lynn C., *The Anglican Rosary*. PRAXIS, Rt./.Box 190B

The Rosary for Episcopalians, Incarnation Priory, 1601 Oxford Street, Berkeley, CA 94709

Anglican prayer beads may be obtained from
Solitaries of De Koven, 1101 County Road 204, Santa Anna, Tx 76878
Internet: www.solitariesofdekoven.org
e-mail: solitariesofdekoven@juno.com

salutations to the WORD
which is present in the earth,
the heavens and that which is beyond.
let us meditate
on the glorious SPLENDOUR
of that DIVINE giver of life;
may he illuminate our meditation.

ancient prayer

Lectio Divina – Praying the Scriptures

The Word of God is very near to you, it is in your mouth and in your heart.

Deuteronomy 30.14; Romans 10.8

An ancient way of praying the Old and New Testament Scripture was known as *lectio divina*. Benedictine monks were encouraged to 'read' up to three hours a day. They did not read for intellectual knowledge, essentially they read to *experience* the word of God, which formed their heart and mind.

It was an experience that affected the whole of their being, body, mind and spirit. They did not read as we do today, principally with the eyes, in a silent, rapid way, but with the lips, mouthing and pronouncing the words; listening with the ear of the heart. In this manner the word is deposited or sown in the heart. When the word of God is received at the level of the heart we experience a profound change in the depth of our being. For the Spirit is already present in our hearts through baptism and so when the word of God reaches the heart, spiritual awakening takes place, thanks to the one Spirit who is present in both. There is a spark or synergistic effect when word and Spirit are one. The eternal spirit of Christ calls out to the Father through being born again in the Word. Born from an imperishable seed, 'we are born anew, not of perishable but of imperishable seed through the living and enduring word of God' (1 Peter 1.23). Thus, born again of the word, we recognize in the word, as in a mirror, our new state of being. 'For if any are hearers of the word and not doers, they are like those who look at themselves in a mirror; for they look at themselves and, on going away immediately forget what they are like' (James 1.23–24). The Divine Presence awakes within us. The word has penetrated to our very depths like a sharp two-edged sword. 'Indeed it is alive and active, sharper than any two-edged sword, piercing until it divides soul from spirit, joints from marrow; it is able to judge the thoughts and intentions of the heart' (Hebrews 4.12).

New life is generated within us as the divine energy of the word spreads through the blood. Our mind-set or rather, 'heart-set', has undergone a profound change. Physicians in ancient times used to recommend reading the sacred Scriptures as an exercise for the good of the physical well-being of their patients because more senses as well as the use of the breath were involved in the process of reading.

Texts were frequently memorized and 'sucked' like a lozenge. Biblical texts were learned by heart for private use in meditation (*meditatio*), an exercise of muttering the sentence rather than mental reflection. Prayer phrases were 'chewed' and 'ruminated' on at will in this way. The main thing is to give oneself up to the word of God. Repeat the word quietly and slowly so that it may become clearer to the eye of the heart. Chew on it, ruminate the word and cradle it in the centre of the heart. By lovingly repeating the word we are 'centring Christ'. The word impregnates the heart and becomes connatural with it. Reborn by the power of the word we are nourished and strengthened and enabled to reshape our life according to the Scriptures.

> We have a consoler, our Lord Jesus Christ. Although we cannot see him with bodily eyes, we keep in written form in the Gospels the things he did and thought while he was bodily among us. If we take care to hear, read and confer with each other about these things, which need to be preserved in our hearts and bodies, we will certainly conquer the obstacles of this age as surely as if the Lord were always standing by us and consoling us.

> *Bede,* Homilies on the Gospels

Lectio – reading in the monastic way – is oriented toward *meditatio* (monastic meditation which is the mouthing or muttering of the word) and *oratio* (praying the word). It is not done for science and knowledge but for the experiencing and wisdom of the word. It then leads toward *contemplatio* – the silent contemplation of the word.

Thus the words are pronounced with the lips in a low tone and the sentence is heard. As Jean Leclerq has written: 'What results is a muscular memory of the words pronounced and an aural memory of the words heard. The meditation consists in applying oneself with attention to this exercise in total memorization; it is, therefore, inseparable from lectio. It is what inscribes so to speak, the sacred text in the body and in the soul.'[58]

Reading and meditation are sometimes described as rumination. In the monastic understanding of the word, to meditate is to attach oneself closely to the sentence being recited and assimilate the context of a text by means of a kind of mastication which releases its full flavour. It is a prayerful reading, savoured by the palate of the heart it develops into a prayer of the heart.

As the Cistercian, Arnoul of Boheriss (AD 1175), advises: 'When he reads, let him seek for savour, not science. The Holy Scripture is the well of Jacob from which the waters are drawn which will be poured out later in prayer. Thus there will be no need to go to the oratory to begin to pray, but in reading itself, means will be found for prayer and contemplation.'[59]

Lord of Creation

AWARENESS EXERCISE

This is an exercise that can help us to be more aware of ourselves and of God.

Choose a time and place in which you are unlikely to be disturbed for ten minutes or so.

Take this exercise slowly and leisurely.

Relax as much as you can. Feel the tensions in the different parts of your body and then let them ebb away.

Be where you are, not where you were or are going to be. Be really present to yourself, right here, right now.

If you are sitting down, feel the weight of your body on the chair.

Feel the floor holding up your feet and legs.

Feel the contact points between your body and the chair.

We all know what happens when we try to be still and quiet. Our mind goes all over the place.

We need a focus to which we can call it back.

An Eastern meditation teacher likened it to training a puppy which sits for ten seconds and then bounds off and has to be called back. Then it sits for maybe twenty seconds and is off again. Our mind is like that. We need a focus to which we can return.

Focus first of all on your breathing. Notice how the body expands when you breathe in and contracts when you breathe out.

Concentrate all your attention on your breathing. (When your mind wanders, bring it back gently to your breathing.)

Keep focusing on your breath.

After two minutes or so, change your focus to the very centre of your being, wherever that is for you. For some it is the head, for some the heart. For many it is around the navel, in the midriff. Find your centre, that deep place within you where everything seems to come together. Focus all your attention there . . . (Again, if your mind wanders, bring it back gently to that deep place within you.)

In that deep place, hear God calling your name. God calls you by name and says, 'Be still'. In the Vulgate, the Latin is *vacate*, 'be empty', 'vacate', 'take a vacation from thinking you are God'. 'Be still and let me be God.' 'Let me be in control. You don't have to be in control all the time. Let *me* be in control.'

Go on hearing God calling you by name and saying, 'Be still.'

Now, in that deep place, call God by name, just one name. It may be God, Lord, Father, Mother, Jesus, Spirit, Love, Life, Light or any other name. Keep repeating it slowly and rhythmically. Every time you say it, let it be a greeting, a meeting with God who is nearer to you than your own breath. Keep calling God by name over and over again.

Then, deep within you, ask yourself what it is that you most desire, what you really, really, really want. Ask God for it.

You may want to go on talking with God.

When you have finished the exercise, review it. Look back and see what has been happening. How have you been feeling, at the beginning, as time went on and what are you feeling now? What word would best describe how you are feeling now? Perhaps you would like to talk with God about that.

This exercise can help orientate us towards God who loves us and is always with us, in us and for us.

Praying a Scripture

The great thing about this kind of meditation is that we don't have to be clever. The less clever we are the better. God will do the work. You just have to be there and, first of all, listen. There is far too much in this Scripture to deal with at one time. You don't have to finish the passage in one sitting. It could last you weeks. Take your time. It's your time, time that God is giving you.

The 6 Rs of praying a scripture are:

Relax
Read
Ruminate
Relish
Respond
Review

So just *relax* for a few minutes both in body and mind. Be where you are, right here, in this present moment. If you are sitting, feel the weight of your body on the chair. Feel the contact points between your body and the chair. *Relax*.

Then read this Scripture once straight through (it is from Isaiah 43):

But now, thus says the Lord who created you, O Jacob, who formed you, O Israel:
'Don't be afraid, for I have set you free.
I have called you by name. You are mine.
You are precious in my eyes, and honoured and I love you.
Don't be afraid, for I am with You.'

Read it again slowly. When you come to 'Jacob' and 'Israel', substitute your own name and hear God speaking to you. When one particular word or phrase strikes you, take it deep within yourself. *Ruminate* on it, chew the cud on it. Let it really sink in. *Relish* it. When you have not only thought about it but felt it in your guts, know it to be true for you, let yourself *respond* and talk with God about it. It may be to be awestruck or to argue with God or to thank him, praise him or to be sorry about something. Have as intimate a conversation with God as you can. Then go on to another word or phrase. But don't be in a hurry.

When you have finished the meditation, *review* the time you have spent on it. What has been happening? What have you been feeling? What are you feeling now? Do you want to talk more with God about it? What do you want to remember and to take with you from this meditation? If you were to do the meditation again, where would you start? What would you want to go back to? Thank God for this time with him.

Two hints:

1 It is useful to read over the passage some time before your period of meditation.
2 Decide how long you will spend in meditation and stick to that time whatever is happening or seemingly not happening. If you give up when nothing seems to be happening, nothing will ever happen!

I am grateful to Bishop Graham Chadwick for permission to use this exercise.

in the Beginning was
silence,
and out of the silence came
sound,
and out of the sound came the
word,
and the word was
vibration,
which took
shape
in the alphabet of
creation.

out of no-thing
god spoke the
word,
which Became
matter,
the order and substance of
cosmos.

thus through the
word made flesh,
all that is created out of silence,
resonates
and returns toward the still, silent
mystery of god,
Before which all words
ultimately fail.

Brendanus scotus

THE PRAYER OF SILENCE

For God alone my soul in silence waits;
from him comes my salvation.
For God alone my soul in silence waits;
truly, my hope is in him.

Psalm 62

It is better to be silent and real than to talk and be unreal.

St Ignatius of Antioch

The Lord speaks in the stillness of nature. He speaks in the still, silent point of our being. Therefore when we are silent in the Presence of God, we most truly pray. God's Presence is reality. Grace 'full-fills' us when we empty ourselves of words, self and imagination. All too often, as Simone Weil said, we fill our inner void with imagination. 'That is why we fly from the inner void, since God might steal into it.'

The art of deep silent prayer, then, is to withdraw gently from all distractions, abandoning all except the *will* to pray, which is the essence of prayer. Then the Spirit of God invades the soul.

And yet,

Prayer is strange in being an activity where no success is possible. There is no perfect prayer – except insofar as it corresponds to one's real situation and represents a total turning towards God. The ecstatic prayer of the mystic is in no way superior to the agonised stumbling of a sinner weighed down by guilt and deformed by a lifetime of estrangement from God. Both attempts represent the upward striving of created nature to find rest in God. Both are real, both are 'successful'. Both remain imperfect, too, because perfection does not belong in this life, it is to be expected in the next. And when God's judgement throws everything upside down and exalts the lowly, who can say which of these prayers has the greater capacity to be raised?

Michael Casey[60]

Above all, we must not judge our prayer to be 'mystical' or not. It is better to pray as we can, rather than to pray as we can't. Essentially, we need to pray even when we find the exercise unattractive and difficult. Julian of Norwich has written that such prayer is very profitable even though we feel nothing. We are to pray with our whole being, even though we feel nothing, even though it feels impossible for us. 'It is in dryness and barrenness, in sickness and in feebleness that your prayer is most pleasing to me, even though you think that it has little savour for you' (Julian of Norwich, *Revelations of Divine Love*).

To express myself briefly: let this thing deal with you and lead you wherever it likes. Let it be the worker and you but the sufferer, look at it briefly then leave it alone. Meddle not with it as though to help it for fear of spilling it all. Be the tree and let it be the carpenter. Be the house and let it be the householder dwelling inside. Be blind in this time and cut away all desire for knowledge, for that will hinder you more than it will help. It suffices that you feel yourself stirred pleasantly with something that you do not know – except that in this stirring you have not thought of anything under God and that all your desire is nakedly directed towards God.

St John of the Cross

The method that leads us further along the path of prayer is to use few words. The fewer the words, the better the prayer. God speaks directly to our hearts in silence. That is his language. We are to dispose ourselves to inner stillness, in order to listen with the ear of the heart to his word.

It is important to be detached. One simple exercise to enable this to come about is to practise a prayer of the breath: as you breathe in silently say: 'I calm my soul'. As you breathe out: 'My soul is calm before the Lord' or 'Be still and know that I am God' (Psalm 46) and 'For God alone my soul in silence waits' (Psalm 62).

When profound silence and stillness descend upon you, rest in the Presence. This is true happiness, for we are not happy because happiness is our sustenance but because our true happiness lies at the still centre of our being. It is the Spirit who dwells in our heart, our source, the Spirit of Love.

The fruit of silence is prayer,
the fruit of prayer is faith,
the fruit of faith is love,
the fruit of love is service,
and the fruit of service
is peace.

Silence

Silence gives us a new outlook on everything, we need silence to be able to touch souls. The essential thing is not what we say but what God says to us and through us. Jesus is always waiting for us in silence. In that silence, he will listen to us, there he will speak to our soul, and there we will hear his voice.

Mother Teresa

Real silence is beautiful.
Everyone needs to find it.
To make silence is to turn your eyes, your ears, your mind to the inside of things, to give all your attention to one thing, to one person.
A beautiful silence is needed to attend to someone whom no one has ever seen.
Silence is a thing that is easily broken.
There are the noises that come from outside.
There are the images, that is the pictures from all my senses, that come from outside and inside.
Distractions break silence.
They kill attention.
By trying hard, little by little,
I can overcome distractions,
not pay attention any more to noises or images.
I can look attentively at just one thing.
I can also shut my eyes.
If a noise penetrates my ears I do not move;
I do not turn my head.
And in this way I become responsible
for my own silence.

To know how to make silence is to know how to make oneself strong and free.
It is to make oneself able to attend to the one thing that matters.

I can make silence alone. I can make silence with some of my friends.
When we reach the point of making silence, all together, to pray, that is even better.
A beautiful silence in the presence of God is already a prayer.

O God, make us children of quietness, and heirs of peace.

St Clement of Alexandria (c. 150–215)

Silence

A very precious way to pray is just through silence. No thoughts or words, just wanting to be silent in the presence of God. Perhaps one of the high points in prayer is where two silences meet: God's silence and our silence. No need for thoughts – and words can get in the way. . . .

To be silent and still is an art to be learned. Be silent and still, and look inwards, first at the darkness within, at conflicting emotions, at the emptiness of the heart, at inner wounds. We are in need of healing, or nearly always, and in need too of being saved from what is base and ignoble. We are not as we should be. When silent and still we can, I believe, hear God's voice speaking to us through our weakness and inadequacy, coaxing our minds to look for one who will bring order into that inner chaos; but most of all giving forgiveness and encouragement.

Cardinal Basil Hume

Silent am I now and still,
Dare not in Thy presence move:
To my waiting soul reveal
The secret of Thy love.

Charles Wesley

Grace fills empty spaces, but it can only enter where there is a void to receive it. We need continually suspend the work of the imagination in filling the void within ourselves . . .

In no matter what circumstances, if the imagination is stopped from pouring itself out, we have a void (the poor in spirit). In no matter what circumstances . . . imagination can fill the void . . . That is why we fly from the inner void, since God might steal into it.

Simone Weil (1909–43)

The true contemplative is not one who prepares his mind for a particular message that he wants or expects to hear, but is one who remains empty because he knows that he can never expect to anticipate the words that will transform his darkness into light. He does not even anticipate a special kind of transformation. He does not demand light instead of darkness. He waits on the Word of God in silence, and, when he is 'answered', it is not so much by a word that bursts into his silence. It is by his silence itself, suddenly, inexplicably revealing, itself to him as a word of great power, full of the voice of God.

Thomas Merton

I kiss my hand
to the stars, lovely-asunder
Starlight, wafting him out of it; and
Glow, glory in thunder;
Kiss my hand to the dappled-with-damson west:
Since, tho' he is under the world's splendour and wonder,
His mystery must be instressed, stressed;
For I greet him the days I meet him, and bless when I understand

G. M. Hopkins[61]

Lord of Creation

song of
creation

now we must praise the guardian of heaven,
the might of the LORD and his purpose of mind,
the work of the glorious father; for he,
god eternal, established each wonder,
he, holy creator, first fashioned
heaven as a ROOF for the sons of men.
then the guardian of mankind adorned
this middle-earth below, the world for men,
everlasting lord, almighty king.

caedmon's song (late 7th century)

Liturgy of Creation

Eucharist for Creation

Introduction or Processional Dance

Sentence
When the spirit makes thin the canvas we see that the universe is a creation.

Gwenallt

In the name of God: Father, Son and Holy Spirit.
Amen

Grace and peace be with you
and keep you in the love of Christ.

Kyrie (Taizé chant)
Lord have mercy
– on your Creation,
– on the world you have made,
– on every living creature,
– we pray to thee, O Lord.

All chant: **Kyrie, Kyrie, Eleison** (repeat)

Christ have mercy
– on all who are suffering,
– on those who are lost,
– on those who stray,
– we pray to thee, O Lord.

All chant: **Christe, Christe, Eleison** (repeat)

Lord have mercy
– on the de-spirited
– on the depressed,
– on the despairing,
– we pray to thee, O Lord.

All chant: **Kyrie, Kyrie, Eleison** (repeat)

or

President	May Almighty God have mercy on us,
	forgive us our sins,
	and bring us to everlasting life.
All	**Amen.**

President	Death is fear, lies, hate, envy, avarice, greed, lust, pride,
	destructiveness, violence, cruelty.
All	**Save us from death.**
President	Life is love, truth, courage, laughter, giving, creativeness,
	tenderness, humility, kindness.
All	**Give us life.**
President	Forgive us
All	**When we choose death instead of life.**
President	Light us
All	**To life – the life of Jesus.**
President	May God forgive us all
	May we forgive ourselves
	And one another.

Gloria

All	**Glory to God in the highest**
	and peace to his people on earth.
	Lord God, heavenly King,
	Almighty God and Father,
	we worship you, we give you thanks,
	we praise you for your glory.
	Lord Jesus Christ, only Son of the Father,
	Lord God, Lamb of God,
	you take away the sin of the world:

Lord of Creation

have mercy on us;
you are seated at the right hand of the Father:
receive our prayer.

For you alone are the Holy One,
you alone are the Lord,
you alone are the most High,
Jesus Christ, with the Holy Spirit,
in the glory of God the Father. Amen.

Opening prayer (see pp. 242ff.)

Let us pray.

Liturgy of the Word (from appropriate lectionary)

Credo

Our God is the God of all humans.
The God of heaven and earth.
The God of the sea and the rivers.
The God of the sun and moon.
The God of all the heavenly bodies.
The God of the lofty mountains.
The God of the lowly valleys.
God is above the heavens;
and he is in the heavens;
and he is beneath the heavens.
Heaven and earth and sea,
and everything that is in them,
such he has as his abode.
He inspires all things,
he gives life to all things,
he stands above all things,
and he stands beneath all things.
He enlightens the light of the sun,
he strengthens the light of the night and the stars,
he makes wells in the arid land and dry islands in the sea,
and he places the stars in the service of the greater lights.
He has a Son who is co-eternal with himself,
and similar in all respects to himself;
and neither is the Son younger than the Father,

nor is the Father older than the Son;
and the Holy Spirit breathes in them.
And the Father and the Son and Holy Spirit are inseparable.

Tírechan's Creed (trans. Thomas O'Loughlin)

Intercession/Bidding Prayers

The Peace

Lord, peace you command, peace you gave us, peace you have left us. Grant us your peace from heaven and order this day and all the days of our life in your peace. We ask this through Christ our Lord. Amen.

Stowe

The peace of the Lord be with you always.
And also with you.
Let us offer one another a sign of peace.

Hymn/chant (or dance)

Offertory

Offering of the bread and wine

President	Thank you, O Lord God Almighty.
	Thank you for the earth and the waters.
	Thank you for the sky, the air, the sun:
	Thank you for all living creatures.
All	**Come, O Lord, in the bread of life.**
President	Praise be to you, our Father and Mother,
	for our homes, and families, our friends, and loved ones.
	Praise be to you for all the
	People around us everywhere
	in this wounded world.
All	**Come, O Lord, in the cup of healing.**

Prayer over the gifts

President	The Lord be with you.
All	**and also with you.**

Lord of Creation

President	Lift up your hearts.
All	**We lift them to the Lord.**
President	Let us give thanks to the Lord our God.
All	**It is right to give him thanks and praise.**

Eucharistic Prayer (Gallican Rite)

The Lord be with you.
And also with you.
Life up your hearts.
We lift them to the Lord.
Let us give thanks to the Lord our God:
It is right to give him thanks and praise.

Blessed are you, strong and faithful God. All your works, the height and the depth, echo the silent music of your praise. In the beginning your Word summoned light: night withdrew and creation dawned. As ages passed unseen waters gathered on the face of the earth and life appeared. When the time had at last grown full and the earth had ripened in abundance, you created in your own image humankind. You gave us breath and speech, that the whole of creation might find a voice to sing your praise; therefore with all the powers of heaven and earth, we chant the ageless hymn of your glory:

> **Holy, holy, holy Lord, God of power and might,**
> **heaven and earth are full of your glory.**
> **Hosanna in the highest.**
> **Blessed is he who comes in the name of the Lord.**
> **Hosanna in the highest.**

How wonderful are the works of your hands, O Lord. As a mother tenderly gathers her children, you embraced a people as your own and filled them with longing for a peace that would last and for a justice that would never fail. Through countless generations your people hungered for the bread of freedom. From them you raised up Jesus, the living bread, in whom the ancient hungers were satisfied. He healed the sick, though he himself would suffer; he offered life to sinners though death would hunt him down. With a love stronger than death, he opened wide his arms on the cross, and surrendered his spirit to you, Father.

Father, let your Holy Spirit move in power over us and over our earthly gifts of bread and wine, that they may become the body and blood of Christ.

On the night before he met with death, Jesus came to table with those he loved. He took the loaf and praised you, God of all creation: he broke it among his disciples and said:

'Take this, all of you, and eat it.
This is my body, which will be given up for you.'

When supper was ended, he poured a final cup of wine and blessed you, God of all creation: he passed the cup among his disciples and said:

'Take this, all of you, and drink from it.
This is the cup of my blood, the blood of the new and everlasting covenant. It will be shed for you and for all so that sins may be forgiven. Do this in memory of me.'

Father, we commemorate Jesus your Son, as we present before you his sacrifice. Death could not bind him, for you raised him up in the Spirit of holiness and exalted him as Lord of creation. May his coming in glory find us ever watchful in prayer, strong in love, and faithful to the breaking of the bread.

Let us proclaim the mystery of faith:

**Dying you destroyed our death,
Rising you restored our life.
Lord Jesus, come in glory.**

Rejoicing in the Holy Spirit, your whole Church offers you thanks and praise together with N. our Bishop, and all those who bring hope to the world.

Remember Lord, your servant N. N. and N.

Lord of the living and the dead, awaken to the undying light of the resurrection those who have fallen asleep in faith, and those who have died alone, unloved and unmourned. Gather them all into communion with Mary, the Mother of Jesus, and with N. and with all your saints.

Then, at last, will all creation be one and all divisions healed, and we shall join in singing your praise through your son, Jesus Christ our Lord.

Through him, with him, in him, in the unity of the Holy Spirit, all honour and glory are yours, almighty Father, now and for ever.
AMEN.

Our Father
As our Saviour taught us we pray:

Our Father in heaven,	Our Father who art in heaven,
hallowed be your name,	hallowed be thy name,
your kingdom come,	thy kingdom come,
your will be done,	thy will be done,
on earth as in heaven.	on earth as it is in heaven.
Give us today	Give us this day
our daily bread.	our daily bread.
Forgive us our sins	and forgive us our trespasses,
as we forgive those	as we forgive those
who sin against us.	who trespass against us.
Save us from	And lead us not
the time of trial	into temptation,
and deliver us from evil.	but deliver us from evil.
For the kingdom, the power	For thine is the kingdom
and the glory are yours	the power and the glory,
now and for ever. Amen.	for ever and ever. Amen.

Fraction

Priest   Just as the loaf which we break was scattered over the earth,
was gathered in and became one,
bring us together from everywhere
into the kingdom of your peace.
For as the wine of many grapes
was crushed to make a single wine,
so we unite in this bloodless
and perfect sacrifice,
then shall we become One
in the Great Light which is Infinite.

All   **O God, thou art one;
make us one.**

Priest   The gifts of God for the people of God.

Didache

Holy Communion
During the distribution of Holy Communion a hymn or chant may be sung.

Post-communion (see pages 249ff.)

or

All   God, who cares for us,
the wonder of whose presence
fills us with awe,
let kindness, love and justice
shine in our world.
Let your secrets be known here
as they are in heaven.
Give us the food and hope that
we need for today.

Forgive us our wrongdoing
as we forgive the wrongs done to us.

Protect us from the pride and from despair
and from the fear and hate
which can swallow us up.

In you is truth, meaning,
glory and power,
while worlds come and go. Amen.

The Blessing

As the earth keeps turning, hurtling
through space, and night falls
and day breaks from land to land,
let us remember people –
walking, sleeping, being born, and dying –
one world, one humanity.
Let us go from here in peace.
Amen.

         Lord of Creation

Contemplative Eucharist

Sentence (from Sentences, pp. 238ff.)

Priest
We gather in the Lord's Name
In the name of the Father, etc.

Gospel reading and meditation (*10 mins*)

Prayer (from Prayers, pp. 242ff.)

Call to repentance.
Merciful God
We have sinned in thought word and deed:
We are truly sorry, repent and turn to you.
Renew our lives by your Spirit
In the image of Jesus Christ our Saviour,
To the glory of your holy name.
Amen.

Priest
May almighty God have mercy on us,
Forgive us and set us free from sin,
And keep us in eternal life.

Pax
Grace and peace be with you from God
Our Father and the Lord Jesus Christ.
And also with you.
We offer one another a sign of Peace.

Offertory and Eucharistic Prayer

The Lord's Prayer

Communion

Interior prayer (silent prayer for several minutes)

Blessing and dismissal

Sentences/Antiphons

Love the creature, as it leads to the Creator.

John Wesley

If you want to know the Creator, first understand and know creation.

Columbanus

God saw everything he had made, and it was very good.

Genesis 1.31

Let us adore the Lord,
Maker of marvellous works,
Bright heaven with its angels,
And on earth the white-washed sea.

Old Irish

Let the summits of heaven praise you
with roaming lightening,
O most loving Jesus, O righteous King
of Kings.

Iona, sixth century

When the spirit makes thin the canvas we see that the universe is a creation.

Gwenallt

The world is changed with the grandeur of God.
  It will flame out, like shining from shook foil;

Gerard Manley Hopkins

Lord of Creation

Happy are those whose refuge is in you,
whose hearts are set on pilgrim ways.

Psalm 84.5

Help us to hear and understand how in the beginning you created heaven and
earth.

St Augustine

Sentences from the Benedicite:

1. Bless the Lord all created things,
    Sing his praise and exalt him for ever.

2. O let the earth bless the Lord:
    bless the Lord you mountains and hills.

3. Bless the Lord, you seas and rivers:
    sing his praise and exalt him for ever.

4. Bless the Lord you waters above the heavens:
    sing his praise and exalt him for ever.

5. Bless the Lord, fire and heat:
    sing his praise and exalt him for ever.

6. Bless the Lord, all winds that blow:
    sing his praise and exalt him for ever.

Praise be thou, O Lord, who hast
made every animal wise in the
instinct thou hast given it.

St Adamnan

As for us, our days are like grass,
we flower like the flowers in the field,
the wind blows and we are gone
and our place never sees us again.

Psalm 103.15–16

For see, the winter is past!
The rains are over and gone;
The flowers appear in the countryside;
The season of birdsong is come.

Song of Songs 2.12

The earth is mother of all for contained in her are the seeds of all.

Hildegard of Bingen

The earth has yielded its fruit
for God, our God, has blessed us.
May God still give us his blessing
till the ends of the earth revere him.

Psalm 67

It is he who fashions the mountains,
who creates the wind,
and declares his thoughts to humankind;
it is he who darkens the dawn with thick clouds
and marches over the heights of the earth –
his name is the Lord, the God of Hosts.

Amos 3.13 (NEB)

They have exchanged the truth of God for a lie, and have offered reverence and
worship to created things instead of to the Creator. Blessed is he for ever. Amen.

Romans 1.25 (NEB)

For anyone united to Christ, there is a new creation: the old order has gone; a new
order has already begun.

2 Corinthians 5.17

God breathes through all Creation,
He is love, eternal love.

Bishop Timothy Rees

Lord of Creation

O Christ, our Morning Star,
Splendour of Light Eternal,
Shining with the glory of the rainbow;
Come and waken us
From the greyness of our apathy
And renew in us your gift of hope.

The Venerable Bede (671–735)

You are my strength Lord, I will love you,
under the shadow of your wings protect me.

The Prayers of Moucan (Welsh eighth century)

Brothers and sisters, be joyful, and keep your
faith and belief, and do the little things
which you have heard and seen with me.

St David

Help us, Unity in Trinity,
Trinity in Unity, take pity.

Laidcenu (Irish, seventh century)

My soul's desire is to see the face of God,
and to rest in his house.

St Columba

The grace of God's love dwells in our hearts
as a jewel of gold is placed in a silver dish.

Iona, sixth century

The King is knocking.
If you would have your share of heaven on earth,
open the door of your heart and let in the King.

Hebridean

O Lord, you have given everything its place in the world, and no one can make it
otherwise. For it is your creation, the heavens and the earth and the stars; you are
the Lord of all.

Latin Antiphon

OPENING PRAYERS

Almighty God,
you have created the heaven and the earth
and made us in your own image:
teach us to discern your hand
   in all your works
and your likeness in all your children;
through Jesus Christ our Lord,
who with you and the Holy Spirit
     reigns supreme over all things
now and for ever.[62]

Almighty God and Father,
you have so ordered our life
   that we are dependent on one another:
prosper those engaged in commerce and industry
   and direct their minds and hands
that they may rightly use your gifts in the service of others;
through Jesus Christ your Son our Lord,
who is alive and reigns with you,
in the unity of the Holy Spirit,
   one God, now and for ever.

Almighty God,
whose will it is that the earth and the sea
   should bear fruit in due season:
bless the labours of those who work on land and sea
   and the grace always to rejoice in your fatherly care;
through Jesus Christ your Son our Lord,
who is alive and reigns with you,
in the unity of the Holy Spirit,
   one God, now and for ever.

Lord of Creation

God our Father,
you never cease the work you have begun
and prosper with your blessing all human labour:
make us wise and faithful stewards of your gifts
that we may serve the common good,
maintain the fabric of our world
and seek that justice where all may share
    the good things you pour upon us;
through Jesus Christ your Son our Lord,
who is alive and reigns with you,
in the unity of the Holy Spirit,
    one God, now and for ever.[63]

Kindle in our hearts, O God,
the flame of love that never ceases,
that it may burn in us, giving light to others.
May we shine for ever in your temple,
set on fire with your eternal light,
even your Son Jesus Christ,
our Saviour and our Redeemer.
Amen.

St Columba

Eternal light shine in our hearts
Eternal goodness deliver us from evil
Eternal power be our support
Eternal wisdom scatter the darkness of our ignorance.
Eternal pity have mercy on us
That with all our heart and mind
and soul and strength we may seek thy face
and be brought by thine infinite mercy to thy presence.

Alcuin

May the heavens and earth
praise Him, the Glorious, and every
creature which is in heaven and
on earth and under the earth, and

the seas and all that are in them.
    Let us praise and exalt Him
above all forever . . . through
Jesus the Christ, our Lord. Amen.

St Francis of Assisi

O God we know that all humankind is grass,
which lasts no longer than a flower in the field,
The grass withers, the flower fades,
when the breath of the Lord blows on them.
Your Word endures for ever,
enable us to breathe your Word
that we may aspire to heaven through Jesus
Christ, Your Son, our Lord.
Amen.

Lord of creation, Lord of fire,
of wind and moon and waters,
protect us in tempest and in storm.
Be with us on our journey to your heavenly kingdom
where you live and reign,
One God, world without end.
Amen.

O God our Father,
we thank you for the little things in life,
and to notice them,
and to remember them,
for all creation lives and flows in ceaseless praise;
for the sake of Christ, Lord of all Creation.
Amen.

Creator of the universe,
watch over us and keep us in the light of your presence.
Let our praise continually blend with that of all creation,
and bring us, with all for whom we pray,

Lord of Creation

to the eternal joys which you promise in your love;
through Jesus Christ our Saviour.
Amen.

Church in Wales[64]

Remember us, gracious God,
when we cannot see your way and purpose,
and renew in us the joy of your kingdom of light and life,
we ask this in the name of Jesus Christ the Lord.

God of light,
teach us to love each other as you love us,
that we may bring peace and joy to the world,
and rejoice in the kingdom of your Son,
Jesus Christ our Lord.

O God,
your name is blessed from the rising of the sun to its setting;
fill our hearts with knowledge of yourself
and our mouths with your praise,
that from East to West all may sing your glory,
with one voice and accord,
in Jesus Christ, your Son, our Lord. Amen.

Let us pray to God the Father, God the Son,
And to God the Holy Spirit
Whose infinite greatness
Enfolds the whole world,
In persons three and one,
In essence simple and triune
Suspending the earth above the waters,
Hanging the upper air with stars,
That he may be favourable to sinners.

Prayers after Communion

God our creator,
by your gift the tree of life was set at the heart of the earthly paradise,
and the bread of life at the heart of your Church:
may we who have been nourished at your table on earth
be captivated by the glory of the Saviour's Cross
and enjoy the delights of eternity;
through Jesus Christ our Lord.

Church in Wales[65]

Lord of all Creation,
with joy we have offered thanksgiving
    for your love in creation
and have shared in the bread and wine of the Kingdom:

by your grace plant within us a reverence
    for all that you give us
and make us generous and wise stewards
of the good things we enjoy
through Jesus Christ our Lord.

God our creator,
you give seed for us to sow and bread for us to eat:
as you have blessed the fruit of your labour in this Eucharist,
so we ask you to give all your children their daily bread,
that the world may praise you for the goodness;
through Jesus Christ our Lord.[66]

We believe, O Lord, that in this breaking of your body and pouring out of your
blood we become redeemed people. We confess that by our sharing in this sacrament we are strengthened to endure in hope until we lay hold and enjoy its true
fruits in the heavenly places.

Stowe Missal

Let us go forth,
In the goodness of our merciful Father,
In the gentleness of our brother Jesus,
In the radiance of his Holy Spirit,
In the faith of the apostles,
In the joyful praise of the angels,
In the holiness of the saints,
In the courage of the martyrs.

From the Gaelic

I beseech you, Jesus, loving Saviour,
to show yourself to all who seek you
so that we may know you and love you.
May we love you alone, desire you alone,
and keep you always in our thoughts.
May love for you possess our hearts.
May affection for you fill our senses,
so that we may love all else in you.
Jesus, King of Glory,
You know how to give greatly
And you have promised great things.
Nothing is greater than yourself.
We ask nothing else of you but yourself.
You are our life, our light, our food and our drink, our God and our all.

From an ancient Irish Prayer

Lord, may we be wakeful at sunrise
to begin a new day for you;
Cheerful at sunset
for having done our work for you;
Thankful at moonrise and under starshine
for the beauty of your universe;
And may we add what little may be in us
to add to your great world

The Abbot of Greve

See that you are at peace among yourselves, my children,
And love one another in Jesus, the Christ, our Lord.

St Columba

Liturgy of Creation   247

Grant within us, Lord, the gift of your glory,
that against all the evils of this present age,
the power of the Eucharist we have received
may be our protecting wall.

Stowe Missal

May this sharing, Lord, in your Son's Body and Blood be the washing away of
our sins, the strength of the weak, and our protection against the dangers of the
world. May it set us free from evil and grant us our share in the joy of your kingdom.

Stowe Missal

Lord you satisfy our longings with this gift from heaven. Cleanse us from our
secret faults and from the assaults of the evil one.

Stowe Missal

Who righteously justifies all who err,
Who ever-living lives.
May God be blessed for ages.
Amen.

Moucan (Welsh, eighth century)

O Holy Jesus
Gentle friend,
Morning star,
Midday sun adorned,
Fountain ever new, ever living, ever lasting
Son of the merciful Father without
    mother in heaven,
Son of the Virgin Mary, without
    father on earth
True and loving brother,
Give, grant and impart to us your holy grace and your Holy Spirit,
to protect and preserve us from all our sins,
present and future.

The Broom of Devotion (early Irish)[67]

Lord of Creation

Celtic Blessings

From sea and manor and nearby mountain,
From depth in the rivers,
God builds all the livelong day
with blessing for the blessed,
and so may God bless you . . .

Early Welsh/Anon.

The holy Lord of creation,
Christ, son of the Holy Mary,
Jesus, beloved pillar –
may he go before the human race.
And the blessing . . .

From Felire Oengusso[68]

May the Creator bless you and keep you,
May the beloved companion face you and have mercy upon you;
May the eternal Spirit's countenance be
turned to you and give you peace;
May the Three in One bless you.

Hebridean

May God give us light to guide us,
Courage to support us,
And love to unite us,
Now and evermore.
And may the blessing of God Almighty . . .

From the Gaelic

May the Lord bless you and protect you.
May the Lord smile on you and show you his favour.
May the Lord befriend you and prosper you.
And may the blessing of God . . .

From the Gaelic

God's grace distil on you,
Christ's grace distil on you,
Spirit's grace distil on you
Each day and each night
Of your portion in the world;
On each day and each night
Of your portion in the world.

Carmina Gadelica

The palmful of the God of Life
The palmful of the Christ of Love
The palmful of the Spirit of Peace
Triune of Grace
Bless you, in the Name . . .

Early Scottish

May the road rise to meet you,
May the wind be always at your back,
May the sun shine warm upon your face,
May the rain fall soft upon your fields,
And until we meet again,
May God hold you in the hollow of his hand.

Gaelic

May the King shield you in the valleys,
May Christ aid you on the mountains,
May the Spirit bathe you on the slopes,
In hollow, on hill, on plain,
Mountain, valley and plain,
May the Three in One bless you . . .

Hebridean

Lord of Creation

See that you are at peace among yourselves,
my children, and love one another.
Take the example of the good people of ancient times
and God will comfort and aid you,
both in this world and in the world
to come. And the Blessing . . .

St Columba

May we all reach the Kingdom of Heaven that is without end,
may we deserve it,
may we dwell there for ages unending. Amen.
And the Blessing . . .

From the Rule of The Céli Dé

My Christ, my shield,
my encircler,
each day, each night,
each light, each dark,
be near me, uphold me,
my treasure, my triumph.

Iona

Salvation is of the Lord,
Salvation is of Christ.
May your blessing, Lord,
be upon your people,
Father, Son and Holy Spirit.
Amen.

Adapted from Nuall Fir Fhio: 'Fer Fio's Cry'

The holy lord of creation,
Christ, son of the holy Mary,
Jesus, beloved pillar –
may he go before the human race.
And the blessing . . .

From Felire Oengusso[69]

Blessing and brightness,
Wisdom, thanksgiving,
Great power and might
To the King who rules over all.

Glory and honour and goodwill,
Praise and the sublime song of minstrels,
Overflowing love from every heart
To the King of Heaven and Earth.

To the chosen Trinity has been joined
Before all, after all, universal
Blessing and everlasting blessing,
Blessing everlasting and blessing.

Irish, ninth century

The Lord bless us, and preserve us from all evil,
and bring us to everlasting life;
and may the souls of the faithful,
through the mercy of God, rest in peace.

Sarum Primer

May the grace of the Lord Jesus sanctify us and keep us from all evil;
may he drive far from us all hurtful things, and purify both our souls and bodies;
may be bind us to himself by the bond of love,
and may his peace abound in our hearts.

Gregorian Sacramentary (sixth century)

May God the Father bless us;
May Christ take care of us;
May the Holy Spirit enlighten us
all the days of our life.
The Lord be our Defender
and Keeper of body and soul
both now and for ever,
to the ages of ages.

Book of Cerne (tenth century)

Lord of Creation

May we all reach the Kingdom that is without end,
May we deserve it,
May we dwell there for ages unending.
Amen.
May Mary Virgin's Son Himself
Be a generous lamp to you,
To guide you over
The great and awful ocean of eternity
And the blessing of God Almighty . . .

Carmina Gadelica

The love and affection of the angels be to you,
The love and affection of the saints be to you,
The love and affection of heaven be to you,
To guard you and to cherish you.
And the blessing of God Almighty . . .

Carmina Gadelica

God's blessing be yours,
And well may it befall you;
Christ's blessing be yours,
And well be you entreated;
Spirit's blessing be yours,
And well spend your lives,
Each day that you rise up,
Each night that you lie down,
And the blessing of God Almighty . . .

Carmina Gadelica

May the peace of the Lord Christ go with you,
Wherever he may send you.
May he guide you through the wilderness,
protect you through the storm.
May he bring you home rejoicing
at the wonders he has shown you.
May he bring you home rejoicing
once again into our doors.

Hebridean

Liturgy of Creation

Prayers in the Celtic Tradition

Lord of Creation

I am the wind that breathes upon the sea,
I am the wave on the ocean,
I am the murmur of leaves rustling,
I am the rays of the sun,
I am the beam of the moon and stars,
I am the power of the trees growing,
I am the bud breaking into blossom,
I am the movement of the salmon swimming,
I am the courage of the wild boar fighting,
I am the speed of the stag running,
I am the strength of the ox pulling the plough,
I am the sap of the mighty oak tree,
And I am the thoughts of all people
who praise my beauty and grace.

From The Black Book of Carmarthen

The collection of Gaelic daily prayers included in this volume are a rare find indeed. They are similar to but not found in the well-plundered collection *Carmina Gadelica*. They too are the prayers of Celts poor in the world's goods but rich in faith, who lived in remote places in Ireland, Scotland and Wales; far removed from the materialism of modern civilization; a people who never lost 'the visionary gleam'. The fisherman casting his nets; the herdsman watching his cattle; the husbandman sowing his seed; the housewife baking bread; it is the thoughts and aspirations of humble folk that are embodied in these prayers; and they are the prayers from which they drew consolation and strength to meet the elements and the trials and temptations of their daily lives.

It is to be remembered that the prayers are practically all traditional and anonymous, which accounts for the occasional obscurity. This collection is only a small fraction of the numerous prayers and pious ejaculations in daily use. They were given to my late father by a Father McHardy of the Braes of Glenlivet in 1924. My father was a young lad at the time and a pupil of Fort Augustus Abbey

School on Loch Ness. He was serving Fr McHardy's celebration of Mass. On coming down backwards after the elevation of the Host my father inadvertently kicked the sanctuary bell (loud) which landed against the altar rails. When he opened the sacristy door for Fr McHardy to go through after Mass the good priest took a swipe at him! Next day the repentant priest gave my father a collection of Gaelic prayers some of which are included in this book. I came across them among my mother's pious effects after her death in 2004. Incredible but true!

Daily Gaelic Prayers

Morning prayers

Prayer on waking

O God, and Virgin Mary
who have brought me and mine
safe from the death of sleep
to the bright sunshine;
bring us whole
from every affliction;
and protect us body and soul
from all evil. Amen.

Connacht

Prayer on rising

I rise up with God,
may he rise up with me,
waking, sleeping, rising,
may His arms around me be. Amen.

Connacht

The grace of God and the blessing of
(name of the Saint of the day)
on all I see and on all I undertake,
from the time I arise in the morning
till I go to sleep at night. Amen.

Connacht

Lord of Creation

Prayers when risen

God's will may we do,
and our own subdue,
our tongue control,
repent in time,
ponder Christ's death,
avoid sin's breath,
our last end face,
and die in grace,
and with angels raise
a hymn of praise
to God. For ever and ever. Amen.

Connacht

O Blessed Jesus, and O Nurse of the Lamb
white and fair,
shelter my soul and be near when
I utter my death-bed prayer;
Saints and angels keep me always
and in every place,
as I put my soul for protection
under the shield of the King of Grace. Amen.

Cno Coilleadh

God guide me; God teach me; God instruct me;
God ever keep me from the habit of sin;
O loving Jesus, full of grace, guide
my feet to the better path of life. Amen.

Cno Coilleadh

God's angels keep and guard us till set of sun:
Protect us God and Mary,
Jesus and the saints
till day be done. Amen.

Connacht

Night prayers

Prayer on lying down

May I lie down with God and may God lie down with me,
may I not lie with evil, nor evil lie with me.
Bridget's girdle around me,
Mary's mantle beneath me;
O Blessed Michael, hold my hand,
and make my peace with the Son of Grace.
If any evil thing pursues me,
may the Son of God protect me
for a year from this night,
and this night itself,
and ever, and always. Amen.

Connacht

Prayer to be said in bed

Four corners to my bed,
four angels round them spread;
should death before morning me o'ertake,
I pray that in Heaven I may awake. Amen.

Åchill

I lie on this bed as I lie in the grave;
firmly I make confession to you, Jesus,
for the deeds of my flesh,
for the thoughts of my heart,
for the looks of my eyes,
for the words of my mouth,
for the wanderings of my feet;
for all that I said which was not true;
for all that I promised and did not fulfil;
for all my sinning against your Law,
or against you Holy Will,
    I ask for forgiveness from you,
    O King of Glory. Amen.

Åchill

Lord of Creation

On falling asleep

I lie down on this bed
in the name of Jesus Christ crucified,
saving and succouring and preserving me.
And when my span on this earth's spent,
may the Eternal Father take me
to the highest Heaven in His Kingdom. Amen.

Áchill

O Blessed Virgin, Mother of God,
O radiant Brightness without speck,
O shining Lamp before God's throne,
be thou with us at the hour of death. Amen.

Connacht

On waking in the night

Have mercy, Lord, and in thy might
bring me safe from death's dark porch;
call me to Thine abode of light,
brighten my darkness, Thou quenchless Torch,
Thou Day that knowest no night. Amen.

Anon.

On passing a church

We rely for our protection upon the God of the Saints,
upon the Apostles, upon Saint Joseph,
and the Holy Sacrament of the Altar. Amen.

T. O'Rahilly

On visiting a church

Hail to thee, O altar,
green leafy tree of the Cross,
let my soul not pass thee by,
keep me in the state of grace;
direct us to our good,
fill us with desire for Heaven,
wet our eyes with tears of sorrow,
and may a share to us be given
of every Holy Eucharist this day
and throughout the world wide. Amen.

Connacht

Prayers in church

I cast myself on the extreme edge of your grace,
doing reverence to the One Church
upon the floor of your Holy Place.
With guileless heart I bend the knee
in affection for the Most High King,
and the other in homage, my God, to you:
From the hosts of woe bring me whole,
O one God in Thee contained;
and may the Blessed Trinity win my soul.

O Lord, who bore the pain and suffered the Passion,
who was scourged with iron from sole to crown,
and then had your palms pierced with wounds;
dear God, I am asking your protection.

From every sin that I have committed
since the day I was born,
may Jesus, Mary's Son
say, 'I grant you pardon.'
May the sweet Child of Sorrows,
who is God and is Man,
save us for ever from the wail of lost souls. Amen.

Connacht

Lord of Creation

Eucharist intentions

I offer my intention with that of the Holy Eucharist,
and my mind, my thoughts, my heart:
to the Heavenly Queen I make my prayer,
of its grace to have a Christian's part. Amen.

I give you my soul, O King of Grace,
give it not back for eternity;
be you my witness, O Blessed Maid,
that I may entrust it to the care
    of your Son.
O Face brighter than the sun,
leave me not long in pain. Amen.

Connacht

Prayers of petition and penance

A thousand welcomes to You, O Body of Christ,
Son of the fair and gentle Maid,
    It was by your blood shed on the Cross,
that sin was overcome
and Eve's children saved.

I come to you as a sinner,
deal not with me as I deserve;
though I merit your anger,
O Jesus, turn to me and save.

Jesus who bought us,
Jesus who blessed us,
do not forget us now,
or at the hour of death.

O Jesus Christ who was crucified on Friday,
who shed your blood for our forgiveness and saving;
may the grace of the Holy Spirit be within us,
may the Son of God grant us mercy. Amen.

O Lord who bore the pain and suffered the Passion,
who was scourged with iron from head to foot,
and was then insulted

and wounded in the palms,
O Lord, I am asking
for your protection.

I am a weak creature under weight of sadness,
who for my great sins would do penance;
the Faith of God I now declare
with heartfelt love and hope sincere.
From the foot of the Cross I cry to thee,
O Jesus, Lord, incline to me. Amen.

I am a sinner, weary and spent,
tho' great my sins I now repent;
with faith I cry to God above,
with hope sincere and heartfelt love;
from the foot of the Cross I cry to thee,
O King, look down and succour me.

May we do God's Holy Will aright,
and hear the songs of angels bright;
and see the blaze of Heaven's light,
    world without end. Amen.

Connacht

Before Holy Communion

Welcome, noble Host,
the food of souls Thou art;
welcome, King of Kings,
to the shelter of my heart.

O Ancient One, 'tis Thou
who art the living Food;
welcome, Bread of Life,
Food of man and God.

Thou didst come in human form,
born of the Virgin Mary;
no son of man e'er lived
who of this deed was worthy. Amen.

Ancient Gaelic MS

After Communion

Protect me, O Body of Christ,
O Sacred Host, my treasure,
ward off from me the darts of vice,
Your might no man can measure.
O Lord you are within my heart,
bless me, with your Face of Flame,
and let my soul and body part
lest I transgress again.

O God of Heaven, O Face sun-bright,
your ear to my prayer incline,
O Architect of boundless might,
conform my will to yours.
O Face sun-bright, O God of Heaven,
Your mercy to me give –
as you have given to every thing
who now with you live.

This heart of mine which holds you
is errant and impure,
and full of human frailty,
O King, its weakness cure.
O Michael, Prince of Heaven's array,
on the narrow path direct me,
be my shelter and my stay;
for Jesus' sake protect me. Amen.

A spiritual communion

O My God, loving beyond measure, it is your love which has made you come to me. It is my hope which has made me receive you. I give you my body as temple, my will as sacrifice, my heart as altar, and my soul as shrine. O innocent Lamb of God, O boundless mercy, house me in your body; shelter me in your heart; hide me in your wounds; wash me in your blood; consume me in the fragrant fire of your friendship; strengthen me in your love; give me new life in your death.

O Lord, O most noble and humble Child, through the merits of your own most Sacred Heart, grant that I may be entirely pleasing to you. Amen.

O'Sullivan

On leaving church

Farewell to you, O house of God,
may his blessing with us remain,
and may his grace not part from us
till we come to his church again. Amen.

Connacht

Occasional Prayers

Before food

May the blessing of the five loaves and two fishes which God divided amongst the five thousand men, be ours; and may the King who made the division put luck on our food and on our portion. Amen.

Seanfhocla Uladh (The Proverbs of Ulster)

After food

Praise to the generous King,
unceasing praise to God,
and praise to Jesus Christ
for what we have had of food. Amen.

Seanfhocla Uladh (The Proverbs of Ulster)

A thousand thanks, O God, for this food given to our bodies, we pray you to give to our souls eternal life in Heaven. Amen.

Before work

O Jesus, teach me to love Thy name,
fill my soul with sorrow's shame,
burn my heart with fervour's flame,
O Jesus, dear God, do not desert me.

Without Thee my thoughts are an idle tale,
without Thee my very members fail,
without Thee my deeds are of no avail;
O Jesus, dear God, be before me and after.

Thou art my love, my King of Kings,
thou art my shield against evil things,
thou art the source whence my happiness springs;
O Jesus, dear God, never part from me.

O Jesus, be in my heart today,
O Jesus, be my intellect's stay,
O Jesus, be in my thoughts always;
O Jesus, dear God, leave me not to myself. Amen.

Douglas Hyde

Before speaking

O Jesus, Son of God, you were silent in the presence of Pilate, do not let me loose my tongue without thinking on what I have to say and how I may say it. Amen.

Anon.

On leaving the house

I will follow, O Lord, wherever you go, since you have the words of Eternal Life. Amen.

Old Irish Prayer

On coming home

Open for me the doors of right living
and on my entrance I will love the Lord. Amen.

Old Irish prayer

Prayer of petition

From the depth of this vale of tears
I call upon Thee, O Lord Jesus;
O Lord Jesus, hear my voice,
let Thine ear give heed to my prayer.
We pray to the Blessed Virgin,
Mother of the God of Angels and of Saints,
that, whatever may be our condition now,
we may be seven times better a year hence,
our possessions prosperous and our people in health,
enjoying the love of God and our neighbours.

Lord of Creation

May we not die in any of seven deadly sins,
but in Penance and blessed with the Holy Oils,
may we obtain a Christian death and
a resting place in Heaven. Amen.

Old Irish

On setting on a journey

In the name of the Father for success,
and of the Son who suffered pain,
may Mary and her Son be with me on my way.
O Mary meet me at the shore,
let not my soul go by Thee,
great is my love of Thy Son.

In the Communion of Saints may we be
listening to the voices of the angels
and praising the Son of God,
world without end. Amen.

Connacht

Journey prayer

Seven prayers seven times said
Mary put to her Son,
Brigid put beneath her mantle,
Michael put beneath his shield,
God put beneath his strength,
between me and the water that would smother me,
between me and the water that would drown me,
between me and sudden death,
between me and the wind of the hills
between me and people's evil hearts,
between me and people's evil eyes,
to shelter me, to save me,
to defend me, to guard me. Amen.

Connacht

On passing a churchyard

Hail to ye, Christ's faithful who here
await a glorious resurrection. May
He who suffered the Passion for your
sakes grant ye eternal rest. Amen.

Old Irish

In time of trouble

O Sweetest Jesus, you are my protection
and my strength in time of trouble:
You are my joy in time of prosperity.
O give relief to me in this difficulty. Amen.

Anon.

In time of peace

Praise for ever to you, O Saviour, for you have brought me safe from this trouble,
although I am not worthy that you should confer prosperity or happiness upon
me. All glory to you for your exceeding mercy. Amen.

Old Irish

Against nightmares

May the Three who are the oldest,
and the Three who are the youngest,
and the Three who are strongest in the glory of Heaven,
may the Father, the Son and the Holy Spirit
save me and guard me for a year from tonight,
and tonight itself.
In the name of the Father, and of the Son,
and of the Holy Spirit. Amen.

An Lóchrann

Lord of Creation

Against drowning

Mary, Christ and the Saints between us and harm.
Mary and her Son,
Patrick with his staff,
Martin with his mantle,
Brigid with her hood,
Michael with his shield,
And God before them all
With His strong right arm. Amen.

From Lady Wilde's 'Folk Lore'

On going fishing

May the luck of John and Peter be upon the nets. Amen.

'Sgea Laidhe Oirghiall'

Prayer to be said in time of temptation

O Blessed Virgin, hear and help me,
I have broken your law through folly of human nature,
But with the help of Jesus I shall keep it yet.
These are the comrades I choose to guard me –
The twelve Apostles and the glorious Redeemer.
O Christ, take my soul to the City of the Trinity,
To the midst of the souls that are clothed in glory.

O Mother Mary, you are my thousand loves,
My help and protection in every need,
You are my doctor of healing, sound and sore,
And my fair blessed guide to The Kingdom of Grace. Amen.

'An Claidheamh Soluis' (the sword of light)

Shepherd's prayer

O Gentle Jesus, guard the sheep,
In the pleasant glens and meadows deep,
Safe from the wolves lead them and keep. Amen.

'Cno Coilleadh'

Liturgy of Creation

Prayer to obtain spiritual help

O King of the Universe
Who early lit the sun,
Who sends the heavy rains
And the crops that come after them:
For You I set down my faults,
To You I turn my face,
O Lord, do not permit me
To fall from the state of grace. Amen.

Connacht

Prayer to obtain grace

We offer these blessed prayers in recognition of the death and Passion of our Saviour; in recognition of the cross you carried to the hill of Calvary, of the crown of thorns which was placed upon your head, of the spear which entered your side, of the blunt nails which pierced your hands and feet. May the blood of your noble head which trickled down over your eyes be upon us; may the favour of God and of the people be upon us; may the dear love of God be upon us, and the warm love of the neighbours. May we have health of body and of soul. May our eyes not see, our hands undertake, nor our hearts think of anything in the world which would deprive us of our share of the everlasting glory of Heaven. Grant that we may not have an unprovided-for death; and give us the grace of the final blessing and penance.

Protect us against the loss of our people or of our goods; against the loathsome diseases of the year; against any one of the seven deadly sins. Well as we are today, may we be still better a year hence, our goods and our people secure – with the greatest graces and the smallest sins, in the love of God and of the neighbours. With this resolution and intentions we offer our prayer for the souls of all who have gone before us to join the hosts of the dead, and for our own souls on the last day; for the soul of every person from whom we have gained much or little, openly or secretly, and to whom we have not made full reparation.

We especially include in this prayer the souls of our own people who have joined the hosts of the dead. If God sees a pain or a penalty unpaid, an imperfect confession or an unfulfilled penance, or any sin whatsoever of which they have not repented, may their glory be increased, their pains lessened, and help, relief and assistance be afforded them this night. If God sees them wandering or straying, O Blessed Virgin, beg and implore your only Son to release and deliver them. With this resolution and intention, glory be to the Father, to the Son, and to the Holy Spirit. Amen.

'An Claidheamh Soluis'

Lord of Creation

Gethsemani prayer

O Blessed Jesus, you were in Gethsemani
To save our souls:
Save us from sin,
From wicked thoughts,
From sudden death,
From judgement to damnation.
You poured sweat
In the Garden of Olives.
Since it was you who brought us,
May it be you who takes us.
Save me, O Lord from thunder, from
hosts and from my enemy. Amen.

MacCrógaigh

Prayer for the goodwill of Christ

Though many a good rider has been thrown in the race,
On the back of the steed shall I now take my place:
From the straight track, alas! I have often gone aside.
Come, Christ, be my judge, for Your goodwill I ride.

In time of trial

Help and friends and grace from God to us:
'Tis this I am asking, help every day to us,
The Sacrament of Penance and strength from God to us,
And, O Mary, Queen protect thou my soul.
O God, O Father, O Lamb,
Banish all wicked thoughts from us,
Be around us when we sleep,
When we stand, when we rest:
Be in our minds and in our company
At the last hour. Amen.

Connacht

Prayer of the passion

O Fair and Bountiful God, O Father of Grace,
Who willingly suffered pain and a death of disgrace,
By the blood from your wounds
we were cleansed from every sin's trace,
set free the poor Gael, nor delay to uplift our race. Amen.

Anon.

On contemplating death

O Body, thy last end regard,
   In debt or in anger do not sleep,
Cold thy sheet in the lone churchyard,
   When thy limbs in clay are buried deep.
To cross beyond the grave, I fear,
   For little of the way I know,
Worse my plight beyond them here,
   Alas! for beyond that I did not plough. Amen.

A prayer to the Blessed Virgin against sudden death

O Glorious Virgin, Mother of God, Lady above all rank and worthy of all praise,
however great, intercede for me with your only beloved Son. O Lady most hon-
ourable, Mother of the King of Angels and Archangels, succour and save me from
every distress and evil. O Flower of the Patriarchs, of the Virgins and of the
Angels, O Hope of Glory, O Beauty of the Maidens, O Chief Thought of the
Angels and Archangels, remember me and desert me not, I pray you, in the dread
moment of death. O Star of the Sea, O Door of Paradise, O Temple of God, O
Palace of Jesus Christ, O Harbour of Health, O Flower of all Nations, O Pearl of
all Sweetness, O Queenly Protectress of the Guilty, O Hope of Believers, O
Brightness of the Virgins and Angels, your converse delights the Angels and
Archangels. Therefore O Mother of Mercy, I place under the protection of your
own blessed hand my going out, my coming in, my lying down, my rising up, the
sight of my eyes, the touch of my hands, the speech of my lips, the hearing of my
ears, so that they may be pleasing to your own beloved Son. Amen.

Connacht

Lord of Creation

Prayer for a holy death

O Blessed Michael, on thy name I call,
   And on thine, O John the Baptist,
On the saints of the world, one and all,
For help in the coming day of battle.

When my mouth is closing and my eye is failing,
And my sense from me is slipping away,
When my term is spent and my cause a-calling,
God with my soul that dreadful day. Amen.

'An Lóchrann'

Before death

O Jesus Christ, O King of Grace,
Creator of Earth and of Paradise,
Your blood the Tree of the Passion has loved
That I from eternal death be saved.

During my life I have ill repaid You,
Reopening Your wounds by my many sins,
Forgetting it was You who gave me health,
My daily bread, possessions, wealth.

What use to me now my worldly store?
My friends, companions and family?
My warrant is signed and Death is calling,
And without Your pardon to Hell I'm falling.

O God, You are the almighty Father,
Give me time to make my will,
My wealth on the poor like dew I'll spend
And a perfume of praise to You shall ascend. Amen.

'Cno Coilleadh'

O Lord, send us not early or sudden death, or death in any of the seven deadly sins, but let us die in our proper mind and senses, and in the love and fear of God. May our last refreshment in this world be the Holy Body of the Lord, holy anointing, penance and our share of the rites of the Church. May we obtain, like St Joseph, a holy death in the state of grace in the arms of the Virgin Mary. Amen.

'An Lóchrann'

On one's deathbed

O Holy Trinity, O Morning Star,
 O Scion from Royal David sprung,
Thy dear child Jesus, earnestly implore
To protect me on my journey home. Amen.

MacCrócaigh

Prayer for the souls in purgatory

We pray for the poor souls who are suffering the pains of purgatory, and especially for the souls of our own relations; for every poor soul for whom there is none to pray; for every soul in great and urgent need; for the soul that has last departed from this world, and for every poor soul burdened with the guilt of imperfect repentance, a forgotten Eucharist, or a penance not performed. We include them all in this prayer: may God release them to-night. Amen.

MacCrógaigh

Prayer for Friday

O King of the Friday,
Whose limbs on the cross were bound;
O Lord, who suffered
Sharp pain in many a wound;
We lay us to rest
Beneath the shield of your might,
May fruit from the tree
Of your Passion fall on us this night. Amen.

Connacht

Prayer for Sunday

A thousand welcomes to you, Blessed Sunday,
Now coming to help us after the week:
My feet guide early to Holy Eucharist,
Part my lips with blessed words,
Out of my heart banish wicked thoughts,
That I may look upon the Son of the Nurse.
Since it was the Son of God who bought us,
I rely for my soul's protection on You, Jesus,
May God establish You within my heart,
May You clear the stain and soil of sin from me
And fill my eyes with tears of repentance. Amen.

O'Sullivan

At Christmas

Welcome, Holy Babe,
Tho' in the manger lowly,
Bright and rich Thou art
This night in Thy halls of glory.

Tiny, mighty Babe,
Young Child, ages old,
small for Thee the manger,
Whom Heaven could not hold.

Motherless ever Thou,
And Fatherless to-night,
Eternal God Thou art
And first made man to-night.

Thy Father, older not than Thou,
Thy Mother, younger she;
Older, younger, the Son,
Older, younger, she than He. Amen.

Connacht

Prayers from Wales and Other Celtic Traditions

To the Trinity

May the grace of the Holy Spirit fill us;
May the true faith ever dwell within us;
May the faithful's example be ever our guide;
In the temple of Christ may we always abide;
The eternal Trinity may we seek;
Our hope in Jesus may we keep;
Relief on the poor may we gladly bestow;
In the path of God's will may we constantly go. Amen.

Connacht

To Jesus Christ

Glory, honour and praise be yours, Our Lord Jesus Christ; may the whole world adore you; blessed be your Holy Name, you who deigned to be born of a humble virgin for the sake of us sinners; and blessed be your incomprehensible goodness which caused you to die on the Cross for our ransom. O Jesus, Son of God, Redeemer of humanity, we implore you to be merciful to us, and to direct our lives here by your grace so that later we shall rejoice in your company in the Heavenly Kingdom for ever. Amen.

'Sgealaidhe Oirghiall'

Prayer in honour of the Holy Name

May the sweet name of Jesus
Be lovingly scribed
On my heart inside.

O Mother of Jesus,
May I with Him be,
And Jesus with me.

May a binding of love
That nothing can sever,
Be between us for ever.
Amen, O Jesus, for ever and ever. Amen.

Cno Coilleadh

O Jesus, only Son of the Father,
O Lamb, who shed your heart's blood to redeem us,
Shelter me, guard me, keep by me for ever,
Whether lying, or sitting,
or standing, or sleeping. Amen.

Sgea Laidhe Oirghiall

Prayer of the Name

Through Jesus is the name of Jesus
On my heart's core graven,
                    Jesu mine.
Through the greatness of His passion,
Through the fervour of His prayer,
Through the abundance of His blood,
Through the sweetness of His sweetness,
Through the bitterness of His death on the Cross
For our sake,
O Lord Jesus Christ,
Make whole our souls
And all the souls in Purgatory:
Thus do God and the Church bid us
To pray unceasing. Amen.

MacCrócaigh

To the Virgin Mary

O Virgin Mary, to us be given
A sight of your household in Heaven.
Obtain for us, too, a glimpse of the Trinity
And the grace of patience in the face of enmity. Amen.

Cno Coilleadh

Prayers at the foot of the cross

From the foot of the cross I raise my eyes,
O Jesus, Lord, incline to me:
The faith of God I boldly sing
With changeless hope and charity. Amen.

Connacht

Hail to thee, O Cross,
Sapling fair and wide;
Hail to thee, O Tree,
Where Christ was crucified;
Hail to Thee, O King,
Who on the Cross didst hang;
O Lord, I do implore Thee
The weakly flesh to blame
For the sin – stains on my soul –
'Twas the flesh that caused my shame. Amen.

Connacht

In honour of St Patrick

Our hope is in Patrick, Ireland's apostle bright,
This glorious and splendid name shines like a beacon-light.

The hart-hearted druids
Our champion o'ercame
Their proud heads he lowered
By the power of God's name.

Ireland's hills and her glens,
And her towns great in story,
He made holy for ever:
To our dear Saint all glory.

We implore you, O Patrick,
For the Irish to pray;
God with us daily,
And our patron always. Amen.

Old Irish Gaelic

Just as a table without bread is a needy one,
so absence of charity is ruin to the soul,
for the soul walks by love,
and the man who does not love abides in death.

The Monk of Farne

Prayer to St Columcille (Columba)

O Friendly Columcille and mild,
In the name of the blessed Trinity,
Through Father, Son and Holy Spirit,
Be a friend and guide to me. Amen.

From the Scottish Gaelic

Prayer to St David

Hail to thee, O blessed David,
I salute thee; hail again!
To thee I come to make my plaint,
Be my friend, O Holy Saint. Amen.

From the Welsh

King of the Friday

O King of the Friday
Whose limbs were stretched on the cross;
O Lord who didst suffer the bruises, the wounds, the loss;
We stretch ourselves beneath the shield of thy might;
Some fruit from the three of thy passion
Fall on us this night.

From the Irish

Amairgen's poem

I am wind on sea
I am ocean wave
I am roar of sea
I am bull of seven fights
I am vulture on cliff
I am dewdrop
I am fairest of flowers
I am boar for boldness
I am salmon in pool
I am lake on plain
I am a mountain in a man
I am word of skill
I am the point of a weapon
I am God who fashions fire
for a head.

Amairgen, early Irish poet (from the Lebor Gabala)[70]

The Tree of Life

King of the Tree of Life with its flowers, the space around which noble hosts were ranged, its crest and its showers on every side spread over the fields and plains of Heaven.

On it sits a glorious flock of birds and sing perfect songs of purest grace; without withering (with choice bounty rather) of fruit and of leaves.

Lovely is the flock of birds which keeps it, on every bright and goodly bird a hundred feathers; and without sin, with pure brilliance, they sing a hundred tunes for every feather . . .

Unknown Irish author, tenth century

Lord of Creation

Psalm to the creatures

Let us celebrate the single-cloaked beings
Content in their coats of fur and feathers,
And the swimmers who wish no other garb than their skins.
Let us sing
The ants who do not reckon the hours of their diligence on their hillock-years
Because a forest of heather-bells
Sweetens their labour;
The common newt who is wiser than men,
And the woolly bear who zig-zags on cabbage wine.

Let us envy
The cormorant who bathes in the precious colours
Of sunset on the sea;
The salmon, sunny is bliss,
Who knows how to breed young without charity;
The moon-drunk owl
Proud because night is the other side of day,
And the squirrel who slinks to Annwfn
to doze away the long barren season.

Let us weave praise
for the birds of legends,
Noah's dove and Brasswen's starling
Who carried the mail across the waters.
And Rhiannon's birds
Who gave merry nights to the dead
And caused birds to dance.

And let us not forget
The hopping gander
Who gave a few quills to Bishop Morgan,
Giving the heaven of its wings to the Welsh language,
And the mother-hens who provided
Welsh beds with their warmth.

Gwilym R. Jones, 'Salm I'r Creaduriaid'

The woodland Mass

A pleasant place I was at today,
under mantles of the worthy green hazel,
listening at day's beginning
to the skilful cock thrush
singing a splendid stanza
of fluent signs and symbols;
a stranger here, wisdom his nature,
a brown messenger who had journeyed far,
coming from rich Carmarthenshire
at my golden girl's command.
About him was a setting
of flowers of the sweet boughs of May,
like green mantles, his chasuble
was of the wings of the wind.
There was here, by the great God,
nothing but gold in the altar's canopy.
I heard, in polished language,
a long and faultless chanting,
an unhesitant reading to the people
of a gospel without mumbling;
the elevation, on the hill for us there,
of a good leaf for a holy wafer.
Then the slim eloquent nightingale
from the corner of a grove nearby,
poetess of the valley, sings to the many
the Sanctus bell in lively whistling.
The sacrifice is raised
up to the sky above the bush,
devotion to God the Father,
the chalice of ecstasy and love.
The psalmody contents me;
it was bred of a birch-grove in the sweet woods.

Dafydd ap Gwilym

Lord of Creation

Blessed be the Lord

Glorious God, all hail.
May church and chancel bless you,
May the three fountains bless you,
Two above the wind, one above the earth;
May darkness and daylight bless you,
May satin and fruit-trees bless you.

Abraham blessed you, the father of the faith:
Life eternal blessed you,
May the birds and bees bless you,
May the stubble and grass bless you.
Moses and Aaron blessed you,
Male and female blessed you,
May the seven days and stars bless you,
Air and atmosphere bless you,
May books and letters praise you,
The fish in the rivers praise you,
May mind and act bless you,
May sand and soil bless you,
Bless you all the good that's done.

I bless you, Lord of Majesty.
Glorious God, all hail.

The Black Book of Carmarthen

Guard my eyes for me, Jesus Son of Mary,
lest seeing another's wealth make me covetous . . .
Guard for me my ears lest they hearken to slander.
Guard for me my tongue lest they listen to slander.
Guard for me my hands, that they be not stretched out for quarrelling . . .
Guard for me my feet upon the gentle earth,
Lest, bent on profitless errands, they abandon rest.

Early Irish Lyric[71]

Praising God

Let's praise God at the beginning and the end of time.
Whoever seeks him out, he'll not deny, not refuse.

The son of Mary queen-bee of kings,
Mary mother of Christ, famed of maidens.
The sun will shift from the east to the north:
out of your great mercy implore your Son to put an end to our sinning.
God above us
God before us.
God rules.

May the King of Heaven give now the portion of mercy.
Regal bosom, let there be peace between us without denial.
May we undo what we have done,
before going to my earth my verdant grave,
all dark without a candle to my tumulus, my nook, my cranny, my resting place.

After horses and drinking new mead, feasting, making love to women,
I don't sleep, I think about my end:
We are in a land where pleasaunce is troubled . . .
Like leaves, we, from the tip of withered trees.

Woe to the miser who amasses great riches
and doesn't give to the glory of God.
Even though he's let off in the bustle of the present,
in danger he will be in the end.
The foolhardy doesn't know, he doesn't tremble
in his time.
He doesn't get up early,
he doesn't greet you,
he doesn't stay put,
he doesn't chant a prayer,
doesn't beg for mercy.
He pays bitterly in the end
for his pride and pomp and sway . . .
    nurtured the body
    for toads
    and snakes,
    and monsters,
    evil done.

And death will come to the door,
greedily collect, take away.
Upon you descend old age, senility;
Hearing, sight, bite, fade away . . .
The skin of your fingers shrivels.
This has ageing
greying wrought.

> May Saint Michael beg for us mercy's portion
> from the King of Heaven.

The Black Book of Carmarthen

I offer thee
Every flower that ever grew
Every bird that ever flew
Every wind that ever blew
Good God!

Every thunder rolling
Every church bell tolling
Every leaf and sod
Laudamus Te!

Every river dashing
Every lightening flashing
Like an angel's sword
Benedicimus Te!

Every cloud that ever swept
O'er the skies, and broke, and wept
In rain, and with the flowerets slept
My King!

Ancient Irish prayer

Celtic idyll

I wish, O Son of the living God, O ancient, eternal King,
For a hidden little hut in the wilderness that it may be my dwelling.
An all-grey lithe little lark to be by it's side,
A clear pool to wash away sins through the grace of the Holy Spirit . . .
A southern aspect for warmth, a little brook across its floor,

A choice land with many gracious gifts such as be good for every plant . . .
A pleasant church and with linen altar-cloth, a dwelling for God from Heaven;
The shining candles above the pure white Scriptures . . .
This is the husbandry I would take, I would choose, and will not hide it:
Fragrant leek, hen, salmon, trout, bees.
Raiment and food enough for me from the King of fair fame,
And I to be sitting for a while praying to God in every place.

Seventh-century Irish poem[72]

I inhabit a wood unknown but to my God
My house of hazel and ash
    as an old hut in a rath . . .
For music I have pines,
my tall music pines
so who can I envy here, my gentle Christ?

Early Irish[73]

Scribes reverie

A hedge of trees surrounds me,
A blackbird's lay sings to me;
Above my script
The trilling birds chant to me.

In a grey mantle from the top of bushes
The cuckoo sings;
Verily – may the Lord shield me –
Well do I write under the greenwood.

Early ninth-century Irish poem[74]

I am the sounding wave
my hand is the voice of the sea.
It swims with the seal in his laughter.
The sacrament of being
you share with me.

Ray Howard Jones[75]

Lord of Creation

Lord of my heart
Give me vision to inspire me
That, working or resting,
I may always think of you.

Lord of my heart
Give me light to guide me
That, at home or abroad,
I may always walk in your way.

Lord of my heart
Give me wisdom to direct me
That, thinking or acting,
I may always discern right from wrong.

Lord of my heart
Give me courage to strengthen me
That, among friends and enemies,
I may always proclaim your justice.

Lord of my heart
Give me trust to console me
That, hungry or well fed,
I may always rely on your mercy.

Lord of my heart
Save me from empty praise
That I may always boast of you.

Lord of my heart
Save me from worldly wealth
That I may always look to the riches in heaven.

Lord of my heart
Save me from military prowess
That I may always seek your protection.

Lord of my heart
Save me from vain knowledge
That I may always study your word.

Heart of my own heart
Whatever befall me
Rule over my thoughts and feelings
My words and actions

Ancient Irish

From *The Spiritual Canticle*

My Beloved is the mountains,
The wooded valleys, lonely and sequestered,
The strange and distant islands,
The loud resounding rivers,
The loving breezes with their gentle whispers.

The still and tranquil night
As it kindles with the coming dawn,
The music that is silent,
The ringing solitude,
The supper that refreshes and awakens love.

St John of the Cross[76]

In praise of creation

Look at the sky, how beautiful it is, and how vast, all crowned with a blazing diadem of stars! For how many ages has it existed? Already it has been there for five thousand years, and shows no signs of ageing. Like some young creature full of sap it preserves all the shining and the freshness of an earlier age, and manifests the beauty it possessed in the beginning, and time has not wearied it. And this vast, beautiful, ageless sky, unchangeable and gleaming, with all its stars, having existed through so many ages – this same God, whom some profess to be able to see with mortal eyes and comprehend with their own pitiable intelligence – this same God created it as easily as a man, throwing a handful of sticks together, creates a hut. And this is what Isaiah meant when he said, 'He stretches out the heavens as a curtain, and spreadeth them out as a tent to dwell in'. Look at the great mass of the mountains, and all the innumerable people who dwell on earth, and the plants, all so rich and wonderfully varied, and the towns, and the vast buildings and the wild animals, and all these the earth supports easily on her back. And yet with all its vastness, it was fashioned by God 'as though it were nothing'. So speaks for us Isaiah, searching for a phrase which will explain the ease with which God created the earth . . . And then look at the inhabitants of earth, of whom the prophet said, 'He sitteth upon the circle of the earth, and the inhabitants thereof are grasshoppers,' and a little while earlier he said, 'Behold the nations are as a drop of water falling from a bowl.' Think of all the people who inhabit the earth: Syrians, Cilicians, Cappadocians, Bithynians, those who live on the shores of the Black Sea, in Thrace, in Macedonia, in all of Greece and the islands of Britain, Sarmatia, India and the inhabitants of Persia, and then of all the innumerable other peoples and races, and all these are 'as a drop of water falling from a bowl'. And what small atom of this drop of water thinks he can know God?

St John Chrysostom, De Incomprehensibili, II, 6 (fourth century)

Adoration

Lord God, we come to adore you.
You are the ground of all that is.
You hold us in being, and without you we could not be.
Before we were born, before time began,
before the universe came into being, you were;
When time is finished, when the universe is no more,
you will still be.
Nothing can take your power from you.
And in your presence we can only be silent
before the mystery of your being, for no words
of ours can do justice to your glory.
(silence)

O Supreme Lord of the universe,
you fill and sustain everything around us:
With the touch of your hand you turned
chaos into order, darkness into light.
Unknown energies you hid in the heart of matter.
From you bursts forth the splendour of the sun,
and the mild radiance of the moon.
Stars and planets without number you set in ordered movement.
You are the source of the fire's heat and the wind's might,
of the water's coolness and the earth's stability.
Deep and wonderful are the mysteries of your creation.
We adore you, you are beyond all form!
You give form to everything. Lord of all creation.

God of all salvation,
you formed us in your own image,
You created us male and female,
you willed our union and harmony.
You entrusted the earth to our care
and promised your blessing to all our descendants.

You gave us the spirit of discernment to know you,
the power of speech to celebrate your glory,
the strength of love to give ourselves in joy to you.
In this wondrous way, O God,
you called us to share in your own being,
your knowledge,
your own bliss.

In the oneness of the Supreme Spirit,
through Christ who unites all things in his fullness
we and the whole creation give to you
honour and glory, thanks and praise,
worship and adoration,
now and in every age, for ever and ever. Amen.

World Council of Churches

When the shadows fall upon hill and glen;
and the bird-music is mute;
when the silken dark is a friend;
and the river sings to the stars:
ask yourself, sister,
ask yourself, brother,
the question you alone have power to answer:

O King and Saviour of all,
what is your gift to me?
and do I use it to your pleasing?

Hebridean

O Son of God, change my heart.
Your spirit composes the songs of the birds and the buzz of the bees.
I ask of you only one more miracle:
Beautify my soul.

Traditional Celtic prayer

Lord of Creation

o god of the
elements
o god of the
mysteries
o god of the
well-springs
o king of
kings
thy joy the joy,
thy light the light,
thy war the war,
thy peace the peace,
thy pain the pain,
thy love the love,
that lasts for ever,
to the end of ends.
and the blessing of
god almighty.

celtic

Psalms of Creation⁷⁷

Psalm 8

1 O Lord our governor,*
 how exalted is your name in all the world!
2 Out of the mouths of infants and children*
 your majesty is praised above the heavens.
3 You have set up a stronghold against your adversaries,*
 to quell the enemy and the avenger.
4 When I consider your heavens, the work of your fingers,*
 the moon and the stars you have set in their courses,
5 What are mortals, that you should be mindful of them?*
 mere human beings, that you should seek them out?
6 You have made them little lower than the angels;*
 you adorn them with glory and honour.
7 You give them mastery over the works of your hands;*
 and put all things under their feet,
8 All sheep and oxen,*
 even the wild beasts of the field,
9 The birds of the air, the fish of the sea,*
 and whatsoever walks in the paths of the sea.
10 O Lord our governor,*
 how exalted is your name in all the world!

Psalm 23

1 The Lord is my shepherd;*
 I shall not be in want.
2 He makes me lie down in green pastures*
 and leads me beside still waters.
3 He revives my soul*
 and guides me along right pathways for his name's sake.

4 Though I walk through the valley of the shadow of death,
  I shall fear no evil;*
  for you are with me;
  your rod and your staff, they comfort me.

5 You spread a table before me
  in the presence of those who trouble me;*
  you have anointed my head with oil,
  and my cup is running over.

6 Surely your goodness and mercy shall follow me
  all the days of my life,*
  and I will dwell in the house of the Lord for ever.

Psalm 24

1 The earth is the Lord's and all that is in it,*
  the world and all who dwell therein.

2 For it is he who founded it upon the seas*
  and made it firm upon the rivers of the deep.

3 'Who can ascend the hill of the Lord?*
  and who can stand in his holy place?'

4 'Those who have clean hands and a pure heart,*
  who have not pledged themselves to falsehood,
  nor sworn by what is a fraud.

5 'They shall receive a blessing from the Lord*
  and a just reward from the God of their salvation.'

6 Such is the generation of those who seek him,*
  of those who seek your face, O God of Jacob.

7 Lift up your heads, O gates;
  lift them high, O everlasting doors;*
  and the King of glory shall come in.

8 'Who is this King of glory?'*
  'The Lord, strong and mighty,
  the Lord, mighty in battle.'

9 Lift up your heads, O gates;
  lift them high, O everlasting doors;*
  and the King of glory shall come in.

10 'Who is he, this King of glory?'*
  'The Lord of hosts,
  he is the King of glory.'

Lord of Creation

Psalm 42

1 As the deer longs for the water-brooks,*
so longs my soul for you, O God.

2 My soul is athirst for God, athirst for the living God;*
when shall I come to appear before the presence of God?

3 My tears have been my food day and night,*
while all day long they say to me,
'Where now is your God?'

4 I pour out my soul when I think on these things:*
how I went with the multitude
and led them into the house of God,

5 With the voice of praise and thanksgiving,*
among those who keep holy-day.

6 Why are you so full of heaviness, O my soul?*
and why are you so disquieted within me?

7 Put your trust in God;*
for I will yet give thanks to him,
who is the help of my countenance, and my God.

8 My soul is heavy within me;*
therefore I will remember you from the land of Jordan,
and from the peak of Mizar among the heights of Hermon.

9 One deep calls to another in the noise of your cataracts;*
all your rapids and floods have gone over me.

10 The Lord grants his loving-kindness in the daytime;*
in the night season his song is with me,
a prayer to the God of my life.

11 I will say to the God of my strength,
'Why have you forgotten me?*
and why do I go so heavily
while the enemy oppresses me?'

12 While my bones are being broken,*
my enemies mock me to my face;

13 All day long they mock me*
say to me, 'Where now is your God?'

14 Why are you so full of heaviness, O my soul?*
and why are you so disquieted within me?

15 Put your trust in God;*
for I will yet give thanks to him,
who is the help of my countenance, and my God.

Psalm 65

1 You are to be praised, O God, in Zion;*
  to you shall vows be performed in Jerusalem.

2 To you that hear prayer shall all flesh come,*
  because of their transgressions.

3 Our sins are stronger than we are,*
  but you will blot them out.

4 Happy are they whom you choose
  and draw to your courts to dwell there!*
  they will be satisfied by the beauty of your house,
  by the holiness of your temple.

5 Awesome things will you show us in your righteousness,
  O God of our salvation,*
  O Hope of all the ends of the earth
  and of the seas that are far away.

6 You make fast the mountains by your power;*
  they are girded about with might.

7 You still the roaring of the seas,*
  the roaring of their waves,
  and the clamour of the peoples.

8 Those who dwell at the ends of the earth
  will tremble at your marvellous signs;*
  you make the dawn and the dusk to sing for joy.

9 You visit the earth and water it abundantly;
  you make it very plenteous;*
  the river of God is full of water.

10 You prepare the grain,*
  for so you provide for the earth.

11 You drench the furrows and smooth out the ridges;*
  with heavy rain you soften the ground
  and bless its increase.

12 You crown the year with your goodness,*
  and your paths overflow with plenty.

13 May the fields of the wilderness be rich for grazing,*
  and the hills be clothed with joy.

14 May the meadows cover themselves with flocks
  and the valleys cloak themselves with grain;*
  let them shout for joy and sing.

Psalm 96

1　Sing to the Lord a new song;*
 　sing to the Lord, all the whole earth.

2　Sing to the Lord and bless his name;*
 　proclaim the good news of his salvation from day to day.

3　Declare his glory among the nations*
 　and his wonders among all peoples.

4　For great is the Lord and greatly to be praised;*
 　he is more to be feared than all gods.

5　As for all the gods of the nations, they are but idols;*
 　but it is the Lord who made the heavens.

6　O the majesty and magnificence of his presence!*
 　O the power and the splendour of his sanctuary!

7　Ascribe to the Lord, you families of the peoples;*
 　ascribe to the Lord honour and power.

8　Ascribe to the Lord the honour due to his name;*
 　bring offerings and come into his courts.

9　Worship the Lord in the beauty of holiness;*
 　let the whole earth tremble before him.

10　Tell it out among the nations: 'The Lord is king!*
 　he has made the world so firm that it cannot be moved;
 　he will judge the peoples with equity.'

11　Let the heavens rejoice and let the earth be glad;
 　let the sea thunder and all that is in it;*
 　let the field be joyful and all that is therein.

12　Then shall all the trees of the wood shout for joy
 　before the Lord when he comes,*
 　when he comes to judge the earth.

13　He will judge the world with righteousness*
 　and the peoples with his truth.

Psalm 97

1　The Lord is king; let the earth rejoice;*
 　let the multitude of the isles be glad.

2　Clouds and darkness are round about him,*
 　righteousness and justice
 　are the foundations of his throne.

3　A fire goes before him*
 　and burns up his enemies on every side.

4 His lightnings light up the world;*
　　the earth sees it and is afraid.

5 The mountains melt like wax
　　at the presence of the Lord,*
　　at the presence of the Lord of the whole earth.

6 The heavens declare his righteousness,*
　　and all the peoples see his glory.

7 Confounded be all who worship carved images
　　and delight in false gods!*
　　Bow down before him, all you gods.

8 Zion hears and is glad and the cities of Judah rejoice,*
　　because of your judgements, O Lord.

9 For you are the Lord: most high over all the earth;*
　　you are exalted far above all gods.

10 The Lord loves those who hate evil;*
　　he preserves the lives of his saints
　　and delivers them from the hand of the wicked.

11 Light has sprung up for the righteous,*
　　and joyful gladness for those who are true-hearted.

12 Rejoice in the Lord, you righteous,*
　　and give thanks to his holy name.

Psalm 98

1 Sing to the Lord a new song,*
　　for he has done marvellous things.

2 With his right hand and his holy arm*
　　has he won for himself the victory.

3 The Lord has made known his victory;*
　　his righteousness has he openly shown
　　in the sight of the nations.

4 He remembers his mercy and faithfulness
　　to the house of Israel,*
　　and all the ends of the earth have seen
　　the victory of our God.

5 Shout with joy to the Lord, all you lands;*
　　lift up your voice, rejoice and sing.

6 Sing to the Lord with the harp,*
　　with the harp and the voice of song.

7 With trumpets and the sound of the horn*

shout with joy before the King, the Lord.
8 Let the sea make a noise and all that is in it,*
   the lands and those who dwell therein.
9 Let the rivers clap their hands,*
   and let the hills ring out with joy before the Lord,
   when he comes to judge the earth.
10 In righteousness shall he judge the world,*
   and the peoples with equity.

Psalm 104

1 Bless the Lord, O my soul;*
   O Lord my God, how excellent is your greatness!
   you are clothed with majesty and splendour.
2 You wrap yourself with light as with a cloak*
   and spread out the heavens like a curtain.
3 You lay the beams of your chambers
   in the waters above;*
   you make the clouds your chariot;
   you ride on the wings of the wind.
4 You make the winds your messengers*
   and flames of fire your servants.
5 You have set the earth upon its foundations,*
   so that it never shall move at any time.
6 You covered it with the deep as with a mantle;*
   the waters stood higher than the mountains.
7 At your rebuke they fled;*
   at the voice of your thunder they hastened away.
8 They went up into the hills
   and down to the valleys beneath,*
   to the places you had appointed for them.
9 You set the limits that they should not pass;*
   they shall not again cover the earth.
10 You send the springs into the valleys;*
   they flow between the mountains.
11 All the beasts of the field drink their fill from them,*
   and the wild asses quench their thirst.
12 Beside them the birds of the air make their nests*
   and sing among the branches.
13 You water the mountains from your dwelling on high;*

Psalms of Creation   299

the earth is fully satisfied by the fruit of your works.

14 You make grass grow for flocks and herds*
and plants to serve us all;

15 That they may bring forth food from the earth,*
and wine to gladden our hearts,

16 Oil to make a cheerful countenance,*
and bread to strengthen the heart.

17 The trees of the Lord are full of sap,*
the cedars of Lebanon which he planted,

18 In which the birds build their nests,*
and in whose tops the stork makes his dwelling.

19 The high hills are a refuge for the mountain goats,*
and the stony cliffs for the rock badgers.

20 You appointed the moon to mark the seasons,*
and the sun knows the time of its setting.

21 You make darkness that it may be night,*
in which all the beasts of the forest prowl.

22 The lions roar after their prey*
and seek their food from God.

23 The sun rises and they slip away*
and lay themselves down in their dens.

24 The labourer goes forth to work*
and to toil until the evening.

25 O Lord, how manifold are your works!*
in wisdom you have made them all;
the earth is full of your creatures.

26 Yonder is the great and wide sea
with its living things too many to number,*
creatures both small and great.

27 There move the ships,
and there is that Leviathan,*
which you have made for the sport of it.

28 All of them look to you*
to give them their food in due season.

29 You give it to them, they gather it;*
you open your hand and they are filled with good things.

30 You hide your face and they are terrified;*
you take away their breath
and they die and return to their dust.

31 You send forth your Spirit and they are created;*
and so you renew the face of the earth.

Lord of Creation

32 May the glory of the Lord endure for ever;*
  may the Lord rejoice in all his works.
33 He looks at the earth and it trembles;*
  he touches the mountains and they smoke.
34 I will sing to the Lord as long as I live;*
  I will praise my God while I have my being.
35 May these words of mine please him;*
  I will rejoice in the Lord.
36 Let sinners be consumed out of the earth,*
  and the wicked be no more.
37 Bless the Lord, O my soul.*

Alleluia!

Psalm 148

1 Alleluia!
  Praise the Lord from the heavens;*
  praise him in the heights.
2 Praise him, all you angels of his;*
  praise him, all his host.
3 Praise him, sun and moon;*
  praise him, all you shining stars.
4 Praise him, heaven of heavens,*
  and you waters above the heavens.
5 Let them praise the name of the Lord;*
  for he commanded and they were created.
6 He made them stand fast for ever and ever;*
  he gave them a law which shall not pass away.
7 Praise the Lord from the earth,*
  you sea-monsters and all deeps;
8 Fire and hail, snow and fog,*
  tempestuous wind, doing his will;
9 Mountains and all hills,*
  fruit trees and all cedars;
10 Wild beasts and all cattle,*
  creeping things and winged birds;
11 Kings of the earth and all peoples,*
  princes and all rulers of the world;
12 Young men and maidens,*

old and young together.

13 Let them praise the name of the Lord,*
    for his name only is exalted,
    his splendour is over earth and heaven.

14 He has raised up strength for his people
    and praise for all his loyal servants,*
    the children of Israel, a people who are near him.

Alleluia!

Postscript

Man offers the first-fruits of his labour to the creator of everything in the universe, stars and cornstalks and grains of dust. This is not to say however that man is simply a brutish breaker of furrows, but he labours well in a variety of trades also, with stone and with loom and with oar and with harp and with law-book and with sweet ordering of words and with prism, towards some end which is likewise a kind of harvest. Well he knows that he could not call himself man at all unless he labours all his time under the sun to encompass the end for which his faculties were given to him. This end, whatever the nature of his occupation, is his harvest time; and he would be a poor labourer that would not wish, among all that broken gold, to offer back a tithe or a hundredth into the hands that formed the original fecund dust.

George Mackay Brown[78]

References, Sources and Acknowledgements

1. G. Murphy, *Early Irish Lyrics* (Oxford, 1956).
2. The *Black Book of Carmarthen* has traditionally been connected with the ancient town of Carmarthen. It has been said to have been produced by one of the Welsh-speaking monks of the Augustinian priory of St John in Carmarthen. It is generally accepted that it was produced around AD 1250. But a lot of material in it is far older than that. These poems are translated by Merion Pennar, published by Llanarch Enterprises, 1989.
3. B. O'Malley, *The Animals of Saint Gregory* (Paulinus Press, 1981).
4. James Finlay, *Merton's Palace of Nowhere* (Indiana: Ave Maria Press, 1978).
5. B. O'Malley, *God at Every Gate* (Norwich: Canterbury Press, 1997).
6. From *Dance Network News*, October–November 1988, p. 7.
7. Clement of Alexandria, *Stromata* 7.7, J. P. Migne (ed.), *Patrologia Graeca* 16.508b.
8. Eusebius of Caesarea, *Ecclesiastical History*, Sources Chrétiennes (Paris: Cerf, 1958), p. 120.
9. Gregory of Nazianzen, *Oratio* II, 5, J. P. Migne (ed.), *Patrologia Graeca* 35.837c.
10. Methodius of Olympia, *The Banquet*, VI. 5, Sources Chrétiennes (Paris: Cerf, 1963), p. 176.
11. *The Acts of John*, in M. R. James (tr.), *The Apocryphal New Testament* (Oxford: Oxford University Press, 1975).
12. Robert Faricy, *Praying for Inner Healing* (London: SCM Press, 1979), pp. 13f.
13. Blanche Gallagher, *Meditations with Teilhard de Chardin* (New Mexico: Bear and Co., 1988).
14. The Prayer of Azariah from which this and subsequent extracts are taken is an addition to the book of Daniel, inserted between 3.23 and 3.24.
15. Gabrielle Uhlein, *Meditations with Hildegard of Bingen* (New Mexico: Bear and Co., 1983).

16. Gallagher, *Meditations*.
17. Matthew Fox, *Meditations with Meister Eckhart* (New Mexico: Bear and Co., 1983).
18. Fox, *Meditations*.
19. Fox, *Meditations*.
20. Fox, *Meditations*.
21. Fox, *Meditations*.
22. Roman Missal, *Rite for the Blessing of Holy Water* (International Committee on English in the Liturgy, 1982).
23. W. Stokes, *Saltair na Rann* (Oxford, 1883).
24. O'Malley, *God at Every Gate*.
25. Gallagher, *Meditiations*.
26. Gallagher, *Meditations*.
27. Gallagher, *Meditations*.
28. Matthew Fox, *Original Blessing* (Santa Fe: Bear and Co, 1983), pp. 142–4.
29. O'Malley, *God at Every Gate*.
30. Gallagher, *Meditations*.
31. Fox, *Meditations*.
32. Neil Diamond, 'Jonathan Livingston Seagull' (Sony, 1992).
33. Fox, *Meditations*.
34. Kathy Galloway, in Jean C. Morrison (ed.), *What on Earth is God Like?* (Wild Goose, 1985).
35. Stokes, *Saltair na Rann*.
36. From Robert Kirchner, 'Supernova – Death of a Star' in *National Geographic*, vol. 173, no. 5 (May 1988).
37. From the unfinished fragment, 'Repeat that, repeat . . . ' in *Gerard Manley Hopkins: A Selection of his Poems and Prose*, ed. W. H. Gardner (Harmondsworth: Penguin Books, 1953).
38. Gerard Manley Hopkins, 'Hurrahing in the HARVEST' in J. Pick (ed.), *A Hopkins Reader* (Oxford: Oxford University Press, 1953).
39. O'Malley, *God at Every Gate*.
40. Teilhard de Chardin, *Building the Earth* (Wiles-Barre, PA: Dimension Books, 1965).
41. From Maura Sée, OSB (ed.), *The Heart at Rest: Daily Readings with St. Augustine* (London: Darton, Longman & Todd, 1986).
42. From Brendan O'Malley, *A Welsh Pilgrim's Manual* (Llandysul, Ceredigion: Gomer Press, 1989).
43. From O'Malley, *Pilgrim's Manual*.
44. Edwina Gately, *I Hear a Seed Growing* (Trabuco Canyon: Source Books, 1992).
45. Sée, *The Heart at Rest*.

46. Gately, *I Hear Seed Growing*.
47. A. Carmichael, *Carmina Gadelica* (Edinburgh and London: Scottish Academic Press, 1976).
48. Robert Frost, *Selected Poems* (Holt, Rinehart and Winston, 1969).
49. From the *Service Book of the Holy Orthodox-Catholic Apostolic Church*, ed. Florence Hapgood (New York: Association Press, 1922).
50. Finlay, *Merton's Palace of Nowhere*.
51. Fox, *Meditations*.
52. 'The Calendar of Oengus', in Whiteley Stokes (tr.), *Translations of the Royal Irish Academy Vol. 1* (Dublin: Hodges, Foster & Figgus, 1880).
53. Uhlein, *Hildegard*.
54. *Daily Gaelic Prayers*. 'Connacht' refers to Dr Hyde's *The Religious Songs of Connacht*. I am not able to trace the provenance of 'Cno Coilleadh', 'Seanfhocla Uladh', The Proverbs of Ulster, 'An Lochrann', 'Sgealaidhe Oirghiall' or 'An Claidheamh'.
55. *Daily Gaelic Prayers*.
56. *Daily Gaelic Prayers*.
57. *Daily Gaelic Prayers*.
58. J. Leclercq, OSB, *The Love of Learning and the Desire for God* (New York: Fordham University Press, 1961).
59. Arnoul of Boheriss, *Speculum Monachorum I.*, J. P. Migne (ed.), *Patrologia Latina*, 184. For useful Scripture texts for *lectio divina*, see B. O'Malley, *A Celtic Primer* (Norwich: Canterbury Press, 2002).
60. Michael Casey, *Towards God* (Triumph Books, 1996).
61. *The Wreck of the Deutschland*, in Gardner (ed.), *Hopkins*.
62. Church in Wales Publications, 1992.
63. *The Christian Year* (Church House Publications, 1997).
64. Church in Wales Publications, 1992.
65. Church in Wales Punlications, 1992.
66. *The Christian Year*.
67. J. Carey, *King of the Mysteries – Early Irish Religious Writing* (Dublin: Four Courts Press, 1998).
68. Carey, *King of the Mysteries*.
69. Carey, *King of the Mysteries*.
70. Amairgen's Poem from R. A. S. Macalister (ed.), *Lebor Gabála Érenn: The Book of the Taking of Ireland*, also known as *The Book of Cougherts*, 5 vols. (London, 1956).
71. Murphy, *Early Irish Lyrics*.
72. O'Malley, *Pilgrim's Manual*.
73. O'Malley, *Pilgrim's Manual*.
74. O'Malley, *Pilgrim's Manual*.

75. O'Malley, *Pilgrim's Manual*.
76. *Poems of St. John of the Cross*, tr. Gerald Brennan (Cambridge: Cambridge University Press, 1973).
77. The psalms are taken from the Standard Book of Common Prayer of the Episcopal Church of the USA, on which no copyright is claimed.
78. George Mackay Brown, *Magnus* (London: Hogarth Press, 1973).

Lord of Creation